The *New* New
CAN-OPENER
Cookbook

Contents

∿∿∿∿∿∿∿∿∿∿∿∿

1

Introduction

A NEW KIND OF COOKING

Sᴏᴍᴇᴛʜɪɴɢ ɴᴇᴡ has been added to the age-old saga of good eating. America, never before gastronomically renowned despite its wealth of excellent ingredients, burgeoning larders, fertile farm lands, herds and flocks, has developed epicurean interests —but with a difference. Our cooking ideas and ideals have their roots in many lands and cultures, but our new way of achieving gourmet food can happen only here—in the land of the mix, the jar, the frozen-food package, and the ubiquitous can opener.

At one time a badge of shame, hallmark of the lazy lady and the careless wife, today the can opener is fast becoming a magic wand, especially in the hands of those brave young women, nine million of them (give or take a few thousand here and there), who are engaged in frying as well as bringing home the bacon.

There has developed among them a pride in preparing and serving interesting meals. It is no longer considered chic, charming, or "intellectual" to be ignorant in the kitchen, but always there is the problem of time, the crowding of many varied interests.

To the rescue comes the manufacturer of so-called ready-to-serve foods. Actually, at least in gourmet terms, they are not *quite* ready to serve, but they do provide the basis for any number of prideful, even complicated, specialties. The modern cook looks at it this way: other people have the responsibility for the selection of my raw materials, the cleaning and preliminary preparation. When I ply my busy little can opener, I move onto the scene the way a chef comes in after a corps of kitchen helpers has done the scullery chores—the drudgery of cooking. Armed with a can opener, I become the artist-cook, the master, the creative chef.

The use of a can opener may not be news, but the gourmet approach definitely is, for our new-style wielder of the can opener is a perfectionist. Gone are the days when anything quick was considered a triumph and concoctions of tuna fish, cream of mushroom soup, and potato chips flourished among the hurry-up menus. Now we are becoming classicists, and are analyzing the complicated, work-consuming recipes of olden days. We are discovering how the canned stews and chicken fricassees, canned gravy, soup, or consommé can be properly employed in today's living.

Escoffier demands over and over again slowly simmered, painstakingly clarified white or brown stock. On the back of every gourmet range, the stock pot never ceased to simmer—that was in the old days. But now, canned consommé or chicken broth provides an admirable answer. For greater economy, bouillon cubes or meat extract, plus hot water, may be used.

In the canned stew department, there is much that is interesting. Although such stews are notoriously underseasoned to appeal to the *average palate* (that much-maligned and underestimated unknown quantity which haunts and hog-ties the average manufacturer), they can be transformed with a rinse of red wine, a clove of garlic, parsley, half a bay leaf, and a flicker of mixed herbs to make something delightfully akin to Le Boeuf en Daube as served in France.

Consider a can of beef gravy. No one in his right mind would wax lyrical over it, but it makes a sound and honest beginning or foundation for a dozen excellent sauces.

Or, take the lowly meat ball—not wildly exciting, certainly, but there is inspiration to be found among the Hindus, where cookery is a sacred ceremony, a recipe for Kofta-Ka-Kari (Forcemeat Ball Curries). This is achieved simply by adding to the meat balls and their gravy the best available curry powder, a well-crushed clove of garlic, dried parsley, thyme, marjoram, and rosemary. Heat and serve inside a ring of cooked rice, decorated prettily with french fried onions (another excellent canned specialty), and pass the chutney, please, and as many other curry accompaniments as are handy: crisp, crushed bacon, coarsely chopped nuts, India relish, grated coconut, chopped hard-cooked eggs, green onion, green pepper.

Jars as well as tins from the ordinary corner store hold gourmet treasure—a jar of real mayonnaise made of whole egg and olive oil, just as any chef would make it, is capable of dozens of interesting variations.

Like the finale in a play, the climax of a meal is the dessert. Far too many meals in this hurried age merely *stop* at a given point—they do not end, they are not climaxed. What a pity, since there are so many uncomplicated yet thoroughly delightful ways to write a lovely finis to a satisfying menu. To be distinctive, a dessert need not be complicated nor even excessively caloric. Consider the canned fruits and their infinite divertissements. Canned cherries, for instance, made into Cerises au Claret (page 246), chilled very well and served from a frosty glass bowl with lady fingers.

On page 251 you will find fresh Pineapple Royale, another impressive dessert, cribbed from Escoffier and adapted to present-day hurried techniques.

It's easy to cook like a gourmet though you are a beginner. We want you to believe just as we do that in this miraculous age it is quite possible—and it's fun—to be a "chef" even before you can really cook.

THE RECIPES

We do not suggest or expect that this be your only cookbook, though it might well be your introduction to the art of cooking. So we have made no attempt to cover in our recipes the whole field of cookery. There is, however, a representative collection of recipes in various categories and a sufficient number of each—appetizers, soups, meats, vegetables, salads, desserts, and beverages—to equip you for any occasion. Armed with these recipes and ideas, you should achieve with the least possible expenditure of work and tension not only excellent eating but also considerable acclaim.

Every recipe includes a short cut—a canned or quick-frozen food, a mix or a new and simplified way to arrive at a particularly delectable result. In each case we have tried with a few lines of introduction to explain our reasons for including each particular recipe. We have tried also to describe as well as mere words can the appearance and the flavor of the various dishes. Far too many recipes—fine recipes, too—are printed to rest unknown, unnoticed, and untasted within the covers of a book simply because modern authors lack the perspicacity of those old-time ladies who in their handwritten recipes more often than not would title a recipe not merely Veal Loaf, for instance, but Aunt Mame's Special Veal Loaf—very light and fluffy. They might add, "Men of this family have always loved a loaf fixed this way with a hard-boiled egg in the center. . . ."

Not only because of the recipe introductions, but also in the listing of the ingredients you will find this book unorthodox. Only the essential ingredients are listed—not salt, pepper, and water. Also, in most recipes the garnishes are included in the ingredients because they are important in making any dish interesting and appetizing.

Because we know that few people outside of home economics classes and TV demonstrations measure before starting to cook, we give the amounts along with the recipe directions so that your eye need not do a jumping-jack act from recipe to ingredients and back again to recipe. For instance, a recipe suggests you will need for Sauce Suprême condensed cream of chicken soup, milk, egg, lemon juice. Later when you start to work you learn that 1/4 to 1/2 cup of milk is required, a can of soup, a tablespoon of lemon juice.

The glossary supplies additional information on ingredients, herbs, spices, seasonings, as well as the addresses of many fine mail-order houses.

AT SERVING TIME

A chef does not serve a dish, he *presents* it; and his presentation is every bit as important as his preparation. Much of the difference between just cooking and epicurean cooking is the *difference in the way the food is served*. In our effort to lift quickly prepared food to extraordinary heights of appeal we have appended to each recipe a few lines titled "At Serving Time," which tell you how to serve, how to garnish attractively and with originality, and, in many cases, what to serve with each particular food for an interesting, well-balanced meal.

Present-day menus have become so simple. Individual and family likes and dislikes are so varied that we find it much more helpful to have suggestions for "what goes with what" instead of a full-scale formal menu plan.

YOU WILL NEED

At least half of the social and culinary success of any hurried epicure depends upon a good stock of supplies. The ability to whip up something wonderful with seemingly miraculous speed and ease often depends more on skill in shopping and management than on skill in cooking. In this book we have confined our recipe ingredients to those products which for the most part can be secured in any ordinary grocery store or delicatessen in small as well as big towns and cities. Occasionally an unusual seasoning or a specialty item is mentioned. You have only to consult the alphabetical glossary at the end of the book to get a complete description of anything that seems unfamiliar and information about where you can find it or order it by mail.

Among those products that are called for most frequently in this book and that it would be well to keep on hand—in addition to the ordinary salt, pepper, milk, bread, and butter—are a collection of canned soups, such as cream of chicken, mushroom, consommé, to be used not only as soups but also in the making of sauces; canned meats and fish to suit your fancy; canned or quick-frozen chicken and chicken fricassee and chicken à la king; canned tomatoes, tomato sauce, and tomato paste; your favorite canned or quick-frozen vegetables; oil, vinegar, and prepared salad dressings; cheese, of course; dehydrated vegetable flakes, such as onion flakes, parsley flakes, mixed vegetable flakes; mixes for pastry, rolls, and cookies, as well as cake, pies, and puddings (vanilla-, chocolate-, and custard-flavored puddings are always good to have on hand); "storable" as well as fresh milk—evaporated, dehydrated, or condensed.

And then the core of all epicurean effort is a treasury of seasonings. You will want all the usual spices, herbs, and flavorous seeds such as: salt, pepper, cloves, nutmeg, cinnamon, allspice, ginger, curry, sage, marjoram, thyme, basil, tarragon, savory, rosemary, paprika, and monosodium glutamate (generally known under various trade names, such as Ac'cent, Zest, etc.). And a few of the less usual ones, too, such as cumin, saffron, cardamon, turmeric; condiments, olives, and pickles to be used not only at the table but in preparation of food; extracts over and beyond the usual vanilla. Kitchen Bouquet or some other condiment with a caramelized sugar base adds rich, homemade color to stews and gravies.

Wines also we have employed frequently—red and white table wines, sherry, port, an occasional dash of champagne, rum and brandy for that glorious and ever-so-easy and dramatic trick of serving food flambé (afire).

Nowadays, most modern cooks have acquired such helpful electrical appliances as the electric can opener, the blender, and the mixer. Occasionally we suggest that these be used. However, all our recipes can be prepared with only a few simple, inexpensive, and helpful hand tools, such as the Mouli grater, the garlic press, and the rotary egg beater.

Although much of your success in contriving the distinguished dish from a ready-to-serve product will depend upon seasoning as well as presentation, it is wise to be light-handed with the spices. A good rule is to add at first when seasoning to taste only about half the amount of seasoning you think will be required, and then, tasting as you go, add bit by bit until the result satisfies you.

Wine is very helpful in glamorizing simple dishes and simple meals, but here, too, it is wise to be cautious as to the amounts used and careful also as to the quality. When improvising your own recipes, add half as much wine as you think you'll need. Taste frequently as you add to be sure the wine will not overpower all other flavors.

Remember that wine is flavoring—that the flavoring is very often one of the least expensive ingredients of the dish as well as the most important one. Perhaps it would be best to forget the term "cooking wine" or "cooking sherry." The wines you use in cooking need not be expensive but they should be well flavored and well made. The same holds true for other liquors—brandy, rum, liqueurs, and cordials. Cooking with wine need not be expensive when you consider how easy it is to open a bottle beforehand, add wine to the sauce, the soup, the stew, or the fish, and drink the rest with dinner.

In a number of instances we have suggested the simple drama of serving ordinary foods flambé, or afire. Too many people feel that such theatrics should be confined to the Christmas pudding or an occasional Cherries Jubilee, but a number of famous restaurateurs have led the procession, and now all manner of foods from appetizers through soups, meats, fish, puddings, and ices acquire a new attractiveness as well as a definite mellowing and blending of flavors by the addition of some type of spirits, which we suggest should be slightly warmed before being set afire.

2

The Quick Gourmet Meal

AND HOW TO PLAN IT

IF METHODS OF COOKING have changed in recent years—and they
have enormously—this change is slight compared to the revolu-
tion in menus. A family dinner as prescribed in the notable *White
House Cookbook* in the early nineteen hundreds consisted of approximately a dozen different items, at least four courses, three
or four different desserts—not including coffee.

Now even for company three courses are considered lavish.
Two-course meals—without an opener—are universally acceptable and in many cases we dine as well at lunch on one main
dish, nibbling at the fruit centerpiece for dessert or content with
"just coffee, please." The planning of the meal is no longer a
problem of "leading up to and away from" the *pièce de résistance*
as it used to be but rather it is a question of combining the right
flavors, colors, textures, as well as getting the proper amount of
nourishment.

Here, as in the planning of the most elaborate meals, the same
basic rules should be observed. First, there must be contrast—
contrast in texture, in color, and in flavor. A smooth and creamy
dish must be served along with something crisp; chicken à la
king, for example, goes well inside a ring of julienne potato
sticks. Crunchy rolls, nuts, carrot sticks, all offer interesting
texture contrast to soft foods. You would not follow creamed
chicken with a creamy dessert. Contrast in color is equally important—green peas, sliced tomato, golden corn—the rich brown
of a grilled lamb chop. A bright green sprinkle of parsley and
lemon slice and chopped egg on black bean soup. The paleness
of pears, a scarlet plum, a vivid apricot, a pale and sunny slice

of pineapple in a fruit compote—such things illustrate the possibilities of color contrasts to provide appetite appeal.

Contrast in flavors is even more important. A bland food requires a piquant accompaniment—a pork chop for example or other rich meat such as ham or goose is at its best with something cool and fruity, such as applesauce or pickled peaches. Sometimes flavor contrasts—sweet and sour, bland and spicy—are combined in a single dish. More often they accompany or follow each other. A hot curry is ringed with rice and served with a number of sharply contrasted accessories—there's cold beer to sip with a hot curry or chili con carne, followed by fresh fruit.

DRAMA AT THE TABLE

If your food is basically good and if you have contrast in texture, color, and flavor, that's more than half the battle. Add drama and you're sure to make yourself a reputation. All of us in our lifetime have eaten honest, nourishing food that is dull as dishwater.

Drama enters not only in your choice of dishes, silverware, and centerpiece but also in the napkins, the tablecloth or mats, the color of the candles, the color and shape of the water glasses. All these things can add tremendously to the enjoyment of a meal.

Use your color sense, your creative imagination, when you buy table linen or mats. Do not be bound to tradition. Dare to dye an old white damask tablecloth a bright shocking pink, a deep leaf green, or a wine red. Have the courage to use a pink plate perhaps on that deep green or red cloth. Consider the possibilities of drapery or curtain material as a tablecloth or runners. If you fear the effect of too much washing on the pattern you might try covering the cloth itself with a clear plastic—but not for formal meals!

Be equally imaginative about the centerpiece. There is no law compelling you to use a brace of candles and a low arrangement of florist flowers. A row of potted geraniums might be far more interesting when you serve a great tureen of party soup. And the centerpiece need not always be dead center. Try the effect of a decorative grouping along one side of the table when there are only three to dinner, or place it at the end of a long buffet.

For those times when you particularly want a meal to be "a

production" you might plan the menu around some particularly effective dish or accessory in your possession. If you have a huge French casserole make it a point to collect several interesting dishes that can be cooked and served en casserole. Is a beautiful salad bowl a prized possession? Make it a habit to include in your menu a number of main dish salads. Perfect your skill as a salad impresario and mix the dressing at the table.

Have you a chafing dish? a crepe suzette pan? a cut-glass punch bowl? Keep them in mind when you begin to think about "what shall we have to eat?" and don't be self-conscious about repeating your specialties or even your menus. Many a fine restaurant and many a clever hostess have built a reputation on a few excellent dishes. If you share the almost universal necessity to be host or hostess as well as cook, learn a few of the tricks of the *métier*. Always allow yourself at least ten minutes alone in the kitchen before dinner is announced. There are various ways whereby guests can be kept happy during this brief interval—with cocktails and canapés or appetizers, television or conversation.

Unless you are exceedingly deft and sure of yourself you may find it wiser to dispense with the first course or to provide one which can properly be set on the table before the guests are called. Make every effort to have by your side either a commodious coffee table or a three-tiered serving table on which extra dishes, accessories, serving spoons, and the like may be set. With a little planning you should be able to arrange matters so that once having sat down to the table you need disappear only once, just before the dessert.

Whether you plan a meal just for yourselves or for company don't attempt too much. Keep it simple—confine your efforts to one or two dishes and make them very, very good.

No matter how simple it is, *never* try out a new dish on a new audience. Even the greatest of chefs has a dress rehearsal before an important dinner.

Serve cold foods cold, chilled foods like salad on plates which have been chilled in the refrigerator, cold drinks preferably in glasses which have been previously filled with ice, frozen desserts on cold plates, too. All this, though it may sound slightly troublesome, is not at all difficult once you become accustomed to the idea. The bowl of salad greens, for example, all washed, dried, and ready for tossing can go into the refrigerator on top of a pile of salad plates. The ice used to chill the glasses can be used later for icing the beverage.

Serve hot foods *hot*. If you have no warming oven (our grandmothers were rather more blessed than we are in this respect what with the old coal range and the warm oven that hung over it), you can use any oven as a warming oven. Keep the temperature somewhere between 150° and 200°—a temperature that should not harm china or silver dishes but will keep plates, serving pieces, coffee and tea cups properly heated. If you are broiling steak or chops and your oven is too hot for the plates, you might use a good-sized top-of-the-stove ovenette such as are sold for baking potatoes, etc. Put an asbestos pad under it and have the heat very low. A steak platter may be warmed on top of the stove on an asbestos pad over a *very* low flame.

To keep your food at its best for second servings it would be wise to invest in some kind of warming equipment. There are a number of inexpensive and attractive warmers on the market on which ordinary serving pieces and casseroles of course may be placed. Most of them use stubby candles—something like votive candles. Ideal, of course, are thermostatically controlled electric warming trays, which come in many sizes.

COMPANY DINNERS

One of the most difficult problems about cooking a meal for guests is that of having everything come out on time—all ready and piping hot or perfectly chilled at the one precise moment when dinner is served. In addition to the hazards of the kitchen you must consider the unpredictability of modern lives. To help the hostess retain her poise we suggest planning the meal around food that can *wait*. Nor need this confine you to the inevitable casserole.

Lamb Chops with Elegance

Liptauer Cheese
(served in the living room)
Baked Lamb Chops Farci
Baby Lima Beans
Sliced Tomatoes Basilica
Sliced Quick-Frozen Peaches with Sherry
Petits Fours
Demitasse

Since the lamb chops are stuffed we have omitted from the menu potatoes or rice.

We have with the lamb green lima beans, and for contrast, there are the bright red tomatoes. As for the dessert, the sliced quick-frozen peaches will be most delicious if they are not entirely thawed, and served with a dash of lemon juice and a bit of sherry or Madeira wine.

Stew with Style

Not merely simple but simply elegant is this menu.

Smoked Salmon with Trimmings and
Canned Sliced Pumpernickel
Beef Stew with Wine
Asparagus with Amandine Sauce
Brown 'n' Serve French Bread
Red Wine
Stewed Figs à la Glacé
Demitasse

Italian with Distinction

With so many ready-to-serve Italian specialties—interesting pastas, prepared sauces, canned ravioli, and quick-frozen pizzas —available, it is easy to plan, on the spur of the moment, a quick meal which would do honor to a proud Italian cook.

Antipasto
(Thin-Sliced Italian Salami, Pickled
Beets, Pimiento, Cole Slaw Topped
with Anchovy Fillets, Sardines, Rad-
ishes, Garlicked Olives, Turkish Spiced
Mushrooms)
Minestra with Pesto
Green Noodles with Meat Sauce
or Alfredo's Noodles or Spaghettini with Meat Balls de Luxe
Tossed Green Salad
Baked Peaches Italienne

SUNDAY BREAKFAST BUFFET

Some people call it brunch and consider it the most modern way to entertain but actually it has classic forebears in the lavish hunt breakfasts of other days. There is no gainsaying the fact that it does offer, especially to the hostess with a weekday job, a unique opportunity to repay social obligations in a leisurely and graceful manner.

Here are two menus. For a large crowd you might combine them—serving two different fruits, hot breads, etc.

I

Large Pitcher of Orange Juice and Melon
Balls, Sliced Bananas, or Sliced Fresh
Pears
Kippers
Potato Balls
Hot Rolls
Assorted Preserves
Plenty of Coffee

II

Exotic Compote
Dried Beef and Mushroom Sauce
Grilled Tomatoes
Sure-Pop Popovers, Coffee Cake
Plenty of Coffee

These menus have the virtue of originality because of the omission of the usual ham or bacon and eggs but these favorites could be added to the buffet or substituted either for kippers or dried beef. Something sweet for dessert is not generally included in a breakfast plan but we have provided a selection of preserves and/or sweet rolls or coffee cake. Large amounts of coffee will be consumed. Be sure to provide at least 2½ cups per person. Instant coffee is a great boon for occasions like this. Make it strong, keep it fiery hot.

FOR IMMEDIATE SERVICE

Certain dishes which actually involve little effort and comparatively little preparation time are often avoided because so many people dread the hazards involved in a dish that must of necessity be served the instant it is ready. However, once you have learned the technique of planning a meal around such a dish you will find many occasions to show off your ability in making a soufflé, for example, or a puffy omelet, a Swiss fondue or a Baked Alaska.

It is easier to manage a meal around a main course soufflé. Just make certain that your guests are seated a minute or two before the soufflé is ready. If you feel that you must have a first course, serve a hearty appetizer in the living room with a cocktail or tomato juice. Make certain that you have all your other food on hand and ready to serve.

> Brandied Liver Pâté with Crusty French
> Bread Served Beforehand
> Neapolitan Cheese Soufflé
> Mixed Green Salad with Fruits
> Chocolate Ice Cream Roll (bought) with
> Chocolate Sauce (canned)

When you serve a soufflé for dessert, it is much better to time it so that the diners instead of the soufflé will be kept waiting for a few minutes. There are two schools of thought in the baking of soufflés. One, the French method, is the quick method in which the oven is quite hot and the soufflé is cooked 20 to 25 minutes. The other method, variously called English or American, substitutes a moderate oven and, in order to slow the cooking even more, it is suggested that the soufflé be placed inside a pan of water.

In our book, we have advised the French method because of the speed and because the quick soufflé, being crisp on the outside and soft in the center, dispenses with the need of an extra sauce. However, if you find that you need an hour or so to eat your dinner, you can put a dessert soufflé into the oven before you sit down and be quite sure of having it ready when the dessert time comes. When your menu is confined to one or two courses and your guests are fairly fast eaters, the 25 minutes allowed by the French-type soufflé should be ample.

In the following menu, we suggest appetizers served in the living room with cocktails.

Ten minutes before the dinner hour excuse yourself and go into the kitchen. It should take you no more than 5 minutes to add the egg whites to a chocolate pudding mixture, which you have already prepared (see page 238), pop the soufflé into the preheated oven. The rest of the menu may include the following:

Paella à la Valenciana
Crusty Rolls
Green Salad with Pimiento Strips
Miracle Chocolate Soufflé with Rum-
Flavored Ready-Whipped Cream
Demitasse

FISH DINNER MENUS

Most people feel that planning a fish dinner presents difficulties. There are, of course, superstitions about certain foods which are presumed not to go with fish but most of these ideas have been proved to be nothing more than superstitions. In making a menu that stars a fish dish, abide by the regular rules. If your fish is rich and fatty, like salmon or swordfish, the accompaniments should not be too hearty. If the fish has a sauce, take care not to include other sauces in the menu. If the fish is bland in flavor, provide extra piquancy—lemon sections, pickles, tartar sauce. If the fish has a great deal of flavor like salt mackerel, provide a bland foil in the way of boiled or baked potato. Observe the usual rules as to color—pale white fish should be accompanied by colorful vegetables. Spinach and beets provide this. Strong-flavored vegetables of the cabbage family tend to overpower the delicacy of fish. Peas are fine but almost too popular. Asparagus is an excellent choice.

Here are two menus suitable for days of abstinence, for no meat or meat extracts are used.

I

Claret Consommé with Lime Slices
Fillet of Perch Baked in Cream
Canned Julienne Potatoes
Green Beans with Mushrooms
Cucumbers in Vinegar
Peach Soufflé Glacé

II

Canned Vegetarian Vegetable Soup
Shad Roe Bonne Femme
Parsleyed Canned Potato Balls
Tossed Green Salad with Diced Beets
and Chopped Eggs, Tart French
Dressing
Apple Snow with Cinnamon Sauce

FESTIVE BUFFET

Although this menu was originally planned as a New Year's
Good Luck Party with a number of traditional New Year's Day
delicacies from several different lands, it is easily adapted for any
festive occasion, and, except for a little help with the dishwash-
ing, you should find it not at all onerous to manage. Provide as
many or as few hors d'oeuvres and appetizers as you feel are
necessary but have them served with cocktails or tomato juice
in the the living-room end of your domain—away from the buffet
table, which should be entirely devoted to solid food:

Ready-to-Serve Smoked Goose or Turkey
Canned Purée of Chestnuts
Buttered Pumpernickel
Buttered Finger Rolls
Cole Slaw in a Cabbage Shell
Sliced Tomatoes with Parsley
Heated Canned Ham Garnished with
Brandied Peaches
Hopping John
Italian Ricotta

Panetone (bought or made from a mix)
Red Wine or St. Louis Glee Wine
Coffee

THANKSGIVING DINNER

A friend whose husband is in television wasn't certain until
the last minute whether or not they would be able to spend
Thanksgiving with her mother in the country. How was she going to prepare for Thanksgiving in their own New York apart-
ment without becoming encumbered with an expensive lot of
perishable foods if they went away? They had almost decided to
solve the problem by eating Thanksgiving dinner bleakly in a
restaurant.

This menu made it possible for them to have on hand everything necessary for a holiday dinner—and precious little which
would go to waste.

Raw Vegetable Hors d'Oeuvres
(celery sticks, raw cauliflower, carrot
sticks, cucumber fingers, radishes, black
olives, green olives)
Rotisserie Roast Turkey, Giblet Gravy
Herb Stuffing (packaged)
Brussels Sprouts and Chestnuts in Mush-
room Sauce
Whole Berry Cranberry Sauce
Sweet Potatoes and Apple en Casserole
New Wave Mince and Pumpkin Pie
Cold Cider

An enormous plateful of raw, crisp vegetables takes the place
of appetizers and salad in this menu. A roast turkey was bought
ready-cooked from a rotisserie (at holiday time, many of these
roasted turkeys are already stuffed, and sold at roadside stands,
supermarkets, and specialty food shops), and stuffed with dressing, made perhaps from a packaged mix. Gravy comes from a
can, enhanced by spices and wine. The Brussels sprouts are
quick-frozen, chestnuts already peeled and cooked in a glass jar
—the sauce made from a can of condensed cream of mushroom

soup. Old-fashioned cranberry sauce with whole berries in it also comes in a can, as do the sweet potatoes and the sliced apples for the casserole. As for the pie, or pies, we suggest buying them at the bakeshop. They will keep admirably in the refrigerator for several days—in the freezer for several weeks.

Wonderful to relate, a Thanksgiving dinner such as this one—even with the scraping and cutting of the vegetables—should not take more than an hour's time, including setting the table!

THE SALAD MEAL

On occasion a hearty salad served generously can provide the main course for an excellent lunch or supper. When planning a meal around a salad, make certain that your salad includes adequate amounts of some stick-to-the-ribs nourishment—eggs, cheese, meat, poultry, or fish. In other words, if you will forgive the inclusion of a bit of nutritional jargon, make certain that there is sufficient *protein* in your salads as well as greens and vegetables or fruits. When such a salad is served with an oil dressing, and with bread, you need have no fears about having a well-balanced meal. Three salad meals follow:

I

Black Bean Soup with Garnishes
Chicken Salad in Tomato Aspic Ring
Hot Biscuits
Mandarins à la Mexico
Cookies

II

Onion Soup or Minestrone with Grated
Cheese
Chef's Salad (made without cheese be-
cause there's cheese with the soup)
Hot French Bread
Quick Crème Caramel with Sliced Peaches
Hot or Iced Tea

III
Petite Marmite Henri IV
Fresh Fruit Salad
Brioches
Coeurs à la Crème
Tea or Coffee

HOT WEATHER MEALS

It is generally conceded that even on the hottest day one hot dish should be included in every meal but the hot food need not necessarily be hearty. It can be a cup of clear hot Madrilène, chicken broth, or just hot tea or coffee. Hot weather food should include plenty of protein foods such as egg, cheese, meat, fish, or poultry. Appearance is particularly important during a hot spell when appetites are inclined to be erratic. When the day is hot serve your most attractive specialties with your prettiest accessories—chill plates and glasses, surround the butter dish with chopped ice. Omit greasy foods. Be careful about candles on the table—they can be extremely heating. On a breathless day choose cool green leaves instead of flowers.

I
Clamdigger Cocktail or Hot Clam Broth
Sliced Beef en Gelée
Tossed Green Salad
Hot Bread
Potato Salad with Chives
Strawberries Romanoff
Demitasse

II
Chicken with White Wine and White
Grapes
Asparagus
Shoestring Potatoes
Fresh Pineapple Royale
Miracle Macaroons
Iced Tea or Coffee

3

EASY AND DRAMATIC
Cocktail Accompaniments
AND APPETIZERS

SHOWCASE—inspiration—source of satisfaction, these party foods, cocktail accompaniments, and before-dinner appetizers are easy to make, delicious, zestfully flavored, and unusual enough to evoke festive feelings, as well as those admiring oh's and ah's and m-m-m's that break the social ice more effectively than many cocktails.

You will find here only a very few canapés or tidbits that are individually concocted and none that require finicky decorating. We suggest rather that your cocktail party guests do most of the work right at the party—and have a fine time doing it!

Any or all of these appetizers may be served before dinner or as party snacks. However, it is a good idea to serve only the simplest appetizers before dinner. The dramatic effects, such as flaming cabbages, and the hot appetizers are most appropriate for parties.

RECIPES

Clamdigger Cocktail
Pink Lady Cup
Tomato Juice Frappé
Brandied Liver Pâté
Smithfield Pâté
Cocktail Cabbage Aflame—
   with Shrimp
Cucumber Canapés
Escargots Bordelaise
Fruit with Prosciutto
Haitian Pâtés de Poulet
Haitian Rissoles
Cocktail Empanadas
International Cheese Board
Liptauer Cheese

Japanese Rumaki
Love Apples Stuffed with
   Tuna Pâté
Mushrooms à la Crème
   George
Sherried Mushrooms
Oyster or Cherrystone Platter
Oysters Herman
Pickled Peas Armenian
Quick Crab Meat Lorenzo
Raw Vegetable Hors
   d'Oeuvres
Red Caviar Pantheon
Smoked Salmon with Trim-
   mings

Clamdigger Cocktail

YOU WILL NEED:
   canned vegetable juice
   clam juice cocktail
   lemon juice (optional)

   vodka (optional)
   lemon or lime

Combine equal parts canned vegetable juice and clam juice cocktail. Or if you like, you may use 1 part vegetable juice, 1 part lemon juice, 1 part clam juice, and 1 part vodka. Mix thoroughly and refrigerate.

AT SERVING TIME:
Pour from silver pitcher into thin goblets filled with shaved ice, or serve on the rocks in Old-Fashioned glasses or small mugs. Garnish with sections or slices of lemon or lime.

Pink Lady Cup

YOU WILL NEED:

canned beet juice
canned carrot juice
buttermilk

crushed ice
seasoned pepper
chives or parsley

Combine 1 cup each of beet and carrot juice with 2 cups buttermilk. Beat or whip in an electric blender with ½ cup coarsely crushed ice. Add salt and seasoned pepper to taste.

AT SERVING TIME:

Serve in chilled cups, sprinkled with chopped chives or parsley.

Tomato Juice Frappé

How dull, how dull tomato juice can be! But when interestingly seasoned, frozen, and imaginatively served, it becomes one of the best beginnings for a meal.

YOU WILL NEED:

canned or quick-frozen
    tomato juice
lemon juice
onion or chives

cayenne pepper or Tabasco
    sauce
parsley or water cress
lemon peel

Season 2 cups of tomato juice with 2 tablespoons lemon juice, 2 tablespoons finely grated or minced onion or chopped chives (with a Mouli grater it's no trick to mince onions exceedingly fine), a few grains of cayenne pepper or 2 or 3 drops of Tabasco sauce. Pour into the freezing tray of your refrigerator and freeze to a mush, about an hour.

AT SERVING TIME:

Spoon into chilled glasses, a footed cocktail or sherry glass preferably, decorate with a topknot of parsley or water cress and a twist of lemon peel. Serve with a demitasse spoon.

Brandied Liver Pâté

Tastes for all the world like one of the homemade pâtés of France.

YOU WILL NEED:

liver pâté	parsley or chives
butter or margarine	Melba toast rounds,
canned chopped mushrooms	pumpernickel, French
brandy or cognac	rolls, or bread sticks

Use equal quantities of canned liver pâté and butter or margarine: a 3-ounce can of liver pâté and 3 ounces, or 6 tablespoons, butter or margarine. Melt the butter in a frying pan and in that melted butter gently brown a 3-ounce can of chopped mushrooms, well drained. Add the liver pâté to the butter and mushrooms and season with 1 tablespoon good brandy or cognac. Mix well and place the mixture in a small but pretty crock. Smooth the top and cover with a generous layer of parsley or chives, finely cut with scissors. Set in the refrigerator for several hours or overnight to blend the flavors.

AT SERVING TIME:

Place the crock in the center of a decorative plate or small platter. Surround with Melba toast rounds, thinly sliced pumpernickel cut into squares, crisp French rolls cut into half-inch slices, or bread sticks. Provide several butter spreaders and let the guests spread their own.

Smithfield Pâté

YOU WILL NEED:

canned minced ham,	butter or margarine
Smithfield ham, or	mustard or mustard pickle
deviled ham spread	India relish or gherkins

With a wooden spoon in a small bowl, combine 1 can minced ham, Smithfield ham, or deviled ham with an equal quantity of butter or margarine—that is, a 3-ounce can minced ham to 3 ounces, or 6 tablespoons, butter or margarine—till smooth and very well blended. Taste the butter and ham mixture before adding extra seasonings. Various brands are variously spiced. Most of these ham spreads or mixtures, however, will be considerably enhanced by the addition of prepared mustard. We use 1 teaspoon Dijon mustard or other mild mustard to 2 teaspoons chopped mustard chow-chow pickles for the 3-ounce can of ham. Place the mixture in a small crock or casserole and set in the refrigerator several hours or overnight, to blend and mellow the flavors.

AT SERVING TIME:
Cover the top of the pâté with a thin layer of well-drained chopped India relish or thinly sliced gherkins. Place the crock on a large decorative plate or platter. Surround with finger lengths of whole wheat or rye bread, bread sticks, or crisp French bread or rolls, cut into half-inch slices.

Cocktail Cabbage Aflame—with Shrimp

If you would like to have a dramatic appetizer at cocktail time, try this.

YOU WILL NEED:

red cabbage
canned or quick-frozen
   cooked shrimp
olive oil

lemon or lime juice or
   vinegar
garlic
curry powder
sour cream

Choose the prettiest cabbage you can find, preferably one with large, loose outer leaves. Cut the stem end so that the cabbage will sit firmly on the platter or plate. Turn back the outside leaves like the petals of a great rose. With a very sharp knife, scoop a round hole out of the top of the cabbage just large enough to hold a can of Sterno.

Drain canned or quick-frozen cooked shrimp. If the black line around the edge of the shrimp has not been removed, take it out with a sharp paring knife. Cover the shrimp with French dressing made by combining 4 parts olive oil with 1 part lemon or lime juice or vinegar; season with plenty of salt and pepper; add 1 clove of garlic, thoroughly crushed. Let shrimp stand, covered by the French dressing, for several hours or overnight. Prepare a dipping sauce by adding ½ teaspoon curry powder to 1 cup sour cream.

AT SERVING TIME:

Drain shrimp, spear with toothpicks, and stud the cabbage with the shrimp. Light the Sterno and allow guests to heat the shrimp over the flame. Some like the shrimp cold, some like it hot. Everybody will enjoy the curried sour-cream sauce.

Cucumber Canapés

Almost any spread for bread or a cracker will take on a special zest when piled on top of a crisp slice of cucumber. Unless the cucumber has a tough skin it's better not to peel it. It looks prettier and the slice has more body.

YOU WILL NEED:

tender young cucumber	paprika
cream cheese or cottage cheese	chives, parsley, or sweet red peppers
horse-radish or Worcestershire sauce	

Cut the cucumber in slices about ¼ inch thick. Since cucumbers become limp on standing, it is best not to slice them too far ahead of time. Top each slice with a cocktail spread of cream cheese, seasoned with horse-radish or Worcestershire sauce, or creamed cottage cheese, mixed with chopped chives or parsley.

AT SERVING TIME:
Arrange on a plate and sprinke with paprika, chopped chives, chopped parsley, or finely chopped sweet red peppers.

Escargots Bordelaise

Escargots now come packaged in all supermarkets and most groceries. The shells, bleached ready to use, usually come about 18 to a see-through tube, which sits upon a can of snails. Put together with a garlicky sauce, they make a wondrously delicious appetizer. Figure on 6 for an appetizer, 9 to 12 as entree.

YOU WILL NEED:

shallots or scallions	dry white wine
garlic	chopped parsley
butter	packaged escargots

Finely chop 2 shallots or scallions and 2 cloves of garlic. Soften in 5 tablespoons butter. Add 3 tablespoons each dry white wine and chopped parsley, ¼ teaspoon salt, pinch pepper. Cook together 1 minute. Put some sauce and then a snail in each shell. Return escargots to remaining sauce and heat 3 to 4 minutes. Serves 2.

AT SERVING TIME:
Arrange each portion of escargots on a small plate, and serve with fresh, crusty French bread to dip up the last bit of sauce.

Fruit with Prosciutto

The combination of melon with prosciutto has been done to death, but the idea is delightful if you bear in mind that many other fruits, fresh or canned, can be substituted for the melon; other meats, sliced paper-thin, can play the role of the prosciutto. We suggest below. Then let your imagination rove.

YOU WILL NEED:

canned mangoes, papayas,	paper-thin slices of
pineapple fingers,	prosciutto, salami,
cantaloupe or honeydew	cervelat, pressed chicken
melon, or fresh bananas	or turkey
(dipped in lemon juice)	fresh coriander or tarragon

Wrap each piece of fruit in a slice of meat and secure with a toothpick. (The bananas should be cut in wedges.)

AT SERVING TIME:

Arrange the meat-wrapped morsels on a large, attractive plate. Sprinkle or garnish with sprigs or bits of fresh coriander or tarragon. Pass the pepper grinder. If you wish to serve fruit and prosciutto (or its stand-ins) as a first course, simply lay the meat over, or beside, the fruit in an attractive arrangement.

Haitian Pâtés de Poulet

We first tasted these delightful tidbits at a reception in the presidential palace at Port-au-Prince in Haiti. I have served them to Haitian diplomats in New York who asked for the recipe to take back home to the islands.

While you are at it, why not make up a quantity and pack them for freezing with 2 sheets of waxed paper between the layers?

YOU WILL NEED:

packaged piecrust mix	pimiento-stuffed olives
sliced white bread	parsley
milk	rosemary
minced chicken pâté	ginger
garlic	lemon juice
onion	Tabasco sauce

To make 45 to 50 cocktail pâtés, prepare 2 packages piecrust according to directions. Roll and cut into 2-inch squares.

To make the filling, soften 6 slices white bread momentarily in ½ cup milk. Squeeze out and place in a bowl along with two 4-ounce cans minced chicken pâté. Season with 1 clove garlic and ¼ small onion finely crushed; add ¼ cup coarsely chopped pimiento-stuffed olives, 1 tablespoon chopped parsley, ¼ teaspoon powdered rosemary, ⅛ teaspoon ginger, 1 tablespoon lemon juice, 2 or 3 dashes of Tabasco sauce, and salt and pepper to suit your taste. Mix thoroughly. Place a scant teaspoonful of this mixture slightly to one side of each square. Fold into triangles; crimp edges with a fork. Pack for freezing or bake immediately about 10 minutes in a moderately hot oven, 375° F. If pâtés are frozen, the time will be a little longer.

AT SERVING TIME:
The pâtés should be served—and kept—piping hot.

VARIATION: Haitian Rissoles
The same mixture and method can be used to make rissoles or turnovers that are delicious for luncheon or supper. For rissoles the pastry should be cut into 4-inch squares. Use a scant tablespoon of the mixture on each square. For a high glaze, brush pâtés before baking with a little cream or beaten egg. Recipe makes 15 to 20.

Cocktail Empanadas

Instead of using minced chicken pâté as in the above recipe, use 2 cans of deviled ham pâté and flavor with 2 teaspoons cumin seed, 1 clove garlic crushed, 1 tablespoon chili sauce.

International Cheese Board

The easiest, most talked about party I ever gave featured cheeses of many lands, set on a cheese board and platters, decorated with green leaves and tiny flags of the countries in which the various cheeses originated. Even in a middle-sized town, you will find cheeses from a number of different countries, in delicatessens, large markets, or department stores with a food department, or you can order them shipped to you by mail.

YOU WILL NEED:
a selection of cheeses   flags
various breads and crackers

An international cheese board—like any other cheese board—
should include cheeses of contrasting colors, flavors, textures—
for instance, creamy white cheese, yellow cheese, hard and soft
cheeses, mellow and sharp.

From France: there are Brie, Camembert, and the more unusual
   Fromage de Foin (cheese of hay), which is actually ripened
   in freshly cut hay and retains that wonderful new-mown hay
   fragrance; Coulommiers, rather like Brie, soft, mellow, and
   easy to spread.
From Italy: Gorgonzola, Bel Paese, Melfino, and Provolone.
From Sweden: Kummel cheese, flecked with caraway; Crème
   Chantilly; Bandost.
From Norway: the famous Gjetost, dark brown goat cheese, made
   with malt; Nokkelost, a Gouda type, studded surprisingly
   with whole cloves.
From Denmark: Danish Bleu and Tilsiter.
From Turkey: Kajmak, soft and mellow, and Kasher Penner, a
   hard, white cheese.
Holland has: Edam, Gouda, and Geheimrath, semi-hard, of a
   deep, golden yellow color.
Greece has: Pheta, often spelled Feta, a snowy white cheese, with
   the salt flavor of the brine in which it is packed.
Portugal: famous for Saloi, a type of hard cheese which comes
   from Lisbon.
From Brazil: pepper cheese.
From England: Cheddar and Stilton.

And don't forget the famous American sharp Cheddar cheese!

AT SERVING TIME:
Arrange the cheeses on a board or platters—a pastry board will
do very well, especially if you cover it with huckleberry leaves,
being sure to leave space around the cheese for cutting. Set the
appropriate flag in each piece of cheese; and if the cheeses are

quite unusual, you might take a moment to write out a card and set it beside the cheese. Be sure to have on hand plenty of knives and spreaders. Provide two or three baskets or plates of bread stuffs. Particularly good with cheeses are: thin, black pumpernickel cut into 2-inch squares; crusty French rolls, cut into half-inch slices; bread sticks, broken into 3-inch pieces; lightly toasted water biscuits; plain, crisp crackers; Melba toast. Bread or crackers should not be too highly or definitely seasoned, but should rather provide a background for the flavors of the cheese.

Liptauer Cheese

This is one of the glories of Budapest, made quickly and easily. Paprika, caraway seeds, and anchovy paste lend color and flavor.

YOU WILL NEED:

cream cheese	caraway seeds
butter or margarine	onion, shallot, or chives
capers	pumpernickel, whole-wheat
paprika	Melba toast, or onion or
anchovy paste	poppy-seed rolls

With a wooden spoon, combine equal quantities cream cheese and butter or margarine: a 3-ounce package of cream cheese to 3 ounces or 6 tablespoons butter. Add 1 teaspoon capers, 1 teaspoon paprika, ½ teaspoon anchovy paste, ½ teaspoon caraway seeds, 1 tablespoon very finely chopped onion, shallot, or chives. Salt and pepper to taste. Press into a small bowl or mold, or form into a roll and wrap in waxed paper or aluminum foil. Place in the refrigerator for several hours to mellow and blend.

AT SERVING TIME:

Set the mold or roll in the center of a plate. Surround with thinly sliced pumpernickel, cut into finger lengths or squares, whole-wheat Melba toast, or even more authentically, serve onion rolls or poppy-seed rolls from a foreign bakeshop or delicatessen, cut into small pieces. Provide plenty of spreaders and let each person spread his own.

Japanese Rumaki

A come-back-for-more appetizer that combines chicken livers, crunchy water chestnuts, and crisp bacon for a succulent mouthful.

YOU WILL NEED:

chicken livers   canned water chestnuts
soy sauce   sliced raw bacon

Cut chicken livers into halves or large chunks. Brush with soy sauce. Drain and wash canned water chestnuts in cold water and cut in halves. Place chicken liver and chestnut half close together. Wrap in bacon strip. Secure each little bundle with a toothpick that has been soaked in water so that it does not catch fire. Broil until bacon is crisp.

AT SERVING TIME:

If you're giving a cocktail party, quantities of these can be made up ahead of time and stored in the refrigerator on broiling foil, ready to pop under the fire. Make lots, for they'll go fast. After they're broiled, transfer to a large serving platter and pass happily. The toothpick serves as a pick-up aid.

Love Apples Stuffed with Tuna Pâté

These delicious little tidbits make a colorful addition to the hors d'oeuvres tray.

YOU WILL NEED:

cherry tomatoes   mayonnaise
canned chunk tuna   chopped parsley
grated onion

Wash cherry tomatoes and hollow out stem, with sharp knife, leaving shell. Drain well a 6-ounce can chunk tuna. Add 1 small onion, finely grated. Mix in enough mayonnaise to form a smooth pâté. Stuff pâté into cherry tomato shells. Chill well.

AT SERVING TIME:
Dip tops of stuffed tomatoes into shallow dish of finely chopped parsley, and place on serving tray.

Mushrooms à la Crème George

Sheer elegance in a silver chafing dish. Marvelous as an appetizer. Excellent for luncheon. Created at Gallatin's restaurant in Monterey, California.

YOU WILL NEED:

canned button mushrooms	sherry
canned mushroom stems and pieces	grated Parmesan cheese
	sour cream
butter	

Sauté 1 can each of button mushrooms and mushroom stems and pieces (drained) in 2 tablespoons butter for 2 minutes. Add 2 tablespoons dry sherry and cook for another minute. Add 1 cup grated Parmesan cheese, 1 cup commercial sour cream, salt and freshly ground pepper to taste. Cook until good and thick. (If sauce becomes too thick for your taste, dilute with a little of the liquor from mushrooms.)

AT SERVING TIME:
Serve on or with toast. Serves 4.

Sherried Mushrooms

YOU WILL NEED:

canned whole mushrooms	Tabasco sauce (optional)
pale dry sherry	
almonds, hazel nuts, cream cheese (optional)	

Drain whole canned mushrooms. Put them into a small bowl and cover with pale dry sherry. Leave them in the refrigerator for several hours or overnight.

AT SERVING TIME:

Bring out the mushrooms in their bowl of wine, provide your guests with toothpicks, and allow them to spear the mushrooms.

You may also drain the mushrooms and fill each little cup with a bit of salted almond, a hazel nut, or a tiny ball of cream cheese seasoned with salt, freshly ground black pepper, or a few drops of Tabasco.

Oyster or Cherrystone Platter

Informal, gay, and very tempting is an enormous plate of iced clams or oysters on the half shell. A fine thing to serve with beer or cocktails.

YOU WILL NEED:

clams or oysters	prepared horse-radish
lemon	sea food cocktail sauce
water cress or green leaves	oysterette crackers
Tabasco sauce	

Count on 6 clams or 4 oysters per person. Unless you have special skill and equipment, it's best to cajole your market man into opening the clams or oysters for you. This should not be done too long ahead of time.

AT SERVING TIME:

On a large platter or deep tray with a rim, arrange the clams or oysters in their shells, tuck nosegays of water cress or green leaves here and there, and make a border of lemon wedges. Provide a number of cocktail forks for those who want them. Most people will take their clams right out of the shell. Plenty of small paper napkins are necessary. The fixings, i.e., Tabasco sauce, cocktail sauces, etc., should go on a separate tray, and there should be several small baskets or bowls of oysterette crackers.

Oysters Herman

Chef Herman Walker, of Ye Olde College Inn in Houston, Texas, gave his name to these crunchy fried oysters, so rich that only 3 make an hors d'oeuvre portion. Chef Herman uses fresh oysters from Bayou Cook; we use canned.

YOU WILL NEED:

canned oysters	lemon juice
flour	A-1 sauce
salad oil	Worcestershire sauce
butter	sherry or Madeira wine

Drain canned oysters. Roll each oyster separately in flour, or toss in a paper bag in which flour has been placed. Lightly butter a pancake griddle or heavy skillet and cook the oysters first on one side, then on the other, until they are lightly browned and just a little crisp. To induce this desired crispness, sprinkle the oysters with a little melted butter or a few drops of salad oil while they are cooking.

Meanwhile, combine 2 tablespoons melted butter with ¼ cup lemon juice, 1 cup A-1 sauce, 2 tablespoons Worcestershire sauce, 1 tablespoon sherry or Madeira wine. Heat thoroughly but do not allow to come to a boil. Blend 2 tablespoons flour into 3 tablespoons water and stir into the sauce. Cook until thickened.

AT SERVING TIME:

Place the freshly grilled oysters on a hot serving dish. Insert frilled toothpicks. Surround with the heated sauce. Sauce can be saved, reheated, and used again.

Pickled Peas Armenian

An Armenian appetizer, spicy and unusual.

YOU WILL NEED:

canned black-eyed peas	garlic
salad oil	onion
wine vinegar	Melba toast or toast fingers

Drain liquid from 2 No. 303 cans black-eyed peas. Place peas in bowl. Add 1 cup salad oil, ¼ cup wine vinegar, 1 clove garlic (whole), ¼ cup thinly sliced onion, ½ teaspoon salt, and freshly ground black pepper. Mix thoroughly. Store in jar in your refrigerator and remove garlic bud after 1 day. Store 2 days more, to allow flavors to mingle. Yields 1 quart.

AT SERVING TIME:
Serve individual portions: a couple of tablespoons on each small plate, accompanied by Melba toast or buttered toast fingers. Or place in a large bowl on a buffet, and let guests help themselves.

Quick Crab Meat Lorenzo

Canned or quick-frozen cooked crab meat mixed with undiluted cream of mushroom soup makes a quick and easy version of one of the world's most famous canapés.

YOU WILL NEED:

cooked crab meat	lemon juice or sherry wine
condensed cream of	butter
mushroom soup	Melba toast
cayenne	grated cheese

Flake and separate 1 cup of crab meat. If there are any large hunks, crumble them. Remove gristle. Moisten with 4 or 5 tablespoons condensed cream of mushroom soup, dipping the soup right out of the can without diluting it. The mixture should be quite thick—thick enough to drop in blobs from a teaspoon. Season with a few grains of cayenne pepper, 1 teaspoon lemon juice or sherry. Brush 1½-inch pieces of Melba toast with melted butter, pile mixture on toast, sprinkle with grated cheese and set in a hot oven, 375° F., just long enough to brown. Makes 20 canapés.

AT SERVING TIME:
Pass the canapés as soon as they are out of the oven. If the browning is done on a heatproof platter that can go into the oven and to the table, all the better!

Raw Vegetable Hors d'Oeuvres

These are a boon to all who must watch their calories or their diets. Hors d'oeuvres made of raw vegetables can be a joy to the epicure, and a treat to the eye as well as the palate. Only the freshest and most perfect vegetables should be used. They should always be crisp, cold, and arranged with an eye to color and design.

For many years a famous New York restaurant has made a specialty of serving raw vegetables in a shiny black bowl filled with crushed ice. A bouquet of celery and finochio is set in the center of the ice; radishes, carrot sticks, black and green olives are set on top of the ice, covering it completely. It is an idea worth copying.

Red Caviar Pantheon

At the Pantheon Restaurant near Broadway, New York's theatrical and literary gourmets feast on the culinary glories of Greece. One of the most popular is this appetizer.

YOU WILL NEED:

red caviar	lemon juice
onion	olive oil
French or Italian bread	

To a half-pound jar of red caviar, add 1 finely chopped onion and stir with a wooden spoon till it looks milky. Cut a loaf of crusty French or Italian bread into hunks. Remove the soft insides, soften in water, and squeeze dry. Add this and the juice of 3 lemons to the caviar, mash, and stir well. Little by little, add olive oil until the mixture is a pale rose color, light and spreadable. This may be done by hand, or in an electric mixer or blender.

AT SERVING TIME:

Heap into a bowl or pile in the center of a plate and surround with black olives, small wedges of iceberg lettuce, and radishes. Serve small chunks of crisp French bread or rolls in a basket and provide plenty of spreaders for your guests. The crusts of the bread used in making the mixture may be used but be sure to trim them so that they look attractive. Serve them in a pretty bowl or basket.

Smoked Salmon with Trimmings

Whether it's lox from the corner delicatessen or smoked salmon
from Nova Scotia or Sweden, here is an elegant way to serve it—
borrowed from "21," New York's notable restaurant.

YOU WILL NEED:

toasted white bread, toasted rye bread, or thin pumpernickel	thinly sliced smoked salmon olive oil pepper in a grinder

For each person provide a thin slice of toasted white bread with
the crust removed. (Toasted rye bread or thin dark pumpernickel, untoasted, is preferred by some gourmets.) This is all
the advance preparation needed.

AT SERVING TIME:

Place one of your prettiest napkins on a plate, arrange the toast
on the napkin, covering it to keep it warm. Pass toast along with
a small platter of well-chilled, thinly sliced salmon. Have on the
coffee table a pepper grinder and a tiny bottle of the very best
olive oil. Each person lays his salmon on the toast, pours on a
golden dribble of olive oil, adds a grind of fresh black pepper.
This salmon ceremony is most appropriate when you're serving
cocktails to a small group around the coffee table.

4

Delicious and Unusual Soups

EVER SINCE ESAU sold his birthright to his brother Jacob for a bowl of savory pottage, which was undoubtedly lentil soup—soup has been one of the mainstays of good eating.

Today, canned soups are probably the most popular and among the finest of ready-to-serve foods. According to recent surveys, a can of soup is America's favorite hot dish for lunch. At the evening meal, it is not only the introduction but often the main course—a most satisfying main course, too, when the soup is hearty and served over toast, crackers, or with rice.

Moreover a fine, thick soup or chowder, served dramatically from a tureen, bowl, casserole, or chafing dish becomes the *pièce de résistance* for informal company meals, or even on the buffet. After years of sampling canned soups in all price ranges, it is a joy to be able to report that the most readily available popular-priced brands are usually the best soups. Since they are intended to appeal to millions of people, they cannot be distinctively seasoned. But this allows plenty of leeway for your imagination.

Always correct the seasoning after the soup has been heated, or just before it goes to the table if it's a cold soup, because heating or mellowing brings out certain flavors, suppresses others. When using herbs or spices, don't be too lavish at first—you can always add more! A quarter of a teaspoon of dried herbs should be enough to impart a subtle flavoring to a can of soup, 3 or 4 portions. It's a pretty good rule of thumb to use three times as much of fresh herbs as dried.

In many of these recipes, wine has been substituted for part of the required milk or water. Here again, you may step up the proportion of wine, but be sure to taste as you go. You don't want your soup to taste like an alcoholic beverage!

The manner in which you serve soup is important. In most cases we have suggested that you bring it to the table in a tureen or casserole and ladle the hot soup into *heated* soup plates or bowls. This is no mere conceit. There is all the difference in the world between a really hot, *hot* soup and one that is wanly lukewarm. To heat plates or bowls, place them in the warming oven or a heated and turned-off regular oven, where the temperature is about 150° F. This amount of heat will not harm even the finest china.

In many cases we have suggested that garnishes be added to the soup as it is served at the table. Sometimes a small decanter of wine is passed so it may be added according to individual fancy.

RECIPES

Apple and Celery Vichyssoise

YOU WILL NEED:

frozen condensed cream of
   potato soup
milk or light cream and
   milk
hot pepper sauce

lemon juice
pascal celery
apples
chopped chives (optional)

To 2 (10½-ounce) cans frozen condensed cream of potato soup add 2½ cups milk, or 1¼ cups each of light cream and milk, ⅛ teaspoon hot pepper sauce, and 1 teaspoon lemon juice. Whir in blender or mix with rotary beater.

AT SERVING TIME:
Serve in chilled cups garnished with circles of pascal (green) celery and very thin slices of unpeeled red apples cut into quarters. A sprinkling of chopped chives is optional. Makes 6 portions.

Bisque with Black Walnuts

YOU WILL NEED:

canned tomato bisque
canned black walnuts

whipped cream

Make up a can of tomato bisque. Follow the directions on the can but add 4 tablespoons finely chopped black walnuts (also from a can). Simmer gently about 15 minutes.

AT SERVING TIME:
Serve with little blobs of salted whipped cream.

Black Bean Soup Guatemala

A garnish of avocado slices adds a Latin-American look and flavor to a glorified black bean soup.

YOU WILL NEED:

condensed black bean soup   lemon or lime
meat extract   hard-cooked egg
Kitchen Bouquet   chives or parsley
onion juice   pepper sauce or Tabasco
sherry or Madeira wine   (optional)
avocado

To a can of condensed black bean soup, add 1 can water, 1 teaspoon meat extract, 1 teaspoon Kitchen Bouquet, 1 teaspoon onion juice. Simmer for a few minutes, and just before taking off the fire, add 2 to 4 tablespoons sherry or Madeira wine. Do not boil after adding wine.

AT SERVING TIME:

Serve from a tureen or bowl, ladling the soup into heated bowls or soup plates, pass the garnishes, which should include very thin slices of avocado, slices of lemon or lime, sliced or chopped hard-cooked egg, chopped chives or parsley, and, if you like, pass around a tiny bottle of pepper sauce or Tabasco. To keep avocado slices from turning dark, brush or sprinkle with lemon or lime juice.

Borsch with Boiled Potatoes Polonaise

An excellent prepared borsch is available in many parts of the country. Served with boiled potatoes (canned or homemade), this soup makes a fine meal all by itself.

YOU WILL NEED:

canned borsch   potatoes
onion   rye bread or pumpernickel
bay leaf (optional)   sour cream

To a jar or can of borsch, add 1 small onion, finely chopped, and a bit of bay leaf if desired. Simmer a few minutes until the onion is very soft.

AT SERVING TIME:
Place a small boiled potato or 2 or 3 well-heated canned Irish potatoes in each plate, ladle the hot borsch over the potatoes and garnish with a large spoonful of sour cream. Heated rye bread or pumpernickel is the ideal accompaniment.

Cold Borsch Polonaise

A jar of prepared borsch can be served in the style of the Polish nobility if a few simple ingredients are added.

YOU WILL NEED:

canned borsch	canned shrimp or salmon
sour cream	(optional)
eggs	fresh dill (optional)
cucumber or dill pickles	

To a quart of ice-cold borsch add 1 cup sour cream.

AT SERVING TIME:
Present the soup frosty cold in a tureen or bowl. Have ready a plate on which you have arranged sliced or quartered hard-cooked eggs, sliced cucumber or dill pickles, well-drained canned shrimp or salmon in small hunks. Place a little of each of the garnishes in the soup plate and ladle the soup over the garnishes. A tiny frond of fresh dill adds a pretty look and an excellent flavor. Don't use too much dill; the flavor is *so* definite.

Small Town Borsch

If your own corner store does not carry canned borsch, you can easily make up your own in a few minutes from the most ordinary kind of ingredients.

YOU WILL NEED:

consommé	vinegar or lemon juice
canned beets	sugar
cabbage	potatoes
onions	sour cream

Combine 2 cans consommé, 2 cans water; add 1 cup canned cut-up or shredded beets, 4 tablespoons beet juice, 1 cup coarsely chopped fresh cabbage, 2 onions, sliced or coarsely chopped, 2 tablespoons vinegar or lemon juice, 1 teaspoon sugar. Cook all together until cabbage is just tender. Do not strain.

AT SERVING TIME:
Ladle into bowls, add half of a boiled potato or a couple of canned whole Irish potatoes to each serving, top with a large spoonful of thick sour cream.

Bouillabaisse

This is a simplified but delicious version of the great fish specialty of Marseilles, which has inspired poets, dazzled gourmets, delighted eaters all over the world. Every single one of the ingredients can be kept on hand on the pantry shelf or in the freezer.

YOU WILL NEED:

onions	canned oysters, clams, or
garlic	mussels (optional)
leeks	canned or quick-frozen
olive oil	cooked shrimp, crab, or
quick-frozen flounder,	lobster meat, or rock
whiting, sole, haddock,	lobster tails
perch, whitefish, or a	canned pimiento (optional)
combination	saffron
canned tomatoes	lemon juice or white wine
bay leaf	French bread
	parsley

Cook 2 medium-sized onions, thinly sliced, 1 or 2 crushed garlic cloves, and 2 sliced leeks in ½ cup olive oil until golden brown. If you can't get leeks in your market, use more onion. Thaw 3 pounds of quick-frozen fish fillets just enough to cut into serving pieces. Add pieces of fish along with 1 cup canned tomatoes, 1 bay leaf, 2 cups water. Simmer about 15 minutes. Add 1 cup oysters, clams, or mussels (these may be omitted, if desired), and 1 cup shrimp, crab meat, or lobster, ½ cup canned pimiento, cut into small pieces. Season with ½ teaspoon saffron, salt, pepper, and the juice of 1 lemon and/or 1 cup white table wine. Heat but do not boil.

AT SERVING TIME:
Bring to the table in a tureen or casserole. Some people pour off the broth, arrange the fish on a platter and combine them once again in the serving dish, but this seems like too much trouble. Place a thick slice of French bread in each soup plate or bowl, spoon the bouillabaisse (fish and broth) on top of the bread, and sprinkle with chopped parsley. This makes 8 servings. Served with a salad and with fruit and cheese for dessert, it's a magnificent meal.

Chicken and Water-Cress Soup, Mandarin Style

A package of dehydrated, or a can of, chicken noodle soup combines with fresh water cress to make a soup with Oriental overtones.

YOU WILL NEED:

canned or dehydrated chicken noodle soup	egg
water cress	butter or margarine or chicken bouillon cube

Make up a package of dehydrated chicken noodle soup according to package directions, or use a can of chicken noodle soup. Simmer to blend all flavors. For extra richness add 1 tablespoon butter or margarine or 1 chicken bouillon cube. Take off the fire, add 1 cup (a large handful) of water cress, leaves and tender sprigs, put the cover on the soup and allow to set in a warm place for about a minute or two, just long enough to wilt the water cress.

AT SERVING TIME:
Ladle into bowls or plates and garnish, if desired, with slices or quarters of hard-cooked egg.

Cream of Chicken Soup Amandine

Almonds, sherry, a beaten egg, and a magical touch of mace transform a popular canned soup into a Viennese specialty.

YOU WILL NEED:

condensed cream of chicken   light cream
  soup   dry sherry
milk or water   almonds
mace   parsley
egg

To a can of condensed cream of chicken soup add 1 can milk or water, add ¼ teaspoon mace, heat over a gentle fire for a few minutes. In the bottom of a tureen or serving bowl, which you plan to take to the table, beat 1 raw egg—it's traditional to use a silver fork—add to the egg a tablespoon of light cream and pour the hot soup slowly onto the egg, stirring vigorously so that the egg does not curdle.

AT SERVING TIME:
Add 2 or 3 tablespoons of sherry. Serve in heated soup cups or plates and garnish with salted almonds, coarsely chopped, and a light sprinkle of parsley.

Cream of Chicken with White Wine and Chestnuts

Chestnuts have always been the gourmet cook's delight, but rather troublesome to shell, blanch, and prepare. They are now available in jars, ready to use. Here they are used as a delightful garnish for a chicken soup.

YOU WILL NEED:

condensed cream of   white wine
  chicken soup   paprika (optional)
milk or water   orange peel
canned cooked chestnuts

Heat but do not boil 1 can condensed cream of chicken soup, ½ can milk or water, ½ can white table wine, ½ cup canned cooked chestnuts, cut into small pieces. If desired, ½ teaspoon paprika may be added to this soup to give it a rosy color.

AT SERVING TIME:
Ladle into heated soup plates and garnish with a twist of orange peel.

New Orleans Chicken Gumbo with Rice

A bit of herb seasoning and a spoonful of rice served in the plate transform a more or less usual soup into a memorable dish.

YOU WILL NEED:

condensed chicken gumbo soup	cayenne pepper or Tabasco sauce
parsley	cooked rice
marjoram	French bread or bread sticks

To a can of condensed chicken gumbo soup, 1 can of water, add 1 tablespoon fresh-chopped parsley, ¼ teaspoon marjoram, a few grains of cayenne pepper or 1 or 2 drops of Tabasco sauce, salt if needed, and a few grindings of black pepper from the pepper mill. Simmer for a few minutes.

AT SERVING TIME:
Bring to the table in a tureen or bowl. Place a large spoonful of cooked rice—white, wild, or brown rice—in the center of a heated soup plate and ladle the soup over this. French bread or bread sticks are particularly good with this soup.

Chilled Clam Broth with Cucumbers

A delightful warm-weather soup with an unusual garnish.

YOU WILL NEED:
- bottled clam juice
- canned vegetable juice
  cocktail
- Tabasco sauce
- crushed ice
- cucumber

Combine equal parts icy cold clam juice and very cold canned vegetable juice cocktail, season with a little extra salt and pepper, if desired, and a few drops of Tabasco sauce.

AT SERVING TIME:

Serve in a glass or china cup or bowl, adding to each portion a spoonful of crushed ice and a spoonful of finely cut, unpeeled cucumber.

NOTE:

If you have no ice-crushing machine you can crush ice cubes by placing them in a small canvas bag and hitting several times with a hammer or any other heavy object.

Chilled Senegalese Soup

YOU WILL NEED:
- apple
- celery
- onion
- butter
- curry powder
- flour
- canned chicken or beef
  broth
- light cream

Peel and dice a small apple, a stalk of celery, and an onion. Lightly gild in 2 tablespoons butter. Add ½ tablespoon each of curry powder and flour. Cook 5 minutes. Add 1 quart chicken or beef broth. Cook 15 minutes longer. Strain. Add 1 cup light cream. Serves 3 or 4.

AT SERVING TIME:

Garnish with white meat of chicken cut into fine strips and bits of raw apple, if desired, and serve hot or cold.

Claret Consommé with Lime Slices

A few drops of red coloring add a great deal to the appearance of this clear soup, which may be served hot or jellied.

YOU WILL NEED:
condensed consommé
claret wine
red vegetable coloring
  (optional)

lime, lemon, or orange
whole cloves

To a can of condensed consommé add ½ can water, ½ can claret wine. To give a deep glowing red to soup, add also a couple of drops of red vegetable coloring. Simmer a few minutes to blend the flavors, but do not boil.

AT SERVING TIME:
Serve in heated cups or soup plates and garnish with slices of lime, lemon, or orange, studded with whole cloves. A perfect soup for your company dinner!

Consommé à la Souveraine

A double consommé, flavored with a little sherry.

YOU WILL NEED:
canned consommé
sherry

seedless white Thompson
grapes

To 1 can undiluted condensed consommé add 2 tablespoons sherry.

AT SERVING TIME:
Serve in demitasse cups garnished with a spoonful of seedless white Thompson grapes.

Manhattan Clam Chowder

Most of the popular brands of canned clam chowder are made with tomato rather than milk. Hence, by definition they are Manhattan clam chowder. A garnish of green pepper rings and caraway seeds adds distinction to them.

YOU WILL NEED:
clam chowder	green pepper
bacon fat or butter	onion
(optional)	caraway seeds

Add 1 can water to 1 can condensed Manhattan-style clam chowder; 1 tablespoon bacon fat or butter may be added if a richer flavor is desired. Bring to a boil and simmer a few minutes.

AT SERVING TIME:
Ladle into heated bowls or soup plates and garnish with green pepper rings, thinly sliced onion rings, and/or a scatter of caraway seeds.

New England Clam Chowder

When milk is used in place of tomato, the chowder becomes New England style and is much admired Down East. White table wine may be substituted for part of the milk.

YOU WILL NEED:
condensed clam chowder	pilot crackers
milk	paprika, chives, or parsley
dry white wine (optional)	

To 1 can condensed clam chowder add 1 can milk, or $\frac{1}{2}$ can milk and $\frac{1}{2}$ can dry white wine. Heat but do not boil.

AT SERVING TIME:
Place a pilot cracker in the bottom of a heated bowl or soup plate, ladle the chowder over the cracker and sprinkle with paprika, chopped chives, or parsley.

Old-Fashioned Bacon and Corn Chowder

When you can't think of a thing you want to eat for lunch or supper, this modern version of an old-time favorite will surely tempt you. Modern households are more likely to have bacon on hand than the salt pork called for in older recipes, so we've used bacon.

YOU WILL NEED:

bacon	Worcestershire sauce
onion	butter
boiled potatoes	paprika
cream-style corn	parsley
milk	crackers

With a pair of scissors or sharp knife cut 6 slices of bacon into small pieces and fry. Leave the bacon bits and the fat in the pan, adding to it 1 medium-sized onion, thinly sliced. Cook 5 minutes over a low flame, stirring often so that the onion does not burn. Add 2 cups of boiled potatoes (canned will do very well), cut into 1/4-inch slices; 2 cups boiling water; 1 can cream-style corn; 4 cups milk. Heat to the boiling point, season with salt and pepper and a little Worcestershire sauce.

AT SERVING TIME:

Pour into a heated tureen or casserole, add 2 tablespoons butter and a sprinkle of paprika and/or parsley. Place a cracker (saltine type) in the bottom of a bowl or a soup plate, ladle chowder over the cracker. This makes a generous amount of chowder. 6 to 8 portions.

Old-Fashioned Fish Chowder

If white wine is substituted for 1/4 to 1/2 of the milk the chowder tastes very French.

YOU WILL NEED:

condensed fish chowder	butter
milk or milk and light	parsley
cream	chives
celery salt or celery seed	paprika
Worcestershire sauce	

To a can of condensed fish chowder add 1 soup can of rich top milk, or ½ can milk and ½ can light cream (1 soup can of liquid in all), ¼ teaspoon celery salt or ½ teaspoon celery seed, and 1 teaspoon Worcestershire sauce. Bring to boiling point but do not boil.

AT SERVING TIME:
Bring to the table in a tureen, casserole, or bowl. Ladle into heated bowls or soup plates, garnish each portion with a thin pat of butter, sprinkle with chopped parsley, chives, and/or paprika.

Onion Soup with Claret

Canned or dehydrated onion soup can be given great distinction by the addition of claret, Burgundy, or sherry.

YOU WILL NEED:

canned or dehydrated onion	garlic
soup	butter or olive oil
claret, Burgundy, or sherry	Parmesan, Gruyère, or
French bread	Romano cheese

For dehydrated onion soup follow the package directions, but substitute for part of the water ½ cup claret or Burgundy or ¼ cup sherry. The same amount of wine may be added to canned, ready-to-serve onion soup. The soup should not be allowed to boil vigorously after the wine is added.

AT SERVING TIME:
Serve in individual casseroles or one large casserole. Top with crusts of garlic bread made by rubbing inch-thick slices of French bread with a cut clove of garlic, brush with melted butter or olive oil, and brown in the oven or under the broiler.

There are two ways of serving onion soup. One school insists that the bread crusts be placed on the soup, sprinkled thickly with grated cheese, and set in a hot oven till the cheese melts and browns slightly—about 5 minutes. Others prefer to dip the soup onto the plates over the toast, and pass freshly grated Parmesan, Gruyère, or Romano cheese.

Flaming Onion Soup

This is one of the most dramatic first courses you can serve. It should be served with theater—the toasted bread flambéed on a heatproof platter at the table.

YOU WILL NEED:

canned or dehydrated onion soup
cognac or brandy
water cress or spinach
pine nuts or blanched almonds

French bread
garlic
olive oil
Parmesan cheese

To 2 cans of onion soup or soup that you have made from a package add ¼ cup cognac or brandy. Heat in the usual manner.

Remove from heat, add 1 cup water cress from which the coarse stems have been removed or 1 cup very young spinach torn into bits, and ½ cup pine nuts or slivered blanched almonds. (Pine nuts can be bought even in very small towns at Italian grocery stores or in many supermarkets. The almonds come in a jar, already blanched and slivered.) In this case the nuts are not toasted.

Cover and allow to steam 1 minute.

Prepare croûtes of French bread (about 2 per person), cutting the bread slightly on a slant about ½ inch thick. Brush with garlic-flavored olive oil, easily made by adding pressed garlic or garlic powder to the olive oil. Brush bread on all sides and toast or set in the oven until golden color.

AT SERVING TIME:

Arrange the croûtes on an attractive heated platter. Have ready ¼ cup cognac or brandy which should be ever so slightly warmed.

Light the liquor with a match and pour while flaming over the croûtes. Place croûtes in individual soup dishes and add the soup. Pass a bowl of freshly grated or freshly opened Parmesan cheese.

Gazpacho

This chilled, refreshing Spanish soup requires no cooking and takes only seconds to prepare.

YOU WILL NEED:

canned tomato soup	fresh tomato
lemon juice	green pepper
olive oil	cucumber
canned beef bouillon	parsley or chives
garlic	croutons or bread sticks
hot pepper sauce	

To a 10¾-ounce can tomato soup, add 2 tablespoons lemon juice, ¼ cup olive oil, 1 cup beef bouillon, 1 clove garlic (crushed), ¼ teaspoon hot pepper sauce, ½ teaspoon salt, 1 finely chopped tomato, 2 tablespoons chopped green pepper, 1 cup chopped cucumber. Chill in refrigerator.

AT SERVING TIME:

Serve very cold with chopped parsley, chives, or other herbs, and croutons of toasted bread, or crumbled bread sticks, to be sprinkled over the top.

Green Pea Soup with Champagne

This recipe came from the Grand Hotel in Stockholm, where the ingredients are wheeled to the table on a silver cart and put together with considerable flourish by the headwaiter in cooperation with the sommelier, who opens the bottle of champagne at just the right moment.

YOU WILL NEED:

condensed cream of green
   pea soup
chicken bouillon cube
mace
dry or fresh tarragon

heavy cream
fresh tarragon or fresh
   mint sprays
champagne

To a can of condensed cream of green pea soup (or even split-pea soup) add ½ can water, and 1 chicken bouillon cube, crumbled and dissolved in a couple of tablespoons of hot water. Add ⅛ teaspoon mace, ¼ teaspoon dry tarragon, *or* 1 scant teaspoon fresh chopped tarragon. Simmer 5 minutes.

AT SERVING TIME:
Bring the heated pea soup to the table in a chafing dish. Have on hand ½ cup heavy cream, slightly beaten, a small bouquet of fresh mint or fresh tarragon sprays, and champagne. Stir the cream into the hot soup, and add at the last minute about ½ cup champagne. This will give a delightfully light texture to the soup as well as a delicate winey flavor. Ladle into heated soup plates and garnish with sprigs of fresh tarragon or mint. Serves 3 or 4.

Minestra with Pesto

Canned minestrone is a fine product, but if you want to achieve something really akin to the great soups of northern Italy, try this one, complete with the basil-blessed *pesto.*

YOU WILL NEED:

Minestra:
canned condensed
   minestrone soup
canned chick-peas
frozen chopped spinach
canned tomato juice
canned condensed noodle
   and ground beef soup

Pesto:
olive oil
butter or margarine
grated Parmesan cheese
dried basil leaves
garlic

To a 10¾-ounce can minestrone, add a 1-pound, 4-ounce can chick-peas, a 10-ounce package frozen chopped spinach, a 12-ounce can tomato juice, and a 10¾-ounce can noodle and ground beef soup. Bring to a boil. Simmer mixture for about 15 minutes.

Pesto: Into a blender put ¼ cup olive oil, 2 tablespoons softened butter or margarine, ½ teaspoon salt, ¼ cup grated Parmesan cheese, ½ teaspoon dried basil leaves, and 4 cloves garlic, crushed. Blend 1 or 2 minutes. You may use a rotary beater if you don't have a blender.

AT SERVING TIME:
Serve minestra from a tureen, stirring about a teaspoon of pesto into each individual bowl. Serves 6 as a supper soup.

Potage of Spring in Cups

During the months of April and May, you might in Ireland make a similar broth from fresh chopped young nettles picked from the fields, which is said to "clear the blood." But in the meantime . . .

YOU WILL NEED:
consommé madrilène   butter
water cress, chives, or
    parsley

Make consommé madrilène from a mix or a can, and when it is boiling, add for each portion ¼ cup finely chopped water cress, chives, or parsley.

AT SERVING TIME:
Stir in a little dab of butter just before serving.

Russian Shchi

The name is pronounced *shchee* to rhyme with *free,* and the soup is similar to some of the borschs but more cabbagy. Served with boiled potatoes and sour cream or yogurt and accompanied by Russian meat pies (see Boats of Beef, page 109), this soup could be the main event for lunch or supper. This recipe should provide six big bowlfuls.

YOU WILL NEED:
sweet and sour red cabbage
  in jars
canned tomatoes
canned beets
onion soup
condensed consommé or
  bouillon
bay leaf
butter, chicken or goose fat

Accompaniments:
boiled potatoes
yogurt or sour cream

Simmer together for 10 to 15 minutes 2 jars sweet and sour red cabbage, 2 large cans tomatoes, 1 can sliced or julienne beets, 2 packages onion soup (made up according to package directions), 2 cans condensed consommé or bouillon, 2 soup cans of water, 1 small bay leaf, and 2 tablespoons butter, chicken or goose fat.

Meanwhile boil 6 potatoes cut in half or heat a can of tiny Irish potatoes along with a bit of onion salt. Drain and shake over fire until they become mealy.

AT SERVING TIME:
Serve soup blazing hot in deep bowls or old-fashioned soup plates. Pass the potatoes, also steaming, in a snowy napkin, and have on hand a bowl of sour cream or yogurt. The potatoes and sour cream or yogurt are added by each person to his portion.

Scotch Broth Garni

A stout and sturdy potage, quite unusual.

YOU WILL NEED:
Scotch broth
canned kidney beans

dry sherry
parsley

Combine 1 can Scotch broth, 1 can water, 1 can cooked red kidney beans, liquid and all; simmer for a few minutes till the flavors are blended, then add 2 or 3 tablespoons dry sherry.

AT SERVING TIME:
Ladle into heated bowls or plates. Sprinkle each portion with about a tablespoon of coarsely chopped parsley.

Soupa Faki

YOU WILL NEED:

canned lentil soup	olive oil
instant minced onions	garlic
orégano	wine vinegar or lemon

To 2 cans ready-to-serve lentil soup, add 2 tablespoons instant minced onions, 1/4 teaspoon orégano, 2 tablespoons olive oil, 1 or 2 cloves garlic, peeled (speared with toothpicks for easy removal). Cook gently about 10 minutes. Retrieve garlic.

AT SERVING TIME:
Pass wine vinegar or lemon to be added ad lib at the table. Makes 4 to 6 servings.

Split-Pea Garbure

The French have a thick and hearty soup made of peas or beans, garnished with sausages and served over garlic-rubbed toast. This is a quick and easy version of that whole-meal soup.

YOU WILL NEED:

dehydrated split-pea soup	French bread for toasting
onion	olive oil
thyme or marjoram	garlic (optional)
cocktail or Vienna sausages or frankfurters	

Make up a package of dehydrated split-pea soup, according to the package directions, adding to the soup as it simmers half of a small onion finely chopped, ¼ teaspoon thyme or marjoram. Drain and brown 1 small can of cocktail sausages or Vienna sausage or frankfurters, cut into ½-inch slices. Cut crusty French bread into slices about 1 inch thick, brush with olive oil, and a cut clove of garlic, if desired. Set in a hot oven 450° F. about 5 minutes, or until golden brown.

AT SERVING TIME:

Bring soup to the table in a tureen or bowl. Have ready on separate plates the browned sausage and the toasted bread. Place a slice of toast in each soup plate, ladle soup over the bread (as for onion soup), and garnish with several slices of sausage or frankfurter.

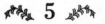

5

Eggs

EGGS WERE PROBABLY the original choice of the original "hurried epicure." Being in its natural state so close to perfect eating, the egg remains, as it must have been throughout history, the favorite recourse of those on the lookout for something good to eat—quick! Yet, despite the fact that speed is the very essence of egg cookery, it is not paradoxical to insist that the basic principle of egg cookery is slow cooking at low temperature. The difference in time between proper and dreadful egg cookery may be only a few seconds, but the difference in taste and texture is enormous.

RECIPES

Eggs Aurora in Patty Shells

A brunch dish that's ready in a trice, magically brought about with hard-cooked eggs, a can of chicken gravy, and ready-baked or frozen patty shells.

YOU WILL NEED:

eggs
canned chicken gravy
lemon juice (optional)

baked patty shells
tomato or marinara sauce

To serve 4, hard-cook 8 eggs. Slice 6. Finely chop the yolks of the 2 remaining eggs. Slice the whites and add all the sliced eggs to a 10½-ounce can of chicken gravy, sparked up, if you like, with 1 or 2 teaspoons lemon juice. Spoon mixture into 4 baked patty shells and set in a moderate oven (350° F.) for about 5 minutes to brown lightly or under a broiler for about 1 minute.

AT SERVING TIME:

Sprinkle with the finely chopped egg yolks and pass a little bowl of spicy tomato or marinara sauce well heated.

Eggs Benedict

Since the poaching of an egg is a mental as well as a culinary hazard for many not-too-experienced cooks, this recipe calls for eggs that are shirred in the oven rather than poached.

YOU WILL NEED:

English muffins
eggs
boiled ham

butter
Mock Hollandaise Sauce
(page 147)

For each person, provide 1 or 2 halves of English muffins. Tear in half crosswise. Scoop out the soft center so as to leave a good-sized hollow deep enough for an egg to rest comfortably. Toast lightly. Provide for each person a thin slice boiled ham as for a ham sandwich. Place the ham on the toasted muffin, pushing it down in the center so that the egg can be accommodated. Break a raw egg into the nest. Pour over it a teaspoon of melted butter. Place on a cookie sheet and bake in a moderate oven (350° F.) about 6 minutes, or until the white is set.

AT SERVING TIME:
Place the muffins complete with egg on individual plates or on a platter. Cover each egg with Hollandaise Sauce, either canned or Mock Hollandaise. Sprinkle with paprika or parsley. Serve at once, 1 or 2 to a person.

VARIATION: Eggs Commodore
Proceed as for Eggs Benedict but, instead of ham, spread English muffin with liver pâté. Serve with canned beef gravy, livened by adding ½ teaspoon Worcestershire sauce, ½ teaspoon Kitchen Bouquet, a dash of cayenne pepper to each cup of gravy.

Eggs en Brioche

For an imaginative Sunday brunch, bake an egg in a brioche, which can now be bought everywhere across the country in frozen food bins. Or you could use an unsplit and hollowed English muffin, or a crusty roll, or even a brown-and-serve French roll. And you needn't brown the rolls ahead of time. The roll and the egg will cook cozily together.

YOU WILL NEED:
brioches, muffins, or rolls	heavy cream or melted
eggs	butter

Provide 1 or 2 muffins and eggs for each person, depending upon size and hunger. Cut off tops and scoop out brioches or muffins, leaving a thick shell, and place on a cookie sheet. Drop in 1 large fresh egg. Sprinkle lightly with salt and pepper. Over each egg, pour 1 teaspoon heavy cream or melted butter. Cover each one with a poaching cap (i.e., a circle of parchment paper or foil with a hole in the center, or 1 large piece with a hole punched with a pencil over each muffin; this cap allows eggs to cook in an atmosphere of moist heat so that the whites will not become hard and rubbery before the yolks are set). Bake in a moderate oven (about 350° F.) for 10 to 15 minutes or until the eggs are set.

AT SERVING TIME:
Serve with Golden Mushroom Sauce (page 146).

Eggs Chasseur

The classic recipe calls for French poached eggs. Our method of
oven poaching gives much the same result.

YOU WILL NEED:

butter	sherry
eggs	cayenne
condensed cream of	onion juice (optional)
chicken soup	grated cheese
canned milk or light cream	

Butter generously 6 individual egg shirrers, tiny casseroles, or
custard cups. Break 1 or 2 eggs into each. Set in a moderate oven,
350° F., for about 6 minutes. If you lay a cookie tin or some other
cover over the top, the eggs will have the appearance of French
poached eggs with the white veil over the yolks. Take from the
heat, pour over a sauce made by heating 1 can condensed cream
of chicken soup with ¼ can evaporated milk or light cream, 1
tablespoon sherry, a few grains of cayenne, and, if desired, ½
teaspoon onion juice. Sprinkle with grated cheese and set back
in the oven or under the broiler just long enough to melt the
cheese.

AT SERVING TIME:
Bring to the table immediately. A few grinds of fresh black pepper or nutmeg from the grinder point up the flavors. Serves 6.

Stuffed Eggs Diavolo

Prepared yellow mustard takes the place of half a dozen seasonings and spices. This is a very simple deviled egg recipe, and very
good.

YOU WILL NEED:

eggs	parsley or mixed fresh herbs
prepared yellow mustard	olives or pimientos

Cut hard-cooked eggs in half, lengthwise. Remove the yolks and put the whites aside in pairs. Mash yolks with a fork, add to each egg yolk 1 teaspoon prepared yellow mustard, salt and pepper, if needed. Refill whites with the mixture.

AT SERVING TIME:
Put together to look like a whole egg and roll in fresh chopped parsley or a mixture of fresh herbs. Or form the seasoned yolks into little balls. Set a ball inside each egg white and garnish with parsley, sliced olives, or pimiento strips.

VARIATION: Eggs Farci
To mashed and seasoned yolks add an equal amount of minced chicken, minced ham, deviled ham, or liver pâté.

Eggs Farci in Aspic

As a first course at a luncheon or dinner or as a main dish at a buffet supper party, eggs in aspic have great elegance.

YOU WILL NEED:

Eggs Farci (see above)	water cress
condensed consommé	radishes
sherry	Sauce Ravigote (page 151)

Set Eggs Farci in a shallow serving dish. Carefully spoon over them a can of condensed consommé, to which 1 tablespoon pale dry sherry has been added. Chill. Do not attempt to unmold since the aspic is far too delicate and tender for handling.

AT SERVING TIME:
Garnish the dish with water cress and radishes. Serve from the same dish. Pass separately a bowl of Sauce Ravigote.

Eggs with Madeira Sauce

Serve as a main dish for lunch or a light supper. The demi-glaze Madeira Sauce is nothing more than canned consommé cooked down.

YOU WILL NEED:

butter

eggs

canned consommé

Madeira or sherry

parsley

Butter generously the required number of custard cups or small ramekins. Break an egg in each. Don't bother to salt or pepper because the sauce is sufficiently seasoned. Place the custard cups in a shallow pan or frying pan with about an inch of warm water. Cover or not, depending on whether you wish the yolks to be veiled with white. Set on a medium fire and allow to cook until whites are set. Serve with Madeira Sauce, made by boiling uncovered a can of consommé until it is boiled down to half its original volume. Add 2 tablespoons sherry or Madeira wine. Simmer 2 or 3 minutes but do not boil.

AT SERVING TIME:

Turn eggs out of the custard cups if you wish, or serve in the custard cups. In either case, spoon 2 or 3 tablespoons of sauce over each egg. Garnish with parsley.

Eggs Ranchero

A wonderful late supper dish, or a spicy eye-opener for an interesting brunch.

YOU WILL NEED:

onion

oil

garlic

oregano

canned Mexican chilis

canned tomato sauce

hot pepper sauce

eggs

hominy grits (optional)

"Wilt" 2 tablespoons minced onion in 2 tablespoons hot oil. Add 1 small clove garlic, crushed; ½ teaspoon orégano; 2 canned green Mexican chilis, mashed and strained (or 2 tablespoons very finely chopped sweet green peppers) ; an 8-ounce can tomato sauce. Cook gently, uncovered, about 8 minutes. Taste and add a little extra salt and a few drops of hot pepper sauce to suit your palate. Into this mixture, drop 6 whole eggs, one at a time. Cover and allow to cook gently about 4 minutes, or until the eggs are poached to your liking.

AT SERVING TIME:

Hopefully, you've poached these eggs in a skillet that can go to
the table. And hopefully, you've provided a huge bowl of hominy
grits to accompany them. If so, spoon a bed of hominy grits onto
each guest's plate and nestle an egg (or two) thereon!

Eggs à la Reine

YOU WILL NEED:

butter	heavy cream or cream sauce
canned mushrooms	grated cheese
cream, sweet or sour	parsley or water cress
eggs	toast

Butter an individual egg shirrer, ovenproof saucer, or custard
cup. Cover the bottom with sliced, drained canned mushrooms
that have been slightly browned in butter then moistened with a
little cream—sweet or sour. On top of the mushrooms, break 1
or 2 eggs. Cover them with thick cream or canned cream sauce.
Sprinkle with 1 or 2 tablespoons grated cheese. Place in a moderate oven, 350° F., about 8 minutes until eggs are set and tops are
brown.

AT SERVING TIME:

Garnish with a topknot of parsley or water cress and serve immediately with triangles of toast.

Eggs Scrambled New York Style

YOU WILL NEED:

uncooked ham	canned sliced mushrooms
butter	eggs
onion	milk

For this dish you make the garnish first: Cut 1 thin slice of uncooked ham into matchlike pieces. There should be about 1 cup.
Heat the ham in 2 tablespoons melted butter along with 2 tablespoons chopped onion for about 5 minutes. Add a 3-ounce can

sliced mushrooms from which the liquid has been drained and saved. Cook about 3 minutes longer. Serve as a border around or on top of eggs scrambled in the following fashion:

Beat 6 eggs slighty with ¼ teaspoon salt, ⅛ teaspoon pepper, ⅓ cup milk, and the juice from the can of mushrooms. Melt 2 tablespoons butter in a pan and add egg mixture. Cook over very low heat, stirring constantly until set and creamy.

AT SERVING TIME:
Turn the eggs onto a warm plate and circle with the ham and mushroom garnish. Serves 4.

Buttered Eggs à la Robert

Since even for the most skillful of cooks, transferring eggs from pan to platter involves some hazard, it's a good idea to prepare eggs in the dish in which you will serve them. A heat-proof, glass pie-pan, for instance, can be used if you cover the heating unit or flame with an asbestos pad.

YOU WILL NEED:
butter

Quick Sauce Robert (page 152)
parsley

Melt 1 tablespoon butter in a frying pan or serving dish. Slip eggs into hot fat. Do not attempt to cook too many at once. Cook over low heat until edges show a faint line of golden brown.

AT SERVING TIME:
Pour Sauce Robert around rather than over the eggs. Garnish with parsley.

Lucanian Eggs au Gratin

A combination of canned cooked macaroni and hard-cooked eggs interestingly seasoned makes a fine dish.

YOU WILL NEED:
    hard-cooked eggs   grated cheese
    canned macaroni in cheese   onion (optional)
        sauce   buttered crumbs

Slice 6 hard-cooked eggs and arrange in layers in a shallow, buttered baking dish along with a can of cooked macaroni and cheese ——first a layer of macaroni, then eggs, and so on. Sprinkle each layer with grated cheese, using in all about ¾ cup. If you like onion, use a medium-sized one, finely chopped. The top layer should be macaroni, the final layer ½ cup buttered crumbs. Bake in a moderate oven, 350° F., until sizzling hot and well browned.

AT SERVING TIME:
Serve from the baking dish along with a green salad and a fruit dessert. Serves 4.

Oven-Poached Eggs in Tomatoes

The beefsteak tomatoes of summer come proudly to brunch, bearing a sunny egg nestled in a spinach cup. When the beefsteaks are gone, simply nest the eggs in spinach and serve with thick slices of canned tomato aspic.

YOU WILL NEED:
    beefsteak tomatoes   canned, cooked ham
    fresh or dried basil   eggs
    frozen spinach   Figaro Sauce (page 145)
    garlic powder

Cut tops off 6 good-sized tomatoes and enough of the bottoms to make them stand straight. Scoop out slightly and sprinkle with seasoned salt and fresh or dried basil, which has been rubbed between your fingers to release the oils. Cook 2 packages of frozen spinach. Season with ½ teaspoon garlic powder, 1 cup finely chopped cooked ham, ¼ teaspoon pepper, and a little salt if needed. Place a mound on each tomato, and with a spoon make a depression to accommodate a poached or a fried egg that has been neatly trimmed.

AT SERVING TIME:
Top with a generous amount of Figaro Sauce.

Scrambled Eggs Creole

Scrambled eggs cooked in a double boiler are tender and delicate. Although the cooking time is longer than scrambling in a frying pan, the method appeals greatly to the hurried hostess because the eggs can cook while other chores are being done. Constant stirring is not necessary.

YOU WILL NEED:

onion	mushrooms (optional)
butter	capers (optional)
canned tomatoes or tomato sauce	eggs
Worcestershire sauce (optional)	parsley or chives

Slightly cook ½ an onion, chopped, in 2 tablespoons butter; add 1 cup canned tomatoes. Season with ½ teaspoon salt, ⅛ teaspoon pepper. A few drops of Worcestershire, 1 tablespoon cooked, sliced mushrooms, and 1 tablespoon capers may be added, if you have them on hand. Cook 5 minutes, then add 5 slightly beaten eggs. Cook over slow heat in top of double boiler until creamy.

AT SERVING TIME:
Take eggs from the fire just *before* they begin to look done. They will then be perfect, because the heat of the pan will continue to cook them even as you are removing them. Serve as quickly as possible. Chopped parsley or chives may be stirred in at the last minute or sprinkled over the eggs as a garnish.

VARIATION: Creole Eggs with Cheese
To the tomato mixture and eggs add ¼ cup grated cheese before cooking.

Shirred Eggs Mornay

A shirred egg is an egg to remember when you're entertaining. They need so little attention, look elegant, are easy to serve. If you have no individual egg shirrers, heatproof glass custard cups will do very well.

YOU WILL NEED:

eggs
canned cream sauce or
    condensed cream of
    chicken soup

grated cheese
parsley (optional)

Butter egg shirrers or individual baking dishes. Break an egg or two into each. Sprinkle with salt and pepper. Cover eggs with sauce made by adding 1 slightly beaten egg to 1 can cream sauce or condensed cream of chicken soup. Sprinkle with grated cheese and bake in a moderate oven, 350° F., about 6 minutes. For easy handling it's a good idea to place the individual small dishes on a cookie sheet or broiler pan, then they can all be taken out together.

AT SERVING TIME:

Place the shirred eggs on individual plates or arrange on a large platter and decorate the platter with bouquets of parsley or green leaves.

Shirred Eggs with Sausage Neapolitan

An exciting dish for late breakfast or supper—Sunday or any day.

YOU WILL NEED:

butter
eggs
pork sausages

condensed tomato soup
basil or parsley

Butter 6 individual egg shirrers, ovenproof saucers, or custard cups; break 1 or 2 eggs in each. Around the eggs, arrange 6 small pork sausages that have been cut in half-inch pieces and browned. Cover eggs and sausages with condensed canned tomato soup, undiluted. Sprinkle with finely chopped fresh basil or parsley. Bake in a moderate oven, 350° F., about 8 minutes.

AT SERVING TIME:
Place the shirrers on individual plates or arrange on a large tray or platter. Garnish with bouquets of parsley or green leaves. Serve in baking dishes. Serves 6.

Mushroom Omelet Flambé

When guests stay unexpectedy for supper and you've said in all honesty that you haven't planned a thing you can in a few minutes appear on the scene bearing this delicate omelet wrapped in fragrant flames.

YOU WILL NEED:

eggs
Worcestershire sauce
butter

canned mushrooms
brandy

Slightly beat 4 eggs just enough to blend yolks and whites. Add 4 tablespoons warm water. Season with ½ teaspoon salt, ⅛ teaspoon pepper, ½ teaspoon Worcestershire sauce. Melt 2 tablespoons butter in a small frying pan or omelet pan. Add eggs. Cook over slow heat. Lift edges with a spatula and tip the pan occasionally so that the uncooked part runs underneath. Do not allow to brown but merely to become firm on the outside. The inside should be creamy. In a separate pan heat 2 3-ounce tins of mushrooms in 2 tablespoons of butter.

AT SERVING TIME:
With the spatula turn ½ of the omelet over the other and serve on a hot platter. In the center, and around the edges of the omelet, place the heated mushrooms. Slightly warm 4 tablespoons brandy, set a lighted match to the brandy and pour while flaming over the mushrooms. Serves 4.

Scotch Woodcock

Neither Scotch nor a woodcock, this dish of creamed eggs dates back many centuries and is as good today as it ever was.

YOU WILL NEED:

condensed cream of chicken
  soup
milk or light cream
hard-cooked eggs
anchovy paste
dried celery flakes
  (optional)

toast or English muffins
anchovy fillets
pimiento
green pepper
paprika

To a can of condensed cream of chicken soup, add ¼ to ½ can milk or light cream. Heat. Add 6 coarsely chopped hard-cooked eggs. Season to taste with about ½ teaspoon anchovy paste, a little coarsely ground black pepper, and 1 teaspoon dried celery flakes if desired.

AT SERVING TIME:

Serve on toast or toasted English muffins. Garnish with crossed anchovy fillets, strips of pimiento, circles of green pepper, and/or a dash of paprika. Serves 4.

VARIATION: Eggs Goldenrod

Chop whites and yolks separately. Add whites to the sauce and pour over toast. Cut yolks fine or put through a strainer and sprinkle over the top. Instead of anchovy paste, season sauce with a tablespoon of pale dry sherry.

Tender Hard-Cooked Eggs

Since so many recipes call for hard-cooked eggs, it's a wise thought to know the best way to produce some.

A hard egg *can* be a good egg, and never, never have whites like rubber, little hard spots all through the yolks, and a line of green between the yolk and the white. Never, that is, if they are not hard-*boiled*—never really boiled at all. Most modern recipes avoid the word—they say hard-*cooked*. Here's how to achieve these paragons of the egg family.

YOU WILL NEED:

eggs   cold water to cover

The French insist that perfect eggs in this particular category are merely covered with cold water to stand 1 inch above the egg. Then the eggs are brought to the boiling point, removed immediately from the heat and allowed to stand, covered, for 20 minutes. To stop the cooking and to avoid any trace of discoloration around the yolks, rinse the eggs in cold water.

AT SERVING TIME:

At this point eggs should be firm enough to slice, but tender, delicate, and ready to be used in a variety of ways for sandwiches, salads, hors d'oeuvres, or in a delicious main dish for Sunday brunch.

Main Dishes

STARRING CHEESE, RICE, AND PASTA

THIS IS A CHAPTER in which we have grouped a number of those dishes which, like many great works of art, are quite unclassifiable. In old-fashioned cookbooks they might have been called entrees. They are for the most part main-course dishes. Several would, with a salad and dessert, constitute one-dish meals.

Among them are such classic dishes as the Welsh rarebit, Swiss fondue, a number of notable pastas—spaghetti in various guises, ravioli, lasagne.

Important rice dishes are here too—pilaf, Spanish rice, Acadian rice.

There are others too, equally indispensable to anyone with an appreciation for good food—polenta for instance, and Philadelphia scrapple.

Each one of these dishes makes use of some short cut—a prepared sauce, a canned product, a quick-cooking rice, a new quick-cooking cereal.

RECIPES

Blushing Bunny

Don't let the whimsical name deceive you—this is a hearty luncheon or supper dish.

YOU WILL NEED:

condensed tomato soup
milk
sharp American cheese
mustard

eggs
toast, crackers, or English
  muffins

Combine 1 can condensed tomato soup, ½ cup milk, 1 cup sharp American cheese finely cut or shredded, ½ teaspoon prepared mustard, the yolks of 2 eggs well beaten. Heat over low heat, stirring constantly until cheese is melted and mixture is thickened.

AT SERVING TIME:

Serve immediately on toast, crackers, or toasted English muffins. Makes 6 servings.

Fondue à la Breakneck Hill

Breakneck Hill is the name of our place in Connecticut, so named they say because the stagecoaches raced down the steep hill toward the Half-Way Inn between Danbury and Norwalk at breakneck speed. Despite our family love of good food, breakneck speed is often necessary in the preparing of it—there is always so much to do.

Chapters have been written about *the true and only way* to prepare, serve, and eat a fondue. The classic recipes call for rather a lot of special cooking equipment. But we, longing for the taste and fun of fondue without fuss, developed one which is completely fail-proof. The knowing ones will raise their eyebrows over the use of a processed Swiss cheese, but therein lies the secret. The processed cheese never gets rubbery. If desired fondue can be reheated; simply add a little more liquid.

YOU WILL NEED:

garlic (optional)	nutmeg
American processed Swiss	brandy or kirsch (optional)
cheese	French bread or hard rolls
dry white wine	

Rub a chafing dish or top of double boiler with a cut clove of garlic. Toss in a half pound of processed Swiss cheese, cut into small pieces. Add ½ cup dry white table wine. Stir until well blended. Season to taste with salt, freshly ground black pepper, and a touch of grated nutmeg. Two or 3 tablespoons of kirsch or brandy may be stirred in, if desired. All this takes less than 5 minutes.

AT SERVING TIME:

Since this fondue is made so quickly and so easily it is a shame not to do it at the table. It should be served from the chafing dish and the eating of it is a ritual. This fondue must be kept bubbling ever so lightly while the guests alternate in dunking cubes of French bread or hard rolls spiked on a fork.

P.S. A candle warmer and any kind of earthenware or serving pan may be used instead of a chafing dish. The idea is to keep the fondue warm and bubbly. Count on this amount to serve 4.

The True Swiss Fondue

This is a dish famed in song and story. Although the fondue uses no canned or ready-to-serve ingredients, it belongs in the repertoire of the hurried epicure because it requires no previous preparation other than the grating of the cheese and the cutting of a loaf of bread or crusty rolls into bite-sized pieces. Furthermore, it's so gay, so different, so everlastingly delicious.

YOU WILL NEED:

In the way of equipment:

A quart-size earthenware casserole with handle or a chafing dish
An alcohol stove with a flame that can be adjusted, Sterno, or an electric plate with an asbestos pad

In the way of ingredients:

garlic	nutmeg (optional)
white wine	kirsch or brandy (optional)
Switzerland Swiss cheese	French bread
flour	

Rub your casserole or chafing dish with a cut clove of garlic. To serve 4—pour in 2 cups dry white table wine and set over a very slow fire. When the wine is hot but not boiling, stir with a fork and add, a handful at a time, a pound (4 cups) shredded Swiss cheese, which has been sprinkled with 3 tablespoons flour. Each batch of cheese should be thoroughly incorporated before the next is added. Keep stirring until the mixture starts bubbling. Season with a little salt, freshly ground black pepper from the mill, and a grating of nutmeg if desired. Also 2 to 3 tablespoons of kirsch or brandy may be stirred in.

AT SERVING TIME:

Remove fondue from the fire and set immediately over a small flame or an electric plate with an asbestos pad or a very low alcohol flame—just enough heat to keep the fondue bubbling lightly. Present to each guest a fork spearing a piece of bread complete with a little crust. The idea is for each to stir the fondue with his bread. If he loses the bread off the fork in the fondue, according to tradition the forfeit is a kiss—or the drinks. Kirsch, brandy, or white wine is usually served with fondue.

Quiche Lorraine

One of the most famous dishes of Alsace-Lorraine is a kind of cheese custard pie, sprinkled with bits of crisp bacon. It may be made without a crust or you can use a prepared crust.

YOU WILL NEED:

bacon
milk or light cream
Swiss cheese
eggs

onion juice or extract
cayenne or Tabasco
plain pastry

Fry 6 slices of bacon until crisp and break into small pieces. Mix with 1 cup milk or light cream, 1 cup grated Swiss cheese, 4 slightly beaten eggs, a few drops of onion juice or extract, ½ teaspoon salt, ⅛ teaspoon pepper, a few grains of cayenne or a couple of drops of Tabasco sauce.

Line a 9-inch pie plate with plain pastry either quick-frozen prepared or made from a packaged mix. Then pour in the cheese and egg mixture. Bake 10 minutes at 450° F., then reduce the heat to 325° and bake until firm or when a silver knife inserted comes out clean. This should take about 30 minutes.

AT SERVING TIME:

Serve neither blazing hot or cold but gently warm. A big bowl of mixed green salad is the traditional accompaniment and with fruit it's all you could possibly want for lunch or supper. Serves 4 to 6.

VARIATION: Quiche Lorraine for Lent

Omit bacon and sprinkle the pie just as it comes from the oven with ½ cup canned French fried onions. If you wish, you can put the onions on the custard after it is set but before it is quite ready to come out of the oven so that the onions will be crisp and warm.

Neapolitan Cheese Soufflé

A soufflé sounds, looks, and tastes tremendously complicated. But when you start with a can of condensed soup, it couldn't be easier.

YOU WILL NEED:

condensed cream of tomato   eggs
   soup   basil, marjoram, or orégano
quick-cooking tapioca   (optional)
sharp cheese

Heat 1 can condensed cream of tomato soup, 2 tablespoons quick-cooking tapioca, and ¾ cup grated sharp cheese in the top of a double boiler, stirring until the cheese melts. Take off the stove and stir in 4 egg yolks, one at a time, beating after each addition. Cool, fold in 4 egg whites beaten until stiff but not dry, season, if desired, in the Italian manner by adding ½ teaspoon dry basil, marjoram, or orégano. Pour into buttered 1½ quart casserole. Bake in a hot oven, 400° F., 20 to 25 minutes. If you prefer a firmer soufflé, place the casserole in a pan of hot water and bake at 300°F. for 1 to 1½ hours.

AT SERVING TIME:

Rush to the table and serve immediately. This recipe makes 6 portions.

Welsh Rarebit with Ale and Basil

Some call it rarebit because it is a rare and tasty tidbit. Others say the right name is rabbit—that it's the only "rabbit" the hunters ate when they caught no rabbits. Since the making of a perfect rarebit has its hazards, our version makes use of a prepared Welsh rarebit. For this particular occasion, choose the kind that is made with ale or beer.

YOU WILL NEED:

jar of prepared Welsh rare-   dry basil
  bit   toast, rolls, or English muf-
milk, ale, or beer   fins

In the top of a chafing dish or double boiler or over a *low* fire, heat 1 jar Welsh rarebit into which you have stirred ¼ to ½ cup milk, ale, or beer. Sprinkle with dried basil. To get the full flavor of the herb, rub it between the palms of your hands to release the oils and so sprinkle it off your hands into the rarebit.

AT SERVING TIME:

Bring to the table in a chafing dish or spoon the hot rarebit over toast, toasted soft rolls, or toasted English muffins. Foaming mugs of beer or ale are the classic accompaniment. An 8-ounce jar of rarebit serves 2 or 3.

Welsh Rarebit with Sherry

Some brands of prepared Welsh rarebit are flavored with tomato and sherry. This rarebit is delicious when the sherry flavor is slightly heightened and the rarebit combined with thick slices of grilled tomato and crisp bacon.

YOU WILL NEED:

tomato-flavored Welsh rarebit with sherry	flour
	butter
sherry or water	toast or English muffins
cayenne	parsley (optional)
tomatoes	bacon (optional)

To a 10-ounce jar of tomato-flavored Welsh rarebit, add 4 tablespoons sherry or water, a few grains of cayenne pepper. Heat in the top of a double boiler or chafing dish, stirring occasionally. Slice a large-sized tomato in thick slices, dip in flour, and sprinkle with salt and black pepper, and brown in 2 tablespoons of butter.

AT SERVING TIME:

Spoon the rarebit, while sizzling hot, over hot toast or toasted English muffins. Top each portion with a thick slice of grilled tomato. Garnish, if desired, with parsley and strips of crisp bacon. Serves 3 or 4.

Macaroni and Ham, Virginia Style

A can of macaroni and cream sauce with cheese is the beginning of great wisdom for the hostess in a hurry. Merely sprinkled with cheese and heated in the oven, it is excellent. Dressed up in the manner of old Virginia, it's superb.

YOU WILL NEED:

butter	mustard (optional)
canned macaroni in cheese	cheese
sauce	bread crumbs (optional)
ham	parsley or water cress

Butter a baking dish. Combine 2 cans macaroni in cheese sauce (yes, it comes canned with its own sauce) with 1 to 2 cups coarsely chopped or finely cut cooked ham. Season with 2 teaspoons prepared yellow mustard. Place in the buttered baking dish. Sprinkle with ½ cup grated cheese and, if desired, 4 tablespoons bread crumbs. Bake at 400° F. or until brown.

AT SERVING TIME:

Set parsley or water cress in the center of the casserole. Serve on hot plates. Serves 6 generously.

Macaroni Ring

An elaborate-looking macaroni ring can be quickly and easily made with canned macaroni.

YOU WILL NEED:

canned macaroni in cheese	eggs
sauce	pimiento, green pepper, or
milk	onion (optional)

Combine a can of macaroni in cheese sauce with 1 cup milk, 2 well-beaten eggs. Various additions, such as a chopped pimiento or green pepper or a tablespoon of chopped onion or onion flakes, may be added if desired. Turn the mixture into a buttered ring mold. Set in a pan of hot water. Bake at 350° F., 30 to 40 minutes.

AT SERVING TIME:

Turn out on a warm plate. Fill the center with chicken à la king, creamed mushrooms, or shrimp. Serves 4.

Green Noodles with Meat Sauce

Green noodles are nothing more than noodles colored with spinach juice. Since the coloring is done by the manufacturer and the noodles are almost as easy to procure as any other type, it's amazing what a sensation they created when they first appeared in this country.

YOU WILL NEED:

green noodles
prepared spaghetti sauce
  with or without meat
basil, orégano,
  Worcestershire sauce, or
  red wine (optional)

garlic
parsley (optional)
grated Parmesan or
  Romano cheese

Cook 2 cups green noodles according to package directions. Be careful not to overcook. Noodles like spaghetti should be cooked *al dente* as the Italians put it—just to the point where it is tender but provides something for the teeth. Drain in a strainer and rinse with hot or cold water to separate the strands.

Meanwhile heat prepared spaghetti sauce. Perk it up by adding a little extra seasoning, basil or orégano or a dash of Worcestershire sauce or a couple of tablespoons of red table wine such as Chianti or Burgundy.

AT SERVING TIME:

Heat a serving dish, rub with garlic, holding the clove with a bit of waxed paper. Pile the drained noodles on the hot plate, make a well in the center and pour the sauce into the well. Sprinkle, if desired, with fresh chopped parsley. Provide a bowl of grated Parmesan or Romano cheese. Crusty bread, green noodles, a green salad, red wine, and a fruit dessert comprise a glorious meal. Serves 4.

Ravioli Gratiné

Ravioli, beloved of the Italians, are nothing more or less than square noodles filled with savory meat, chicken, vegetables, or cheese. When homemade, they take hours and hours. But you can buy them complete with tomato sauce in a jar. In most cases the sauce can take a little doctoring, but ready-to-serve ravioli sprinkled with grated cheese and fresh-chopped parsley, heated in a shallow casserole, make a good and filling dish.

YOU WILL NEED:

olive oil	cheese
jar of ravioli in tomato	parsley, chives, onion tops,
sauce	or finochio

In a shallow ovenware casserole or heatproof glass pie pan, pour a tablespoon of olive oil. Add the ravioli with sauce. Sprinkle generously with grated cheese, using about 4 tablespoons of cheese to an 8-ounce jar of ravioli. Set in a hot oven, 350° F., for about 20 minutes or until the ravioli are bubbly hot, the cheese melted and delicately brown.

AT SERVING TIME:

Sprinkle with chopped parsley, chives, finely cut green onion tops, or the finely chopped fronds from a bunch of finochio (something like celery with an anise flavor) .

Venetian Spaghetti with Clam Sauce

This masterly sauce, formerly a labor of much love and many hours, now cooks in 5 minutes—thanks to a can of minced clams, another can of tomato sauce.

YOU WILL NEED:

vermicelli, spaghetti, or	canned tomato sauce or
any other type of pasta	condensed tomato soup
garlic	parsley
olive oil	canned minced clams

Start cooking your vermicelli or spaghetti, according to package directions, before you begin the sauce, since spaghetti will take 10 to 15 minutes. Brown 1 or 2 well-crushed cloves of garlic in 4 tablespoons of hot olive oil in a saucepan. Add 1 can tomato sauce or 1 can condensed tomato soup, diluted with ½ can water, add 1 tablespoon chopped parsley, a little freshly ground black pepper. Cook about 3 minutes. Add a 7- or 8-ounce can of minced clams with their juice. Cook for only 2 minutes. Too much cooking toughens the clams.

AT SERVING TIME:
Pour hot sauce over cooked spaghetti in a well-heated shallow bowl or platter. Garnish with parsley. Grated cheese is not generally passed with this dish but it is not forbidden!

Spaghettini with Meat Balls de Luxe

For the greatest speed use the thinnest spaghetti. The thinner the spaghetti the faster it cooks. Vermicelli and spaghettini, being very thin, cook in about 6 minutes if you like them *al dente* which all connoisseurs insist is the only way.

YOU WILL NEED:

thin spaghetti, spaghettini, or vermicelli
canned meat balls in spaghetti sauce
garlic
basil
green olives
capers (optional)
grated Parmesan or Romano cheese

Cook 1 pound spaghetti or its thin cousins, spaghettini or vermicelli, according to package directions. When tender but not soft, drain and arrange on a hot platter.

Meanwhile, open a can of meat balls in spaghetti sauce. Remove the balls and cut in halves. Put back in the sauce and heat along with one well-crushed clove of garlic, ½ teaspoon basil, 2 tablespoons chopped green olives, 1 tablespoon capers if desired.

AT SERVING TIME:
Pour hot sauce over spaghetti. Sprinkle with grated cheese— Parmesan or Romano cheese. Serve very hot with green salad, crusty bread, fruit for dessert. Serves 4 to 6.

Acadian Rice

This is the great dish of the Acadian farmers who came from Nova Scotia to Louisiana, as told by Longfellow in his tale of Evangeline. Once it required half a day's cooking, but no more. Instant rice and canned giblet gravy make the difference.

YOU WILL NEED:

canned giblet gravy
canned tomato soup
instant rice
instant minced onions

hot pepper sauce
canned boned chicken
Spanish or Italian sausages

Combine 1 can giblet gravy, 1 can condensed tomato soup, 1 soup can water, 3 cups instant rice, 2 tablespoons instant minced onion, ¼ teaspoon hot pepper sauce. Bring to a boil on top of the stove. Add ½ cup each of canned boned chicken and sliced hot Spanish or Italian sausages. Place in a buttered casserole and set in a moderately hot oven (375° F.) about 15 minutes. Serves 4 to 6.

AT SERVING TIME:

This dish stands alone for a hearty Saturday night supper, needing only a salad and crisp bread to accompany it. Or it can replace potatoes to serve with pork, ham, or chicken.

Gilded Rice

Rice with a golden glow adds a party touch to any meal. Because it's so easy to achieve perfectly cooked rice *every time*, we suggest using quick-cooking rice.

YOU WILL NEED:

quick-cooking rice
saffron

curry powder or turmeric

Prepare a small package, 1⅓ cups, quick-cooking rice according to package directions. But add to the water ½ teaspoon saffron, ¾ teaspoon curry powder *or* turmeric.

AT SERVING TIME:
Fluff with a fork. Makes 3 cups, 4 to 5 servings.

Pilaf Indienne

One of the ladies of the Indian embassy was a guest on my television show when we cooked this pilaf. She asked for the recipe
to give to her chef. That's why we know that though our method
is unorthodox, the flavor must be authentic.

YOU WILL NEED:

quick-cooking rice	cinnamon
chicken bouillon cubes	bay leaf
saffron or curry powder	cardamon seeds (optional)
onions	nutmeg
butter	leftover chicken, lamb, beef,
raisins	or ham (optional)
almonds	garnishes (optional)

To a package of quick-cooking rice, add 1½ cups cold water,
1 teaspoon salt, 3 chicken bouillon cubes, dissolved in ¼ cup
hot water (this trick of dissolving bouillon cubes in a small
amount of hot water is well worth remembering when a recipe
calls for cool liquid). Add ¼ to ½ teaspoon curry powder or
½ to 1 teaspoon saffron. Bring to a full boil, cover and let stand
in a warm place 10 minutes

In the meantime, fry 2 small, sliced onions in 4 tablespoons
butter to a golden brown. Add 4 tablespoons raisins, 2 tablespoons coarsely chopped salted almonds, ¼ teaspoon cinnamon,
a bay leaf, 2 or 3 cardamon seeds if you have them, a dash of
nutmeg, salt, and freshly ground black pepper to taste. (If you
wish to serve this as a main dish rather than as an accompaniment add 1 cup leftover chicken, beef, lamb, or ham, cut into
small pieces.) Mix with cooked rice. Heat a minute or two.

AT SERVING TIME:
Heap on a heated platter. Garnish in the Oriental manner with
chopped crisp bacon sprinkled over the top, French fried onions
(from a can), chopped chives or parsley, salted almonds, and/or
sliced hard-cooked eggs. Serves 4 to 6.

Ring of Rice

Nothing is dressier than rice molded in a ring—filled with chicken à la king, lobster Newburg, or any creamed vegetable. It is especially easy when you use quick-cooking rice.

YOU WILL NEED:

quick-cooking rice	nutmeg (optional)
butter	

Place 3 cups cooked rice (5-ounce package or 1⅓ cups quick-cooking rice, prepared according to package directions) in a well-greased 8-inch ring mold. Pour on 4 tablespoons melted butter. Set in moderate oven, 350° F., 10 minutes.

AT SERVING TIME:

Loosen the edges of the mold by running a knife blade around it. Place a warm plate over the mold. Turn upside down and shake slightly to loosen the mold. If you wish sprinkle the top with nutmeg. Fill center with any desired creamed mixture. Serves 6.

Spanish Rice à la Minute

YOU WILL NEED:

quick-cooking rice	butter or olive oil
canned meat balls in	chili powder, cayenne, or
tomato sauce	Tabasco
dehydrated mixed	grated cheese (optional)
vegetable flakes	parsley
dehydrated onion flakes	

To a 5-ounce package of quick-cooking rice (1⅓ cups), add 1 cup water, 1 can meat balls with their sauce. The balls may be sliced or cut up into pieces so that they "go further." Add 2 tablespoons mixed vegetables flakes, 1 teaspoon salt, 2 tablespoons dehydrated onion flakes. Add 2 tablespoons butter or olive oil. Bring to a full rolling boil, uncovered. Cook 2 minutes. Season to taste with chili powder, cayenne, or Tabasco sauce. Cover and let stand about 10 minutes. If desired, the Spanish rice may be sprinkled with 4 tablespoons grated cheese and set under the broiler for a minute or so until the cheese melts.

AT SERVING TIME:
Garnish with parsley and serve with grated cheese. Serves 4.

Corny Cornmeal Mush

Our forefathers swore by cornmeal mush for breakfast. A sophisticated version adds canned cream-style corn to make it even cornier. When made plain, as we give it below, it becomes a super-porridge. If you add grated cheese, butter and pepper, it becomes a sort of polenta to serve with meats.

YOU WILL NEED:

quick-cooking cornmeal	wheat germ (optional)
cold water	melted butter
canned cream-style corn	hot milk
butter	honey

A quick and easy way needs no slow and careful mixing, cooks speedily without lumps. In a large saucepan, gradually stir 1 cup quick-cooking cornmeal (yellow or white) into 1 cup cold water. Add 1 medium can (about 2 cups) cream-style corn with liquid and 3 more cups of cold water and 1 teaspoon salt. Bring to a boil, stirring occasionally, and then continue to cook and stir until thickened. May be served immediately, but is even better if allowed to stand covered in a warm place for about 15 minutes. To prevent a film from forming, add a little butter and allow to melt over the top.

AT SERVING TIME:
A couple of tablespoons of toasted wheat germ adds an interesting look and texture, whether stirred in or not. Present in large bowls (perhaps Chinese lotus bowls?), accompanied by a trio of squat pottery pitchers holding melted butter, hot milk, and warmed honey.

Italian Polenta

Popular brands of packaged yellow cornmeal cook in about ⅓ of the time that an old-time Italian cook would have devoted to making one of her country's beloved national dishes. Polenta is nothing more than cornmeal mush combined with grated cheese. Ideal with stews, fish, or meat.

YOU WILL NEED:

water
yellow cornmeal
butter

Parmesan cheese
parsley (optional)

Boil 3 cups water in a saucepan. Mix 1 cup yellow cornmeal and 1 teaspoon salt with 1 cup cold water. Pour into the boiling water, stirring constantly. Cook until thickened, stirring frequently. Cover and continue cooking over low heat 10 minutes or longer. Stir in 3 tablespoons butter, 1 cup grated Parmesan cheese. Season with a little freshly ground black pepper, mix thoroughly.

AT SERVING TIME:
Serve very hot. If desired, polenta may be poured into a buttered ring mold. Set in a warm place for 10 minutes, then unmold. The center may be filled with stew, chicken à la king, or any creamed mixture. Garnish or sprinkle with parsley if desired. Or if you'd rather not bother with a mold simply spoon the polenta around the dish making a casual kind of ring.

VARIATION: Baked Polenta with Sausage
Drain and brown canned cocktail or quick-frozen sausages. Place in a shallow oven-proof dish. Cover with polenta prepared as above. Bake 15 minutes in a hot oven, 400° F. If ingredients are already hot, sprinkle with grated cheese and set under the broiler until the cheese melts and browns.

Scrapple for Brunch

Philadelphia scrapple ready for browning can be secured in cans, but since it is not universally available, it's good to know about one that can be put together quickly with wheat cereals that cook in 5 minutes or less. The use of minced ham instead of fresh pork may be unorthodox but makes the scrapple taste good.

YOU WILL NEED:

quick-cooking wheat cereal	thyme or sage
small can minced ham	butter or bacon fat
onion	syrup or applesauce

Prepare quick-cooking whole-wheat cereal according to package directions. To 2 cups cooked cereal, add a small jar or tin (3 or 4 ounces) minced ham, 2 tablespoons finely chopped onion, 1/4 teaspoon powdered thyme or sage, salt and pepper to taste. Cook over boiling water about 5 minutes to blend the flavors. Pack into a well-greased refrigerator tray to chill thoroughly and harden.

AT SERVING TIME:

Slice 1/2 inch thick. Fry in butter or bacon fat until crisp and brown on both sides. Serve with syrup or applesauce. Leftover cooked cereal may be utilized very well in this way. Makes about 8 or 10 slices.

7

Fine Fish Dishes

VIA CAN AND FREEZER

IN THE PAST, what has been difficult for most modern and harried householders has been the primary admonition "first, catch your fish." Even when you weren't compelled to catch it yourself there was the ever present problem of getting the fish *when* you wanted it and the even greater problem of cleaning, boning, skinning, and otherwise preparing it for the pan.

Enter the quick-frozen fillet and the sad tale is ended. Quick-frozen fish has the advantage of being at least as fresh as the freshest since the best brands are generally frozen within an hour or so after being caught. Equally important—such fish comes to the frozen-food lockers all ready to cook.

The quick-frozen fillet is presented here in a number of interesting classic guises.

Each one of these dishes is achieved with a minimum of effort in the fewest possible minutes.

In using quick-frozen fish, it is not necessary to thaw beforehand. In several recipes we have suggested thawing only enough to separate the fillets. By this method the utmost in flavor is achieved and, furthermore, there is no possibility of deterioration. In case you should thaw fish completely before cooking, remember that quick-frozen fish spoils as promptly as fresh.

Never refreeze fish and if you have leftover cooked fish, use it within twenty-four hours because it does not keep.

In addition to quick-frozen sea food there are of course the canned varieties, some of which are probably among the best known and most popular of canned foods. A large number of new products have within the last few years been added to this category—shad roe, for example, and prepared fish cakes. Salted, fresh and dried fish in several forms are now presented so that they no longer require soaking or freshening.

So wide is the choice, so delicate are the flavors that many individuals and families who once insisted "we're not much for fish or sea food" have now completely changed their way of thinking. Whether you are a fish fancier or nonfancier try some of our short cuts. They may well become some of the most prized and often-repeated dishes of your repertory.

RECIPES

Codfish Puff Balls
Curried Crab Meat
    Amandine
Quick Baltimore Deviled
    Crab
Quick Crab Meat Mornay
Fish Soufflé
Norwegian Fish Pudding
Fillets of Perch Baked in
    Cream
Fillets of Perch in Mushroom
    Sauce
Quick Fillets of Sole
    Marguery
Oven-Fried Fillets
Swedish Fish Balls

Seafood Gumbo
Kedgeree
Kippers in Rum
Baked Lobster
    Tails à la Diavolo
Quick Lobster Newburg
Airborne Salmon Soufflé
Salt Mackerel, Virginia
    Breakfast Style
Scalloped Oysters
Shad Roe Bonne Femme
Spiced Salmon
Baby Shrimp
Shrimp Jambalaya
Tuna à la Grecque

Codfish Puff Balls

Breakfast need not be confined to the usual standbys. Experiment with a different and unusual entree, such as fish. Light and airy codfish puff balls will make that welcome difference—and nothing could be more interesting served in a chafing dish at a Sunday brunch!

YOU WILL NEED:

canned, ready-to-fry
  codfish cake mixture
Worcestershire sauce
hot pepper sauce

eggs
oil or shortening
chili sauce or catsup

To a can of ready-to-fry codfish cake mixture, add ½ teaspoon salt, 1 teaspoon Worcestershire sauce, 2 drops hot pepper sauce, 2 slightly beaten egg yolks. Mix well and then fold in lightly 2 stiffly beaten egg whites. Drop by tablespoonfuls into hot shortening or salad oil that stands about 1½ inches deep in the skillet. Fry at 370° F. about 2 or 3 minutes, or in a regular skillet until crisp and brown. Drain on paper towels. Makes about 24.

AT SERVING TIME:

Serve with chili sauce or catsup. May be escorted to the table by creamy scrambled eggs, liberally strewn with chives.

Curried Crab Meat Amandine

In less than 15 minutes, you can have this delicious curried crab dish on its way to the table!

YOU WILL NEED:

butter
curry powder
canned chicken gravy
canned Alaska crab meat

canned bean sprouts
salted almonds
brown rice

Melt 2 tablespoons butter. Add 1 tablespoon curry powder. Stir over heat about 2 minutes. Add 1 10½-ounce can chicken gravy,

1 7-ounce can crab meat cut into chunks, and 1 can bean sprouts, drained. Cook gently 10 minutes. Sprinkle lavishly with toasted salted almonds. Serves 6.

AT SERVING TIME:
Serve with brown rice.

Quick Baltimore Deviled Crab

If this be treason—to concoct Baltimore's own deviled crab from quick-frozen crab meat and cream of mushroom soup—make the best of it, and very good it is!

YOU WILL NEED:

canned or quick-frozen crab meat	Worcestershire sauce
onion	parsley
butter	melted butter or salad oil
condensed cream of mushroom soup	egg
	dry mustard
chili sauce	lemon juice
	bread crumbs

To fill 6 medium-sized crab shells you will need 2 to 2½ cups of crab meat. Sauté 2 tablespoons of minced onion in 1 tablespoon of butter until golden. Combine crab meat with 1 cup undiluted condensed cream of mushroom soup heated in the top of a double boiler and add sautéed onion. Season with 1 tablespoon chili sauce, 2 teaspoons Worcestershire sauce, 1 teaspoon chopped parsley, dash of pepper. Place the mixture in 6 crab shells, or individual baking dishes, cover with a paste made of an egg beaten with ½ teaspoon dry mustard, 1 teaspoon lemon juice, ¼ teaspoon salt, and ½ cup fine bread crumbs. Brush liberally with melted butter or salad oil and bake until a rich brown.

AT SERVING TIME:
Garnish with a sprig of parsley in the middle of each crab. Serve warm or cold. 6 servings.

'Quick Crab Meat Mornay

YOU WILL NEED:

condensed cream of chicken
  soup
milk, water, or white wine
egg

butter
crab meat
grated cheese
chives or parsley

Heat in the top of the double broiler 1 can condensed cream of chicken soup, ¼ can milk, water, or white wine. Simmer 2 or 3 minutes; cool 5 minutes; add 1 slightly beaten egg. Butter a shallow casserole or 6 small oven-proof ramekins or custard cups. Place in each a thin layer of crab meat, using about 1¼ cups for the 6, cover with sauce, sprinkle with grated cheese, using about ½ cup grated cheese. Set under the broiler just long enough to melt the cheese and give a delicate brown.

AT SERVING TIME:

Sprinkle or garnish with chopped chives or parsley and serve immediately. Makes 6 portions.

Fish Soufflé

A fine main dish for a meatless day, this simple soufflé is made with a canned soup base.

YOU WILL NEED:

canned flaked fish, such as
  salmon or tuna
condensed cream of celery
  soup
lemon juice

onion, onion juice or
  extract
Worcestershire sauce
eggs
Mock Hollandaise Sauce
  (page 147)

Combine 2 cups canned flaked fish with 1 can condensed cream of celery soup. Season with 2 teaspoons lemon juice, a little finely chopped onion, onion juice, or onion extract, ½ teaspoon Worcestershire sauce. Add, one at a time, 3 egg yolks, beating well after each yolk is added. Gently fold in 3 stiffly beaten egg whites. Turn into a buttered 2-quart baking dish which can go to the table. Bake the quick French way in a hot oven, 450° F., about 25 minutes or if you like a firmer soufflé, bake the American way in a moderate oven, 350° F., for 1 hour or until firm.

AT SERVING TIME:
Rush to the table and serve immediately with Mock Hollandaise Sauce. Makes 6 servings.

Norwegian Fish Pudding

A modernized, quick version of a famous Scandinavian dish—deserving an honored place on your party table.

YOU WILL NEED:

fish	sugar (optional)
condensed cream of	cracker meal or flour
mushroom soup	butter
milk	lemon juice
eggs	

Start with 2 cups of canned flaked fish well drained. Combine with 1 can condensed cream of mushroom soup and add ½ can milk. Heat together and simmer a few minutes, stirring occasionally. Set aside to cool. Three-quarters of an hour before eating time add the yolks of 4 eggs, very well beaten, and if you want the true Scandinavian touch, add ½ teaspoon sugar. Now gently ease into the mixture the whites of 4 eggs, beaten stiff but not dry. Butter a baking dish or casserole and dust with 2 tablespoons very fine cracker meal or flour. Bake in a medium oven, 350° F., about 30 minutes, until it is puffed and firm and lightly browned.

AT SERVING TIME:
Like any of the soufflés, to which class this pudding belongs, it should be served immediately. Serve with melted butter to which lemon juice has been added. Serves 6.

Fillets of Perch Baked in Cream

A *plat* comparable to this one is prepared by many a fine chef by first poaching the fish, then preparing a cream sauce, later combining fish and sauce. Here is a short cut using quick-frozen fillets of red perch. Sole or flounder may be substituted.

YOU WILL NEED:

fillets of perch, sole, or flounder	anchovy paste or Worcestershire sauce
cream	parsley or water cress

Thaw a pound package of quick-frozen fillets, just enough to separate. With scissors cut the fillets into serving pieces. Arrange on a shallow baking dish that can be brought to the table. Cover with 1 cup light cream which has been delicately flavored with ½ teaspoon anchovy paste. (Lacking anchovy paste, use Worcestershire sauce.) Bake 10 to 15 minutes in a hot oven, 450° F., until the fish is done—flakes off readily when touched with a fork.

AT SERVING TIME:
Serve from the dish in which it was baked. Garnish with parsley or water cress. Serves 3.

VARIATION: Fillets of Perch in Mushroom Sauce
Instead of cream, use 1 can condensed cream of mushroom soup. Omit seasonings, but garnish with celery leaves.

Quick Fillets of Sole Marguery

This unorthodox version of probably the most famous of all French fish specialties is delicious and unbelievably quick. In place of the lemon sole or flounder, any delicately flavored fillets can be used.

YOU WILL NEED:

fillets of lemon sole or flounder	egg
	canned shrimp
paprika	Little Neck clams
white wine or water and lemon juice	lobster meat (optional)
	Parmesan cheese
condensed cream of mushroom soup	(optional)

Thaw 6 to 8 small fillets (about 3 pounds) just enough to separate and place on a shallow buttered baking dish, preferably one that can go to the table. Sprinkle with salt, pepper, and paprika, and pour over ⅓ cup white wine. Cover with waxed paper, parchment paper, or aluminum foil and bake 10 to 15 minutes in a moderate oven, 350° F. When the fish is done, carefully pour off the liquid in the pan. You will want about ½ cup of this liquid. Add it to 1 can condensed cream of mushroom soup. Heat, season with salt and pepper. Beat 1 egg slightly, add a little of the hot sauce to the egg, stirring it well, and then incorporate egg into the sauce. Pour sauce over the fillets. Garnish with canned and drained shrimp, Little Neck clams, and/or pieces of cooked lobster meat. Sprinkle with grated Parmesan cheese, if desired, and broil 3 minutes, or until thoroughly heated and very lightly browned. Water and lemon juice may be used in place of wine.

AT SERVING TIME:
Serve immediately in the same dish in which it is baked. This makes 6 or 8 servings.

Oven-Fried Fillets

When you don't want to go to the trouble of deep-fat frying, or when you want to fix quite a few servings all at once, try the quick trick of oven frying. This method is adaptable for all types of fillets and for small fish that are fried whole, such as smelts or porgies.

YOU WILL NEED:

fillets of fish	butter or oil
milk	parsley or water cress
soft bread crumbs	lemon or lime
paprika (optional)	

Thaw a pound box of quick-frozen fillets just enough to separate. Dip in milk, using about ¼ cup, roll in bread crumbs seasoned with salt and pepper. A little paprika added to the bread crumbs provides an extra pretty brown. Place the fish in a buttered or oiled baking dish, preferably one that can go to the table. Sprinkle with 2 tablespoons melted butter, salad or olive oil. Bake in hot oven, 450° F., about 20 minutes or until done.

AT SERVING TIME:
Garnish with parsley or water cress and wedges of lemon or lime.
Serves 3.

Swedish Fish Balls

The making of these from scratch is quite a chore, so we suggest
that you use several excellent brands that are available either at
department store food counters, Swedish delicatessens or by mail
order.

YOU WILL NEED:

canned fish balls	melted butter
parsley	lemon juice

Gently heat fish balls in their liquid.

AT SERVING TIME:
Sprinkle liberally with chopped parsley and pass melted butter,
seasoned with freshly ground black pepper and lemon juice.

Seafood Gumbo

Although gumbo is quite generally accepted as a Creole invention
—part French, part Spanish—its distinctive ingredient, filé
powder, was originally made and brought to the New Orleans
market by the Choctaw Indians on Bayou Lacombe. This filé
powder is nothing more than the tender young leaves of the sassa-
fras bush dried, powdered, and sieved. Nowadays, it can be
bought at almost any good food store in various parts of the
country—or it's well worth ordering a jar by mail from New
Orleans.

Gumbos usually have an alarmingly long list of ingredients.
Certainly they have been extravagant as to shopping time and
length of simmering. The 5-minute version is a boon, therefore,
to the busy cook of today.

YOU WILL NEED:

condensed chicken gumbo   filé powder
  soup   rice
canned or quick-frozen
  shrimp, crab meat,
  lobster, oysters or cooked
  canned or leftover
  chicken or turkey

To a can of condensed chicken gumbo soup add 1 cup canned
or quick-frozen sea food or cooked chicken or turkey cut into
1-inch pieces. Heat and simmer 3 or 4 minutes. Add 1 teaspoon
filé powder—more if you like a very spicy gumbo. Gumbos must
never be boiled *after* adding the filé powder, otherwise they will
become ropey.

AT SERVING TIME:

Serve with rice in a soup plate, as the main dish for a simple meal
which need include nothing more than a salad and a dessert of
fruit and cheese or cookies.

Kedgeree

The original of this recipe is said to have been brought by the
captains of the clipper ships. Certainly it has an East Indian
name and an Oriental flavor. In the Franklin D. Roosevelt
family it was for years a favorite Sunday night supper dish.

YOU WILL NEED:

rice   light cream
eggs   curry or Worcestershire
parsley   sauce
canned or cooked flaked fish   grated cheese

To 2 cups cooked rice add 4 hard-cooked eggs, chopped; ¼ cup
chopped parsley; 2 cups canned or cooked fish (salmon, tuna,
codfish, or halibut may be used); ½ cup light cream. Season
with plenty of salt, pepper, a little curry powder or a tablespoon
of Worcestershire sauce. Heat in a double boiler or chafing dish,
or place in a buttered casserole, sprinkle with grated cheese and
heat in a moderate oven, 350° F., about 20 minutes.

AT SERVING TIME:
Serve from a chafing dish or casserole. Kedgeree, a big green salad, and dessert make a fine supper menu. Serves 4 to 6.

Kippers in Rum

For brunch at Sunday noon or high tea Sunday at six, nothing is more dramatic than this quick and simple dish of kippers.

YOU WILL NEED:

butter	rum
canned kippered herrings	toast
(not the tomato sauce	lemon or lime
variety)	

In a shallow pan, preferably one which can be brought to the table, melt 1 tablespoon of butter, lay kippered herrings side by side in the pan. Sprinkle with freshly ground black pepper. Add enough white or golden rum to half cover. Let stand to warm slightly, then light the rum, and spoon the burning rum over the herrings until it burns out.

AT SERVING TIME:
The burning may be done right at the table, or the dish may be brought blazing into the room. Serve with triangles of fresh but tered toast and be sure to provide sections of lemon or lime.

Baked Lobster Tails à la Diavolo

Easier to handle than whole fresh lobster, lobster tails are meaty, inexpensive, can be prepared and served exactly like whole live lobsters. Baking in a hot oven is much less trouble than regular broiling and the tails won't curl up.

YOU WILL NEED:

lobster tails	parsley, water cress, or
olive oil and/or butter	lemon
Diavolo Sauce (page 144)	

Have 1 lobster tail for each person. Cut tails open with a scissors on the soft underside. Brush the lobster tails fore and aft with olive oil and/or butter. Place in a shallow pan and bake 15 minutes in a hot oven, 450° F. While they are baking make the Diavolo Sauce.

AT SERVING TIME:
Place the baked lobsters on individual plates. Pour sauce over and around lobster and garnish with parsley, water cress, or lemon sections.

Quick Lobster Newburg

Lobster à la Newburg has a French sound, but actually it belongs to the New York of Delmonico's and the old Waldorf Peacock Alley. As the story goes, this dish was composed by one of Delmonico's chefs for an expansive gentleman whose name was Wenburg. Came a parting of the ways between Mr. Wenburg and his erstwhile favorite haunt. The restaurant, still wishing to feature the glorious concoction on their menu, changed the Wen to New and so it has been Lobster Newburg to this day. Our recipe is not the classic version, and it may not be authentic Wen- or New-burg, but it is powerfully good. Furthermore this is not nearly so rich or calorific as the straight cream and butter version.

YOU WILL NEED:

canned lobster meat	egg
condensed cream of	nutmeg or paprika
mushroom soup	(optional)
sherry	rice or toast or canned
milk or light cream	julienne potato sticks
(optional)	

Start with 2 cups cooked, canned lobster meat. The pieces should be good sized, about ¾ of an inch at least. Combine with 1 can condensed cream of mushroom soup, ¼ to ½ can dry sherry, or you may use equal parts of milk or cream and sherry. Heat but do not boil. Beat 1 egg slightly with a fork. Dip a little of the hot sauce into the egg and stir. This is to prevent the egg from curdling. Add the egg and sauce mixture to the lobster. A touch of paprika may be added, just enough to make the sauce pink.

AT SERVING TIME:
Serve at once, if possible from a chafing dish and add to each portion a few grains of nutmeg. Served with rice or on toast, or garnished with heated julienne potato sticks (canned). Serves 6.

Airborne Salmon Soufflé

One of the airiest and most delicate of soufflés, but very dependable.

YOU WILL NEED:

canned salmon	canned mushroom soup
butter or margarine	sherry or light cream
eggs	canned shrimp (small)
heavy cream	hot pepper sauce

Remove any bones, flake and mash a medium-sized can of salmon. Add ½ cup softened butter or margarine. Blend well. Add, one at a time, the yolks of 4 eggs. Blend 30 seconds in electric blender on high or beat until light, gradually adding ½ cup heavy cream. Pour into a buttered and floured straight-sided 1-quart soufflé dish or pan. Bake in a moderately hot (375° F.) oven, about 25 minutes or until puffed and slightly firm to the gentle touch. Meanwhile to a can of condensed cream of mushroom soup add ¼ cup sherry or light cream, ¼ cup tiny cooked shrimp, and 2 drops hot pepper sauce. Heat but do not boil.

AT SERVING TIME:
Serve instantly accompanied by the shrimp and mushroom sauce.

Salt Mackerel, Virginia Breakfast Style

No doubt there are a few underprivileged Northerners who have never experienced the delight of eating delicate plump fillets of salt mackerel with tiny boiled potatoes on a lazy Sunday noon!

YOU WILL NEED:
fillets of salt mackerel   parsley (optional)
onions

If your grocery store has never heard of salt mackerel fillets (this could happen), you may order them in small wooden kegs by mail. Since the fillets are very salty, it is necessary to soak them in water overnight, then drain, before cooking. To cook, place the fillets in the pan, cover with thinly sliced onions, using 1 medium-sized onion to each pair of fillets. Sprinkle with freshly ground black pepper. Pour about ½ inch of water into the bottom of the pan. Cover and allow the fillets to steam and heat thoroughly until done.

AT SERVING TIME:
Sprinkle if you wish with chopped parsley and serve with tiny boiled potatoes and hot biscuits.

Scalloped Oysters

This is a speeded-up version of the old-fashioned New England recipe for scalloped oysters.

YOU WILL NEED:
canned oysters   prepared herb-flavored
butter   stuffing

Drain oysters and reserve liquid. Mix ½ cup of melted butter with 1½ cups prepared stuffing. You may wish to crush the crumbs a little if they seem too coarse. Put a layer of the stuffing in the bottom of a shallow buttered baking dish, cover with oysters, add 3 tablespoons of oyster liquid, repeat and cover top with remaining crumbs. Bake 30 minutes in a hot oven, 450° F. It is best not to have more than 2 layers, for if 3 layers are used the middle layer will be underdone.

AT SERVING TIME:
Serve from the baking dish in which it is baked. Cole slaw is a traditional accompaniment. Serves 4.

Shad Roe Bonne Femme

Shad roe are the eggs of the fish, a pair of new-moon-shaped crescents held together inside a gossamer-thin but sturdy veil. In most markets at most seasons, canned shad roe are less expensive than fresh. Usually they come packed two pairs to a can, making two large à la carte servings. The canned roe have already been poached, so they require very little extra cooking.

YOU WILL NEED:

canned shad roe	fresh mushrooms
butter	white wine or vermouth
shallots or onion	heavy cream
parsley	

To serve 4, you will need 2 cans of shad roe. Place the roe in a deep skillet along with 2 tablespoons butter, 3 chopped shallots, or ¼ of a small white onion finely chopped, or 1 tablespoon freeze-dried shallots or instant onion. Add 2 teaspoons finely chopped parsley, fresh or dried; a dozen fresh mushrooms, sliced; 1 teaspoon salt, ¼ teaspoon pepper; about 1 cup dry white table wine or vermouth. Bring to a boil and let cook gently about 10 minutes if the roe is fresh, about 5 minutes if canned. Remove shad roe to a heatproof serving dish. Boil down liquid in the skillet to just about a third of its original quantity. Stir in 4 tablespoons heavy cream and, bit by bit, 2 more tablespoons butter. Season to taste with salt and pepper.

AT SERVING TIME:

Just before serving, whip up ¼ cup heavy cream, adding a bit of salt and pepper. Spoon on top of the roe and set the dish low under the broiler for a couple of minutes—just long enough to get puffy and lightly browned. Very rich, but delicate and sumptuous. Makes 4 servings.

Spiced Salmon

Canned salmon may sound dull. Prepared in this spicy manner, it is anything but! In fact, it is so flavorsome that it may well be used as an appetizer, too.

YOU WILL NEED:

canned salmon	bay leaf
vinegar or white wine	romaine, chicory, lettuce
cloves	radishes or green pepper
allspice berries	potato chips or canned
peppercorns	julienne potato sticks

Drain a can of salmon and set in a shallow bowl that can be brought to the table. Meanwhile bring to a boiling point 1 cup vinegar or dry white table wine, 1 teaspoon whole cloves, ½ teaspoon allspice berries, several peppercorns, a little salt, a bay leaf. Pour over the fish, cover and let stand in the refrigerator several hours, or overnight.

AT SERVING TIME:

Decorate the bowl with crisp romaine, chicory, or green lettuce leaves. Garnish with radishes or green pepper rings, and serve with heated potato chips or julienne potato sticks from a can.

Baby Shrimp

Baby shrimp are usually thought of as an appetizer. Here they are a main dish, served with a crisp Italian salad, hot, crusty bread, an appropriate vegetable, and dessert.

YOU WILL NEED:

canned shrimp	fresh orégano or basil
olive oil	parsley
garlic	

Drain tiny canned shrimps and sauté just until heated in olive oil with 2 cloves garlic, crushed; and 1 teaspoon each of fresh chopped orégano or basil, and parsley. If you can't get fresh herbs, use dried but only half as much.

AT SERVING TIME:

If you use this as an appetizer, provide toothpicks or tiny forks and thin slices of Italian or French bread; if as an entrée, pile the shrimp on thin slices of Italian or French bread, brushed with garlic butter and lightly toasted.

Shrimp Jambalaya

Truly one of the great Creole dishes of Louisiana. Probably the original French name was *Jambon au riz*. Many ingredients, such as New Orleans breakfast sausage, oysters, and a large variety of spices, can go into a jambalaya. Our simplified version uses ham, shrimp, and rice.

YOU WILL NEED:

onions
butter or bacon fat
slice of ham
canned shrimp
garlic
tomato juice or canned
   vegetable juice

red pepper or Tabasco
   sauce
parsley or parsley flakes
thyme
quick-cooking rice

Brown 2 medium-sized onions, chopped, in 2 tablespoons of butter or bacon fat, add 1 cup ham cut into ½-inch squares or into thin julienne strips, 2 cups canned shrimp. Allow this mixture to simmer in a covered pan about 5 minutes, then add 1 clove garlic, mashed, 2 cups tomato juice or canned vegetable juice, a few grains of red pepper or 3 or 4 dashes of Tabasco sauce, 1 tablespoon freshly chopped parsley or 1 teaspoon parsley flakes, ½ teaspoon thyme, 1⅓ cups quick-cooking rice, salt to taste. Bring to a full boil uncovered, allow to cook 2 to 3 minutes. Cover and let stand 10 minutes longer. (Cooked ham may be used, but the flavor is not so rich.)

AT SERVING TIME:
Fluff with a fork. Serve with a tossed salad and dessert. This makes a full and satisfying meal. Serves 6.

Tuna à la Grecque

In Greece, they preserve tuna by laying it in crocks and pouring hot olive oil over it. This tuna dish, served with fresh cucumbers in an olive oil vinegar dressing, is a favorite. It makes a quick and deliciously refreshing lunch.

YOU WILL NEED:

canned solid tuna   olive oil
parsley   vinegar
fresh cucumber

Drain 2 8-ounce cans solid tuna. Arrange in 2 cakes on serving
plate. Surround with parsley. In a separate bowl, slice 1 or 2
(depending on size) young, crisp cucumbers thinly, leaving on
green rind. Sprinkle with salt and freshly ground black pepper.
Pour over dressing made by mixing ½ cup olive oil with ¼ cup
vinegar. Chill in refrigerator.

AT SERVING TIME:
Pass cucumbers to be spooned over tuna.

8

Double-Quick Meats

BECAUSE THE MEAT of the meal is frequently the most time-consuming as well as the costliest part of the menu, the time- and money-saving recipes and suggestions in this chapter will, we hope, be of great help to you. Within this field great strides have been made in the past. Your local chain store or favorite delicatessen has a wide variety of meat specialties—lamb and veal as well as beef stews—several types of meat balls presented in a variety of sauces—all sorts of meat pies, pot roasts, meats in gravy. If you are careful to select some of the best-known brands you should be agreeably surprised at the good flavor of many canned meats.

In a number of cases manufacturers have been singularly successful in avoiding or disguising a canned flavor. But even the best, in our opinion, may be greatly improved—taste freshened and flavor heightened by herbs, spices, and/or wine or sour cream.

Most canned meats and gravies are not particularly attractive to look at. Too often they have a grayish or drab brick color but this can easily be changed into the deep glossy brown of a French ragout by the addition of widely available bottled gravy darkeners, such as Kitchen Bouquet or Gravy Master. These products contain some spices but the base is caramelized sugar which does not sweeten food. However, if you use too much you might get a slight bitter taste. So add it little by little.

Canned meats are by no means the whole story. There are quick-frozen meats too. And also most helpful to the hurried cook with a small family are ready-cooked meats—sliced roasts and baked hams—that are generally available at delicatessens, whose owners always seem to prefer to sell them in sandwiches but can sometimes be persuaded to omit the bread. Buy thick slices and you can embark on a series of dishes that were formerly possible only to those who must first "roast a joint."

May we reiterate that many of the recipes included in this group are economical and need no last-minute fussing.

RECIPES

Beef Stew with Wine
Boats of Beef
Cold Roast Beef Martinique
Dried Beef and Celery Sauce
Beef Stroganoff
Irish Stout Beef
Sliced Beef en Gelée
California Chili
Baked Ham Flambé
Ham in Champagne Sauce
Baked Corned Beef Hash de Luxe
Crunchy Brown Hashburgers
Pizza Hash
Baked Lamb Chops Farci

Breaded Lamb Chops aux Fines Herbes
Butterfly Barbecued Lamb
Quick Swedish Meat Balls
Baked Stuffed Pork Chops with Apple
Intoxicated Pork Chops
Ragout with Black Olives
Country Sausage with Fried Apples
Lamb Pasty
Shepherd's Pie au Gratin
Hasty Tamale Pie
New Warrington Scouse

Beef Stew with Wine

Several good beginnings for beef stew are available in cans. Few are savory enough to serve as is. But the additions suggested here will improve them.

YOU WILL NEED:

canned beef stew
Kitchen Bouquet
red wine

garlic
marjoram or orégano
parsley (optional)

To a can of beef stew, add ½ teaspoon Kitchen Bouquet, 1 to 2 tablespoons red wine, or a little more if you wish, ½ to 1 clove garlic well crushed, and/or ½ teaspoon dried marjoram or orégano. Simmer (do not boil) at least 5 minutes to blend the flavors.

AT SERVING TIME:
Serve in heated casserole. Stew should be bubbling hot. A tablespoon of finely chopped parsley may be sprinkled on the top to give that homemade appearance and a fresh flavor.

Boats of Beef

This is a quick version of piroshki, the boat-shaped meat pies that are made all over eastern Europe. Often they are served as an adjunct to a rich consommé or chicken broth or along with a hearty borsch (see pages 40–42). Or they may be used as an entree for lunch or supper.

YOU WILL NEED:

oven-ready packaged biscuits, regular or buttermilk type
chopped cooked beef
onion
raw egg
hard-cooked egg
butter, chicken or goose fat
parsley

To make 10 piroshskis, open a package of unbaked refrigerated biscuits, either plain or made with buttermilk. Flatten the biscuits with your hands or rolling pin until they are only about ¼ inch thick. Allow to stand at room temperature while you make the filling:

Use 1 cup chopped cooked beef (chopped junior food beef, canned chopped beef, delicatessen beef, or leftovers). Add 1 small onion finely chopped, 1 whole raw egg, 1 chopped hard-cooked egg. Add 1 tablespoon softened butter or chicken or goose fat, season to taste with salt and pepper, and add 1 tablespoon fresh chopped parsley or 2 teaspoons dry parsley.

Place a spoonful of the filling in the center of each biscuit. Bring the edges up together to form a boat shape, open at the top. Brush with beaten egg. Bake in a hot oven (450° F.), for 15 or 20 minutes.

AT SERVING TIME:
Serve hot as an accompaniment to soup or as an entree with a leafy green vegetable. Also good cold. A nice change from the usual sandwiches.

Cold Roast Beef Martinique

Leftover or delicatessen roast beef looks and tastes delicious when served like this.

YOU WILL NEED:

cold roast beef	mustard or curry powder
olive oil	parsley or green pepper
vinegar	

Arrange 6 slices beef on a platter. Pour over Martinique French dressing made of ½ cup olive oil, ¼ cup vinegar, ½ teaspoon salt, ¼ teaspoon pepper, ½ teaspoon dry mustard or curry powder, 1 tablespoon chopped parsley and/or chopped green pepper.

AT SERVING TIME:
Garnish with lettuce or escarole, stuffed olives or pickles, celery sticks and leaves. Serves 4.

Dried Beef and Celery Sauce

This is a fine main dish for a late breakfast or a light supper.

YOU WILL NEED:

dried beef
condensed cream of celery
    soup
water, milk, or light cream

dehydrated horseradish
brandy (optional)
toast or English muffins
parsley, chives, or almonds

Cover ¼ pound dried beef with a little cold water and bring to a boil. Take from the stove and let stand for about 5 minutes. This removes the excess salt from the beef and softens it. Drain the beef and add it to a can of condensed cream of celery soup that has been diluted with ½ can of water, milk or light cream. Stir in ½ teaspoon dehydrated horseradish. The addition of 1 tablespoon brandy to the sauce will add piquancy for a particularly elegant effect with no suggestion of a liquor flavor. Heat slowly, stirring once or twice.

AT SERVING TIME:

Serve on toast or English muffins. Sprinkle with chopped parsley, chives, or whole toasted almonds. Serves 4.

Beef Stroganoff

Chip steaks are ideal for the making of this delicious entree.

YOU WILL NEED:

chip steaks
canned beef gravy
tomato juice

sour cream
butter
onion

Cut chip steaks into strips, allowing at least 2 steaks for each portion—3 for heartier appetites. To 6 chip steaks allow 1 can beef gravy. Bring gravy to a boil, stir in 1 tablespoon tomato juice, 2 to 4 tablespoons sour cream and meanwhile lightly brown beef strips in 1 tablespoon butter with a little chopped onion. This should not take more than 1 minute. Overcooking toughens the meat. Put the pieces of meat in the sauce, simmer 5 minutes.

AT SERVING TIME:

Stir well and serve with rice, julienne potato sticks from a can, or noodles.

Irish Stout Beef

The original recipe from Ireland calls for Guinness' stout, a
black-brown ale, but you might substitute dark beer.

YOU WILL NEED:

onions	canned beef consommé
bacon fat	flour
chopped beef	Kitchen Bouquet
Guinness' stout or dark	parsley
beer	mashed potatoes

Slice 2 good-sized onions very thin and lightly brown in 4 tablespoons bacon fat. When the onion is golden add to the skillet
2 pounds chopped beef. Brown lightly. Pour in 1 cup Guinness'
stout or dark beer and 2 cups canned beef consommé. Cover and
cook gently 10 minutes. Meanwhile, mix to a paste 3 flat tablespoons flour with a little cold water. Add 2 teaspoons Kitchen
Bouquet. Bring to a boil and cook while stirring for 5 minutes or
until flour entirely loses any raw flavor. Combine the meat and
the gravy. Sprinkle liberally with parsley. Serves 6. Can easily be
doubled or tripled.

AT SERVING TIME:

Serve inside a border of mashed potatoes.

Sliced Beef en Gelée

This is a quick, easy version of a classic French specialty. It can
be made from sliced roast beef (delicatessen beef slices are fine),
pot roast, or leftovers. This is one aspic that does not require
troublesome unmolding. It is served right out of the dish in
which it jells.

YOU WILL NEED:

sliced roast beef	Worcestershire sauce
orégano or thyme	carrots
condensed consommé	green peppers
plain gelatin	

Have your beef cut in slices slightly thicker than for sandwiches.
Season well with salt, pepper, a little orégano or thyme. Lay 6

slices of beef overlapping in a shallow serving dish. For the aspic combine 2 cans condensed consommé and 1 can water. Soak 2 envelopes plain gelatin in ½ cup water and dissolve in 1 cup hot water; add 1 teaspoon Worcestershire sauce and pour over beef. Garnish the top of the dish with circles of thinly sliced carrots and green peppers. You can make a flower using 5 circles of carrots as petals, strips of green pepper as the stem. Put in the refrigerator to jell. This aspic should set in about an hour.

AT SERVING TIME:
Bring the dish to the table, cut into serving pieces. A tossed green salad dressing flavored with a little tarragon vinegar is particularly good with the beef. Serves 4 to 6.

California Chili

A little extra garlic and paprika, a teaspoon of cumin seed provide flavor for canned chili.

YOU WILL NEED:

canned chili con carne
with beans or a can of
chili and a can of red
kidney beans

garlic
paprika
cumin seed (optional)
parsley or chives

Crush well 2 cloves of garlic and combine with 2 cans of chili con carne with beans *or* 1 can chili (meat) and 1 can cooked red kidney beans. Season with 1 tablespoon paprika, 1 teaspoon cumin seed. Heat, stirring occasionally.

AT SERVING TIME:
Serve with celery, dill pickles, and crackers. Or place the chili mixture inside a ring of cooked rice or cooked yellow cornmeal mush. Sprinkle with chopped parsley or chives.

Baked Ham Flambé

For a buffet supper, nothing is more dramatic than a lordly baked ham ceremoniously flared, if you wish, with rum or brandy. A canned ham is a good stand-by. Whether precooked, home boiled, or canned the procedure for baking is the same.

YOU WILL NEED:

cooked ham   honey
dry mustard   brandied or spiced peaches
cloves   rum or brandy

Use a whole ham or for a smaller group a half or quarter ham.
Rub about 1 tablespoon dry mustard into the ham. With a knife,
score the rind into diamond shapes. Stud each diamond with a
whole clove. Pour over plenty of honey, 1 or 2 cupfuls, depending
upon the size of the piece. Bake in a moderate oven, 350° F.,
long enough to heat through and glaze prettily. Baste 2 to 3
times with the juices from the bottom of the pan.

AT SERVING TIME:

Set on a large platter. In this case, the platter need not be
warmed, for ham is best served neither piping hot nor chilled
but merely warm. Garnish with brandied or spiced peaches. To
flambé a ham, warm very slightly ½ to 1 cup rum or brandy. Set
fire to the liquor and pour around the ham. Always serve ham in
paper-thin slices.

Ham in Champagne Sauce

A delicate champagne sauce is an excellent dress-up for canned
ham! If you are temporarily out of champagne, you may substitute grape juice (white) or white wine.

YOU WILL NEED:

canned ham   lemon juice
cornstarch   champagne
canned consommé or   green seedless grapes
    chicken broth

Slice a canned ham in ½-inch thick pieces. Meanwhile make
sauce by mixing 1 tablespoon cornstarch in ¼ cup water. Add 1
cup hot canned consommé or chicken broth. Pour into wide
skillet and cook, stirring constantly, until clear and slightly
thickened. Then add 3 tablespoons lemon juice and 1 cup
champagne. Bring to a boil. Lower flame and tenderly place ham
slices in sauce. Allow to heat gently 5 minutes.

AT SERVING TIME:
Sprinkle, if you like, with small green seedless grapes.

Baked Corned Beef Hash de Luxe

Many and varied are the varieties of corned beef hash on the market. Shop around for a brand with a low proportion of potato. Dress it up like this.

YOU WILL NEED:

canned corned beef hash	canned beets (optional)
onion	butter
milk, ketchup, or chili sauce	parsley

To a 6- or 8-ounce can of corned beef hash, add 2 tablespoons finely chopped raw onion, 2 tablespoons milk or ketchup or chili sauce. Add ½ cup finely diced cooked beets if desired. Butter generously a shallow casserole or pie pan. Spread hash in the pan. Dot with butter. Bake in a moderate oven, 350° F., until piping hot and crusty underneath, about 20 to 25 minutes.

AT SERVING TIME:
Sprinkle with chopped parsley and serve piping hot from the baking dish. Serves 4.

Crunchy Brown Hashburgers

YOU WILL NEED:

canned corned beef hash	corn bread or English muffins
prepared mustard	chili sauce
Kitchen Bouquet	bottled steak sauce

Chill canned hash and open on both ends. Push out the cylinder. Cut into 4 patties. Brush with prepared mustard and then very lightly with Kitchen Bouquet, and cook on a heavy, well-greased griddle or frying pan over moderate heat at least 12 minutes on each side—slowly—so that a good crust has a chance to form.

Split squares of hot corn bread, or toasted English muffin, and slip patty on each half.

AT SERVING TIME:
Have ready a sauce, hot or cold, made by combining 4 tablespoons chili sauce with 3 tablespoons bottled steak sauce. Spoon over patties and pass more of the sauce if you like.

Pizza Hash

A can of corned beef hash, glorified with cheese, tomato sauce and mushrooms, provides a swift and delicious luncheon or supper dish.

YOU WILL NEED:

canned corned beef hash	canned chopped mushrooms
sharp processed American cheese	garlic salt
	orégano
canned tomato sauce	grated Parmesan cheese

Chill a 1-pound can of corned beef hash. Open on both ends and carefully push out the cylinder. Cut into 6 slices and arrange in a baking dish. Sprinkle with 1 cup shredded sharp processed American cheese. Combine an 8-ounce can tomato sauce, a 3-ounce can broiled chopped mushrooms drained, ½ teaspoon garlic salt, and ½ teaspoon crushed orégano. Spoon over hash. Sprinkle with 2 tablespoons grated Parmesan cheese. Bake in a moderately hot (375° F.) oven about 20 minutes, or until the hash is well heated, the cheeses melted, and the sauce all bubbly. Makes 3 servings.

AT SERVING TIME:
Serve from its own baking dish while piping hot. Assorted fresh vegetables, relishes, and crusty garlic bread go well with this . . . or you might even want to serve the portions atop a thick slice of toasted garlic bread.

Baked Lamb Chops Farci

Because these chops need no watching while they are baking in the oven, they are a perfect choice for the hostess cook.

YOU WILL NEED:

thick lamb chops
prepared poultry stuffing
flour
egg

canned beef gravy
  (optional)
dehydrated mixed
  vegetable flakes
  (optional)

Have chops cut about 1½ inches thick and slit through the lean meat right to the bone. Prepare packaged poultry dressing according to directions, reserving about ½ cup for coating the chops. Place inside the chop as much as the space will hold. Press together lightly. Skewer with a toothpick if you wish. Dip chops in flour, slightly beaten egg, and poultry dressing. If the crumbs are coarse roll them out. Set chops in a buttered baking dish that can be taken to the table. Bake in a hot oven, 425° F., about 30 minutes, at which time the meat should be sufficiently cooked and the crumbs deliciously browned.

AT SERVING TIME:

Serve plain or with Sauce Jardinière made by heating 1 can beef gravy with 2 tablespoons dehydrated mixed vegetable flakes. Makes 1 cup sauce—enough for 4 to 6 chops.

Breaded Lamb Chops aux Fines Herbes

An herb-scented prepared poultry stuffing makes a quick and flavorsome coating for lamb chops. If the crumbs are coarse, crush them a little. If fine, use as they are.

YOU WILL NEED:

thin lamb chops
flour
egg

prepared poultry stuffing
salad oil or shortening

Do not sprinkle lamb chops with salt and pepper. The prepared stuffing is probably seasoned enough. Dip the chops first in flour, then in slightly beaten egg, then in the prepared poultry stuffing. In a heavy frying pan, heat about an inch of salad oil or shortening to 385° F., hot enough to brown an inch cube of bread in 40 seconds. Cook not more than 4 chops at a time from 5 to 8 minutes. Drain on paper towels.

AT SERVING TIME:

Serve on heated platter or plates. Garnish with curly lettuce leaves or escarole.

Butterfly Barbecued Lamb

This is new, startling, wild: a leg of lamb cooked in 30 minutes! The secret is to have all bones removed. Lamb emerges from grill, broiler, or oven gloriously crusty brown on the outside, rose-pink in the middle. And the special marinade adds a memorable taste.

YOU WILL NEED:

a leg of lamb, boned and slightly flattened (have your butcher do this)	bottled garlic salad dressing soy sauce onions

Have your butcher (even the impersonal type at your supermarket will do it) remove bones from, and slightly flatten, a leg of lamb. Marinate the boned leg of lamb in a bottle of garlic salad dressing along with ½ cup soy sauce and 6 sliced onions. The marinating may be brief, only about 20 minutes, or it can be long, even overnight. No extra seasoning is needed on the meat, not even salt and pepper. Drain the meat, saving the onions and marinade. Broil meat over charcoal and hickory chips about 15 minutes on each side, or until done to suit your taste, basting occasionally with the marinade. The cooking can, of course, be done under the broiler indoors (or the meat may be roasted in a hot oven—400° F.). In any case, the length of time required will be about the same and must be adjusted according to the degree of doneness you prefer. (We like our lamb pink!)

AT SERVING TIME:

This leg of lamb is as easy to slice as a filet mignon. Additional hints: If the leg of lamb is fair sized when you buy it, you might want the butcher to remove a couple of hefty double-thick lamb chops, which you can wrap for the freezer. Take the bones home with you, too, and freeze them to make lamb broth for another day. And the roast itself can be divided into 2 parts, one or both to be grilled, according to the crowd.

Quick Swedish Meat Balls

It is possible to transform canned meat balls in spaghetti sauce into a delicious prototype of the famous Swedish köttbullar.

YOU WILL NEED:

canned meat balls in spaghetti sauce	Kitchen Bouquet allspice heavy cream

To meat balls and their sauce, add ¼ teaspoon allspice, ½ teaspoon Kitchen Bouquet, simmer 5 or 6 minutes.

AT SERVING TIME:

Stir in about 4 tablespoons heavy cream. Serve in true Swedish fashion with boiled potatoes and pass lingonberries or whole berry cranberry sauce. Green beans are the traditional accompaniment to this combination.

Baked Stuffed Pork Chops with Apple

YOU WILL NEED:

pork chops	canned sweet potatoes
onions	canned apples
prepared poultry stuffing	nutmeg or mace (optional)
butter	rum (optional)

Place 4 pork chops on a large oven-proof platter. On top of each chop, place a mound of onion stuffing made by adding 4 boiled and coarsely chopped onions to 1 package prepared poultry stuffing and as much butter or liquid as the package directions indicate. Bake in a moderate oven, 350° F., about 1½ hours or until almost cooked. Take from oven; arrange around the chops canned drained sweet potatoes and canned baked apples. Brush potatoes and apples with melted butter, a very small amount of nutmeg or mace, if desired. Put back into the oven 15 or 20 minutes longer.

AT SERVING TIME:

Serve from the platter on which they were baked. If desired, you can make this dish most dramatic by serving it flambé—simply

warm slightly about 1/2 cup rum. Pour over the meat and set fire
to the rum.

Intoxicated Pork Chops

Doused with a generous quaff of Marsala, these pork chops are a
marvel for speed and elegance, especially if you use the thinly
sliced brown 'n' serve type.

YOU WILL NEED:

brown 'n' serve pork chops	garlic
butter	tomato paste
olive oil	canned consommé
Marsala wine	parsley

Season 8 thin brown 'n' serve pork chops with salt and pepper.
Brown in 1 tablespoon butter, 1 tablespoon olive oil about 5
minutes on each side. Add 1 Cup Marsala wine; 1 clove garlic,
crushed; 1 tablespoon tomato paste; 1/2 cup condensed canned
consommé, undiluted. Cook about 5 minutes longer.

AT SERVING TIME:
Sprinkle generously with chopped parsley and serve immediately.
Serves 4.

Ragout with Black Olives

This is an interesting and quick dish to make from leftover
meats.

YOU WILL NEED:

canned beef gravy	leftover or delicatessen
Worcestershire sauce, claret,	cooked veal, pork, or
or Marsala wine	lamb
cayenne or Tabasco sauce	canned mushrooms
(optional)	(optional)
Kitchen Bouquet (optional)	black olives

To a can of beef gravy, add 1 teaspoon Worcestershire sauce or
2 tablespoons claret or Marsala wine. Season with a few grains of

cayenne or a few drops of Tabasco if desired. For a darker, richer color add ½ teaspoon Kitchen Bouquet. To the heated sauce add about 2 cups cooked veal, pork, or lamb, cut into ¾-inch cubes. One 3-ounce can sliced mushrooms may be added if desired. Simmer 2 or 3 minutes.

AT SERVING TIME:
Garnish with black olives and serve with rice.

Country Sausage with Fried Apples

Sausage and apple slices make a combination beloved in old-time plantation kitchens.

YOU WILL NEED:

pork sausage	nutmeg or cinnamon
canned sliced apples	(optional)

Shape sausage meat into flat round cakes at least ½-inch thick. They will shrink as they cook. Put into a cold frying pan without grease. Cook slowly about 15 minutes, turning to brown evenly. Pour off fat and save it. Keep sausages warm. Drain canned sliced apples and dry on a paper towel. Put back into the frying pan enough fat to cover the bottom of the pan. Heat the fat and put in the apples. Brown quickly on one side and carefully turn with a pancake turner to brown the other side.

AT SERVING TIME:
Arrange the sausage cakes in the center of a heated platter with the browned apple slices around the edge. The apples may be lightly sprinkled with nutmeg or cinnamon.

Lamb Pasty

A generous hearty lamb pie. Poppy seeds on the crust add unusual savor.

YOU WILL NEED:
   canned lamb stew   Kitchen Bouquet
   canned peas   piecrust mix
   canned white onions   poppy seeds

To 2 1-pound cans lamb stew, add a 1-pound can each of green peas and white onions, drained; and 1 teaspoon Kitchen Bouquet. Pour into a 9-inch pie pan. Cover with crust made from piecrust mix (directions on back of package), and sprinkle with 2 tablespoons poppy seeds. Cut slit in top to form a design. Bake at 400° F., for 25 minutes.

AT SERVING TIME:
Serve steaming hot, accompanied by a bowl of glistening mint jelly, and a fruit compote for dessert. Serves 6 to 8.

Shepherd's Pie au Gratin

A new way to prepare a very old-time dish.

YOU WILL NEED:
   quick-frozen mashed   onion juice or onion
      potatoes   grated cheese
   canned hash
   catsup, chili sauce, or
      steak sauce

Heat a package of quick-frozen mashed potatoes according to package directions. Cover the bottom of a baking dish with half of the potatoes. On top of the potatoes, place a thick layer of hash, well seasoned and moistened with catsup, chili sauce, or steak sauce and onion juice, or you may use 2 tablespoons finely chopped raw onion. Top with the rest of the potatoes. Sprinkle generously with grated cheese and bake in a hot oven, 425° F., about 20 minutes or long enough to heat thoroughly and brown delicately.

AT SERVING TIME:

Serve from the baking dish with a green salad or crisp carrot sticks, celery, and radishes. Serves 6.

Hasty Tamale Pie

Three canned specialties combine happily to make a perfect dish for a supper or buffet. Try to have the ripe olives. They add a lot.

YOU WILL NEED:

garlic

canned chili con carne or
   canned chili and canned
   red kidney beans

whole kernel canned corn

ripe olives

canned tamales

sharp cheese

Butter a shallow baking dish, rub well with garlic. Put into the dish a can of chili con carne, or 1 can chili (meat) and 1 can red kidney beans, a small can, about 1¼ cups, whole kernel corn— the kind that comes complete with pimientos and green pepper is particularly good. Sprinkle with ½ cup pitted ripe olives. Lay on top canned tamales (with the husks removed if there are husks). Sprinkle with about ¾ cup grated sharp cheese. Bake in a moderately hot oven, 350° F., until hot and brown—about 20 to 25 minutes. For even greater haste, heat ingredients separately on top of stove. Combine, sprinkle with cheese and set under the broiler just long enough for the cheese to melt and brown.

AT SERVING TIME:

Bring to the table in the dish in which it was cooked. If it's a Mexican dish all the better! We know a man who makes a specialty of tamale pies. He uses a copper pan with handles and ties on two bright colored napkins of different hues. Serves 6 to 8 generously.

New Warrington Scouse

This version of a Lancashire-type lamb stew is, quite unbelievably, ready in less than 30 minutes.

YOU WILL NEED:

lamb stew meat	canned potatoes
meat tenderizer	canned chicken gravy
butter or margarine	cooked turnip or rutabaga
canned white onions	(optional)
canned whole baby carrots	vinegar

Trim away excess fat and gristle from 3 pounds lamb stew meat, then cut each chunk into 1-inch pieces or smaller. Sprinkle with meat tenderizer (following directions on jar). Sauté meat in 3 tablespoons butter or margarine until very lightly tanned, about 5 minutes. It will still be a little pink inside. Add 1 can drained cooked white onions, 1 small can or jar whole small baby carrots (with liquid), 1 small can potatoes, well drained, 1 10-ounce can chicken gravy, 1 cup diced cooked turnip or rutabaga, if desired. If you think you need more liquid, you may add a little more chicken broth or water. Allow to cook slowly, uncovered, at least 15 minutes longer or until meat is tender and flavors well blended. Taste and correct the seasonings, adding salt and pepper if needed.

AT SERVING TIME:

A teaspoonful of vinegar added at the last gives a little sparkle without any suggestion of sour. Serves 6.

9

Poultry

SOME OF THE BEST and also some of the worst of the ready-to-serve canned and quick-frozen foods are chicken products. Perhaps one reason for the wide disparity in quality may be the enormous variety of brands, manufacturers, and techniques. Find a good brand and once you have found it never give it up—or at least don't give it up unless it should become evident that there has been a change in management and a consequent change in quality. (Sad to say—this sometimes happens.)

In addition to the ubiquitous canned and quick-frozen chicken à la king, which is so useful in so many guises, you should acquaint yourself with canned chicken fricassee, in which, as in the old-time Sunday dinner, the chicken is left on the bones.

Still another boon to the time-pressed is quick-frozen poultry which is cleaned, cut up and all ready to be thawed and cooked. And blessings on the practical genius who first thought of selling chicken parts!

You no longer need to own a poultry farm or shares in a fancy restaurant in order to be able to enjoy breast of chicken suprême —whenever you have a mind for it.

RECIPES

Asopao

Casserole à la King

Chicken au Gratin

Chicken Divan

Chicken Flambé with Black Cherries

Chicken Livers Stuffed in Fresh Tomato

Chicken Mumbled

Chicken Paprika

Chicken Soufflé with Almonds

Chicken Timbales

Chicken with White Wine and White Grapes

Artichokes with Minced Chicken

Molasses Chicken with Artichoke Hearts

Duck in Aspic au Cointreau

Roast Duck Bigarade

Pheasant in Wine

Paella à la Valenciana

Chestnut Stuffing

Mushroom Stuffing

Asopao

As the name implies, this is a "soupy" stew.

YOU WILL NEED:

canned stewed tomatoes

bay leaves

garlic

dried orégano

olive oil

canned Spanish rice

canned chicken, lobster, shrimp, or tuna

canned peas

hard-cooked eggs

To 1 large can stewed tomatoes (which include green peppers, onions, and the like), add 2 very small bay leaves; 1 or 2 cloves garlic, crushed; ¼ teaspoon dried orégano; 2 tablespoons olive oil. Cook 5 minutes. Add 2 cans Spanish rice, 1½ cups canned chicken, lobster, shrimp, crabmeat, or tuna. Stir with a fork. Allow to become blazing hot.

AT SERVING TIME:

Fish out the bay leaves. Arrange the *asopao* in a shallow serving dish. Make a wide border of drained canned peas (1 can). In the center, arrange a "flower" made of 2 hard-cooked eggs cut into quarters or slices. In the heart of the flower, place the 2 bay leaves. Makes 6 servings.

Casserole à la King

YOU WILL NEED:

canned macaroni in cheese
   sauce
canned chicken à la king
grated cheese

bread crumbs
butter
parsley or water cress

Heat separately on top of the stove canned macaroni and canned chicken à la king. Arrange in layers in a shallow casserole. Top layer should be macaroni. Sprinkle with 4 tablespoons grated cheese mixed with 4 tablespoons packaged bread crumbs. Dot with butter. Set under the broiler just long enough to become bubbly and brown.

AT SERVING TIME:
Garnish with parsley or water cress. Serve from its own dish. Serves 4.

Chicken au Gratin

Start with a small cooked chicken, barbecued, boiled, or roasted either by yourself or at your kindly delicatessen.

YOU WILL NEED:

cooked chicken
canned sliced mushrooms
canned stewed tomatoes

condensed cream of
   mushroom soup
dry vermouth
sharp Cheddar cheese

Cut the meat off the bones of a small cooked chicken and slice it into julienne strips. Add 2 4-ounce cans sliced mushrooms and 1 large can stewed tomatoes, both well drained, 1 can cream of mushroom soup, undiluted, 1/2 cup dry vermouth. Mix lightly and place in a buttered casserole. Set in a moderate oven (350° F.) until bubbling hot, about 25 minutes. Remove, sprinkle with a heavy layer of good sharp Cheddar cheese. Set low under the broiler and brown until puffy and golden, about 3 minutes. Serves 6.

AT SERVING TIME:
Serve immediately, in its own casserole accompanied by a crisp green salad and crusty French bread.

Chicken Divan

A certain New York restaurant has become famous for a dish that is quickly achieved at home. Though the recipe below may not be exactly the same, it is a delicious facsimile.

YOU WILL NEED:
broccoli or asparagus   mayonnaise
chicken or turkey   grated cheese
egg white

On a buttered heatproof dish arrange 4 stalks lightly cooked broccoli or 8 stalks cooked asparagus. Cover with 4 thin slices chicken or turkey (from the delicatessen, if you have no leftovers). Top with Sauce Divan made by adding 1 stiffly beaten egg white to 1 cup mayonnaise. Sprinkle lightly with 4 tablespoons grated cheese. Set in a moderate oven, 325° F., just long enough for the dish to heat thoroughly and the sauce to brown slightly—about 10 minutes.

AT SERVING TIME:
Bring to the table immediately and serve from the same dish. Serves 2 to 4.

Chicken Flambé with Black Cherries

A bird, bought ready cooked from a rotisserie, covered with canned cherries and flamed with brandy makes a dramatic entree.

YOU WILL NEED:
a roast chicken   brandy or rum
butter   canned pitted black Bing
Kitchen Bouquet   cherries

Place chicken on an ovenproof dish, preferably one that can be brought to the table. Combine 4 tablespoons melted butter or salad oil with 2 teaspoons Kitchen Bouquet. Thoroughly brush the bird with this mixture. Sprinkle bird with salt and freshly ground pepper (usually rotisserie chickens are lacking in seasoning) and a tablespoon of brandy or rum. Set in a hot oven (400° F.) long enough to heat thoroughly (time depends upon the size of the chicken). Meanwhile heat and drain a small can of pitted black Bing cherries. A few minutes before serving time arrange cherries around chicken, pour on about ¼ cup of juice.

AT SERVING TIME:
Have on hand ¼ to ½ cup brandy or golden rum. To ensure a good flambé, the liquor should be slightly warm. Set ablaze. Pour over the chicken and cherries. Serve as soon as the flames have died down.

Chicken Livers Stuffed in Fresh Tomato

A delightful lunch or supper dish, or if you use small tomatoes, it could be a first course at dinner.

YOU WILL NEED:

fresh tomatoes	canned sliced mushrooms
fresh chicken livers	A-1 sauce
flour	parsley
onion	dry sherry (optional)
butter	coarse bread crumbs

Begin by cutting off the tops and hollowing 6 medium tomatoes. Sprinkle with salt and turn upside down to drain for a few minutes. Meanwhile, cut 1 pound of chicken livers in halves. Lightly dust with flour and sprinkle with salt and freshly ground black pepper. Sauté 4 tablespoons finely chopped fresh (or 3 tablespoons minced, dried) onion in 4 tablespoons butter. Add a 6-ounce can sliced mushrooms, drained. Add the chicken livers, cooking about 1 minute on each side (just long enough to turn color so that no blood shows). Add 1 teaspoon A-1 sauce. Scatter generously with chopped fresh or freeze-dried parsley. Add 1 or 2 tablespoons dry sherry if desired.

Spoon the mixture into the tomatoes. Set on a buttered oven-proof serving dish, preferably one that can go on the table. Sprinkle with coarse bread crumbs. Dot lightly with bits of butter and broil about 5 inches below heat only about 4 minutes, or until bread crumbs are toasty brown. The tomatoes will be barely heated, but this is as it should be.

AT SERVING TIME:
Serve from the dish in which they were baked, accompanied by fresh broccoli and bread sticks.

Chicken Mumbled

As a change from all the usual long-cooked chicken stews, try this accelerated version of an old English dish done fast as a polka because you start with such young and tender birds, 2 or 2½ pound broilers, cut into quarters.

YOU WILL NEED:

young broilers	canned white onions
canned chicken broth	canned peas
celery	canned baby carrots or
onion	canned button
bay leaf	mushrooms (optional)
flour	fresh parsley
heavy cream	buttered toast

To serve 4 sumptuously, you will need 2 birds. Cover chicken pieces with 1 quart hot canned chicken broth. Add 2 stalks celery cut into inch pieces, 2 tablespoons minced onion, ½ bay leaf. Bring to a boil; half-cover the pan and allow to cook until the chicken is fork-tender. This should take only about 20 to 25 minutes. Meanwhile, smooth 3 tablespoons flour into 4 table-spoons heavy cream. Pour a small amount of the chicken broth into the creamy mixture. Stir again. There should be no lumps. Then turn the whole thing into a casserole. Allow to cook about 5 minutes longer, or until the sauce has the look and texture of light coffee cream. Add 1 can white onions, drained, and 2 cups canned drained peas. Canned baby carrots or button mushrooms may be added if desired. Bring to a boil again and serve.

AT SERVING TIME:
Lavishly sprinkle with fresh parsley, decorate with toast that has been buttered and cut into triangles, and serve from casserole.

Chicken Paprika

This is an unorthodox but delightfully flavored version of a famous Hungarian specialty.

YOU WILL NEED:

onion	canned chicken fricassee
butter	sour cream
paprika	

Thinly slice and gently fry in butter 1 medium-sized onion. Add 1 flat tablespoon paprika and 4 tablespoons water. Allow the onion to become thoroughly soft, then add 1 can chicken fricassee. Heat thoroughly and stir in carelessly and streakily, ¼ cup thick sour cream. Do not boil after the cream is in.

AT SERVING TIME:
Serve immediately with buttered wide noodles scattered with poppy seeds or slivered almonds, which are available in tins.

Chicken Soufflé with Almonds

"Something elegant" for a luncheon party. Have guests seated at the table—keep them happy with a chilled soup or other first course—it won't matter if they have to wait a few minutes for the soufflé. It's worth waiting for.

YOU WILL NEED:

condensed cream of chicken soup	canned chicken
quick-cooking tapioca	eggs
	almonds or Brazil nuts

Heat slowly 1 can condensed cream of chicken soup. Add 2 tablespoons tapioca and 1 cup finely diced cooked canned chicken.

Heat thoroughly. Take from fire. Cool 5 minutes. Add 6 well-beaten egg yolks. Fold in 6 stiffly beaten egg whites. Pour into ungreased 2-quart casserole. Bake in a hot oven, 400° F., for 25 minutes or until soufflé is tall and puffy, firm and golden brown.

AT SERVING TIME:
Sprinkle with ½ cup toasted buttered and slivered almonds or Brazil nut chips. Serve immediately. Makes 6 servings.

Chicken Timbales

They sound and look very fancy. Made with canned cooked chicken, they are prepared almost as easily as they are eaten.

YOU WILL NEED:

condensed cream of	parsley
mushroom soup	eggs
cooked chicken	Sauce Suprême (page 154)

To 1 can condensed cream of mushroom soup, add 1 cup finely chopped cooked chicken, 1 tablespoon freshly chopped parsley or 1 teaspoon dried parsley flakes. Heat preferably in double boiler. Off heat, add 3 slightly beaten eggs. Place mixture in 6 custard cups, which have been slightly buttered, filling them about two-thirds full. Place in a pan of hot water and bake 20 minutes in a moderate oven, 350° F., or until firm. Allow to stand in a warm place about 5 minutes.

AT SERVING TIME:
Unmold by running a knife around the edges and turning upside down on a plate. Serve with Sauce Suprême. Serves 6.

Chicken with White Wine and White Grapes

YOU WILL NEED:

canned chicken fricassee	white seedless grapes, fresh
dry white table wine	or canned
curry or turmeric	canned wild rice or saffron
	rice (optional)

Open and empty a can of chicken fricassee with its gravy into a pan. Rinse the tin with 4 tablespoons dry white table wine such as Riesling, Rhine wine, or Moselle. Add about ½ teaspoon curry powder or turmeric. Season with a little extra salt, freshly ground black pepper. Mix thoroughly. Bring to boil, simmer about 2 minutes but do not boil. Add ½ cup tiny white seedless grapes. If canned seedless grapes are used, drain them first and heat for a minute in 2 tablespoons of butter.

AT SERVING TIME:
For the utmost in elegance serve with wild rice, which can be bought canned and ready for heating, or saffron rice. Serves 2 or 3.

Artichokes with Minced Chicken

An interesting main dish for luncheon is made from canned French artichokes. Despite its luxurious sound and taste, this "specialty" costs less than lamb chops!

YOU WILL NEED:

canned artichoke hearts	milk
canned minced chicken	parsley and pimiento
butter or grated cheese	(optional)
condensed cream of mushroom soup	

Plan to have 3 or 4 artichoke hearts for each person. Set artichoke hearts in a shallow baking dish or piepan which can come to the table. Hollow slightly at the top and place in each artichoke a small ball of minced chicken—the kind that is generally used for a cocktail spread. Top each with a tiny dab of butter or a bit of grated cheese. Pour around 1 can condensed cream of mushroom soup diluted with ½ can milk. Set in a moderate oven, 350° F., about 15 minutes or until thoroughly heated. Baste once or twice with the sauce.

AT SERVING TIME:
Garnish with parsley and strips of pimiento if desired. Serve with hot, crisp French bread or rolls.

Molasses Chicken with Artichoke Hearts

Chicken with molasses sounds rather startling. Doesn't taste at all strange! During the cooking, the molasses seems to disappear, leaving a wonderfully rich, almost unidentifiable savor and providing a beautiful deep-brown glaze.

YOU WILL NEED:

2 frying chickens	dark molasses
olive oil	sherry
peanut oil	canned artichoke hearts
butter	

To serve 6 to 8, have 2 frying chickens cut into pieces or into quarters. Remove the skin. This procedure is necessary; otherwise the fat directly under the skin imparts a different taste. In a large heavy skillet or Dutch oven, heat 2 tablespoons olive oil and 4 tablespoons peanut oil to about 360° F. Brown the chicken on one side and then the other and cook until just about half done. Add 1 tablespoon butter. Pour in 1 cup each dark molasses and dry sherry. Bring to a boil and cook about 10 minutes. Add 2 cans artichoke hearts, drained. Cook about 5 minutes longer, or until chicken is very tender and the juices have cooked down to less than half.

AT SERVING TIME:

Serve with a cool fruit salad, and provide a jug of well-chilled California white wine.

Duck in Aspic au Cointreau

For a summer buffet, this dish is outstanding and very easy to prepare.

YOU WILL NEED:

duckling	consommé
orange	cointreau or sherry
onion	canned plums, black
cloves	cherries, or pear halves
honey	cinnamon
Kitchen Bouquet	

Thaw quick-frozen duckling (3½ to 5 pounds). Stuff with 1 orange quartered and 1 onion quartered. Spear each onion quarter with a clove. Roast uncovered in a shallow pan, 1½ to 2 hours at 375° F. About 15 minutes before duck is done, brush with 2 tablespoons honey combined with ½ teaspoon Kitchen Bouquet to give the bird a beautiful golden-brown gloss. Cool to room temperature. Cut with poultry shears into serving pieces.

Arrange in a shallow serving dish about 10 by 6 inches. Pour over duck 2 cans undiluted condensed consommé to which you have added 3 tablespoons cointreau. If you do not have cointreau, use pale dry sherry. Allow to stand in the refrigerator until consommé has jelled.

AT SERVING TIME:
Bring to the table in the same dish in which it has jelled. Decorate with canned plums, black cherries, or pear halves. Sprinkle delicately with cinnamon. A bouquet of crisp escarole or water cress looks pretty at one side or in the center.

Roast Duck Bigarade

Since quick-frozen Long Island ducklings have become so widely available, they are an excellent choice for the company dinner.

YOU WILL NEED:

duckling	cayenne
onions	Seville orange marmalade
cloves	canned beef gravy
Kitchen Bouquet	brandy (optional)
orange juice	

Thaw frozen duckling (3½ to 5 pounds). Instead of stuffing the duck, place inside it 2 onions peeled and quartered, each quarter studded with a single clove. Roast uncovered 1½ to 2 hours at 375° F. About 15 minutes before the duck is done, brush lightly with Kitchen Bouquet.

Bigarade Sauce:

Meanwhile prepare Bigarade Sauce by beating together ¼ cup orange juice, ½ teaspoon Kitchen Bouquet, a few grains of

cayenne, 1 tablespoon Seville orange marmalade, and 1 can prepared beef gravy. If desired, 1 or 2 tablespoons brandy may be
added to the sauce. Simmer gently about 4 minutes.

AT SERVING TIME:
Duck Bigarade may be served in either of two ways—brought to
the table whole and carved like any poultry or it may be cut into
serving pieces beforehand, arranged on the serving dish with the
sauce poured around the duck. A bouquet of fresh watercress
makes a pretty garnish. Thin slices of unpeeled orange are also
used.

Pheasant in Wine

The queen of birds, pheasant, prepared as easily as chicken in a
red wine sauce.

YOU WILL NEED:

pheasant	red wine
seasoned flour	bay leaf
oil or shortening	dried or fresh tarragon
canned beef bouillon	parsley

Cut your pheasant into serving pieces just as you would chicken
—in fact, chicken can be substituted if you lack pheasant—and
toss in paper bag with flour seasoned with salt, pepper, and
paprika for color. Fry until about three quarters done. Remove
and keep warm. Into the skillet where pheasant was fried, pour
1 can condensed beef bouillon and 1 cup red wine. Add 1 bay
leaf, ½ teaspoon dried tarragon or 1 teaspoon fresh. Cook, uncovered, until reduced by half. Put bird back into pan and cook
gently about 15 minutes or until tender, and imbued with savor.
Or, transfer all to casserole and bake in moderately slow oven
(325° F.) for 45 minutes to an hour, if that is more convenient.

AT SERVING TIME:
Arrange on a handsome platter, scatter with chopped parsley,
and serve with heated canned wild rice.

Paella à la Valenciana

Since this Spanish dish gets its name from the special pan in which it is cooked and served, it seems most appropriate to make it in a pan which can come to the table. Our approximation uses canned chicken fricassee and quick-cooking rice.

YOU WILL NEED:

quick-cooking rice
saffron
bay leaf
garlic
canned chicken fricassee
Kitchen Bouquet
cooked shrimp, crab meat,
  and/or lobster, clams or
  mussels

peas
canned green beans
canned artichokes
  (optional)

To 1 small package (1⅓ cups) quick-cooking rice add 1¾ cups water, ¾ teaspoon salt, ¼ teaspoon saffron, ⅛ teaspoon black pepper, ½ bay leaf, 1 clove garlic very finely chopped. Bring rice quickly to a full rolling boil. Add 1 can chicken fricassee with its gravy, ½ teaspoon Kitchen Bouquet to lend a rich brown look and flavor, 1 cup cooked shrimp, crab meat, and/or lobster, clams or mussels, if desired. Also ½ cup lightly cooked peas and green beans. If you have some canned artichokes, cut them into quarters and add them also. This dish, as you see, can be as simple or as elaborate as you choose. Heat everything together and simmer 2 or 3 minutes. Cover tightly, let stand in a warm place 10 minutes longer so that the rice absorbs the varied flavors.

AT SERVING TIME:
Bring to the table in the pan in which it was cooked. Serve with a green salad, crusty bread, and cheese for dessert. This serves 3, 4, or more, according to the number and quantity of "trimmings."

Chestnut Stuffing

A good packaged poultry stuffing and canned cooked chestnuts combine to make a delicious poultry dressing. Most poultry stuff-

ing is put up in packages large enough for a chicken. Two packages are generally needed to stuff a turkey. However, if ready-
cooked chicken or turkey is used it is generally better to cook
the stuffing in a separate pan.

YOU WILL NEED:
    packaged poultry stuffing   cooked chestnuts

To 1 package poultry dressing prepared according to package
directions, add 1 cup boiled Italian chestnuts cut into small
pieces.

VARIATION: Mushroom Stuffing
Instead of chestnuts, drain 2 3-ounce tins broiled-in-butter mushrooms, chopped. Drain and dry mushrooms on a paper towel and
brown in 3 tablespoons butter. Add to 1 package prepared poultry dressing and proceed according to package directions.

10

Sauces for a Gourmet

IN A HURRY

Top rank in the hierarchy of culinary artists has always been reserved—and most properly—for the *saucier,* the chef who makes the sauces. The perfect sauce is the zenith, the ne plus ultra of gastronomic accomplishment and appreciation. Up to now the art of sauce-making has always been long and demanding. Formerly a great deal of time was consumed in the reduction, or the boiling down, of liquid necessary for the rich concentration of flavors which is the essence of the fine sauce. More time and skill were consumed in the slow simmering required for the perfect blending of various ingredients.

The requirements of a good sauce are still the same as they have always been—the methods used in the accomplishment of the *saucier's* aims also remain the same. But in a small and inexpensive can of condensed soup it is possible to find almost the same concentration of flavor, the same blending of ingredients—all done for you!

In addition to the sauces made from various canned condensed soups or from canned beef gravy or canned spaghetti sauce, you will find in this chapter a number of cold sauces with a prepared mayonnaise base. Some of these such as Ravigote, Vinaigrette, and Gloucester are particularly valuable to add an extra note to canned cooked or quick-frozen sea food or to delicatessen cold cuts.

RECIPES

New Allemande Sauce
Amandine Sauce
Béarnaise Sauce
Short-Cut Béchamel Sauce
Yellow Béchamel Sauce
Brown Sauce or Gravy
Chestnut Sauce
Curry Sauce
Diavolo Sauce
Estragon Sauce
Figaro Sauce
Giblet Gravy
Golden Mushroom Sauce
Gloucester Sauce
Mock Hollandaise Sauce
Sour Cream "Hollandaise"
Mint Sauce
Modern Mornay Sauce

Quick Mousseline Sauce
Sherry Newburg Sauce
Rarebit and Rarebit Sauce
Ravigote Sauce
Quick Sauce Robert
Salmi Sauce
Italian Spaghetti Sauce with
    Meat
Sauce Rouennaise
Cheese Sauce Soubise
Sauce Suprême
Sweet and Sour Sauce
Tartar Sauce
Savory Tomato Sauce
Quick Velouté Sauce
Suprême or Poulette Sauce
Vinaigrette Sauce

New Allemande Sauce

The name attributes this sauce to Germany but the taste is
Parisian.

YOU WILL NEED:

condensed cream of
    mushroom soup
light cream
chicken bouillon cube

egg yolk
lemon juice
nutmeg (optional)
Parmesan cheese

To a can of condensed cream of mushroom soup, add ½ can
light cream, 1 crumbled chicken bouillon cube. Heat in the top
of a double boiler stirring occasionally.

AT SERVING TIME:
Stir in 1 slightly beaten egg yolk diluted with a little hot sauce, add ¾ teaspoon lemon juice, a few grains of nutmeg, if desired, and 3 tablespoons grated Parmesan cheese.

Amandine Sauce

With sautéed fish or over such vegetables as asparagus, broccoli, and cauliflower, nothing is better than a sauce of almonds. To save yourself the trouble of blanching, soaking, and shredding the nuts, why not buy a can of sliced, blanched almonds?

YOU WILL NEED:

butter	lemon juice
almonds	parsley or chives (optional)

Use the fat remaining in the pan after frying fish or meat; add enough butter to make about ½ cup. Stir until well browned. Add 4 tablespoons coarsely chopped salted almonds, 2 or 3 teaspoons lemon juice, salt and pepper to taste.

AT SERVING TIME:
Pour over or around fried fish, chicken, or cooked asparagus, cauliflower, or broccoli. A sprinkle of chopped parsley or chives may be added if desired.

Béarnaise Sauce

This notable sauce is actually nothing more than a super-seasoned Hollandaise. It is traditional with grilled filet mignon but is equally good with minute steak or a grilled hamburger.

YOU WILL NEED:

prepared or Mock   onion or chives
   Hollandaise Sauce (page   parsley and fresh
   147)   tarragon
tarragon vinegar

To 1 cup Hollandaise Sauce add 1 tablespoon tarragon vinegar, 1 tablespoon very finely chopped, or scraped, onion or chopped chives. Keep warm over hot water but do not heat or boil.

AT SERVING TIME:
Add 1 teaspoon each finely chopped parsley and fresh tarragon leaves.

Short-Cut Béchamel Sauce

This is one of the classic sauces of the great French cuisine. Formerly the perfect Béchamel Sauce required considerable doing and more than a little skill. But now that we have condensed cream of chicken soup, it couldn't be simpler.

YOU WILL NEED:

condensed cream of chicken   milk or water
   soup

To a can of condensed cream of chicken soup, add ¼ to ½ can of milk or water, depending on how thick a sauce you want. Heat and stir, preferably in the top of a double boiler. Strain if you wish, though actually it isn't necessary.

AT SERVING TIME:
Pass in a separate heated bowl or pour over chicken, fish, or vegetables.

VARIATION: Yellow Béchamel Sauce
To the above sauce add one slightly beaten egg or egg yolk, diluted with a small quantity of the hot sauce. The sauce should not be cooked after the egg is added or it will curdle.

Brown Sauce or Gravy

Many and varied are the methods for preparing this basic sauce. We will leave to the other cookbooks the chore of preparing gravies from scratch and concentrate on the glamorizing of the canned variety.

YOU WILL NEED:
canned beef gravy
Kitchen Bouquet

red wine or ketchup
parsley or chives (optional)

Canned beef gravy actually needs nothing but heating. However, for a richer color and a more interesting flavor we suggest that you add to a can of beef gravy ½ teaspoon Kitchen Bouquet, 1 tablespoon, or more, of red wine, or 1 tablespoon tomato ketchup. Heat thoroughly before using.

AT SERVING TIME:
Serve with or over sliced cooked or roast meats. Especially good with leftovers. A sprinkle of chopped parsley or chives is always attractive.

Chestnut Sauce

With cooked, ready-to-serve chestnuts available, this sauce, formerly long and bothersome to prepare, becomes as quick as it is delectable. A fine sauce for stretching leftover or delicatessen chicken or turkey!

YOU WILL NEED:
cooked chestnuts
canned beef gravy
Kitchen Bouquet
(optional)

sherry or Madeira
(optional)

Cut ½ cup peeled, cooked chestnuts into small pieces, add to 1 can beef gravy. One-half teaspoon Kitchen Bouquet may be added if desired. Simmer gently 3 or 4 minutes.

AT SERVING TIME:
Add 2 or 3 tablespoons sherry or Madeira wine. Serve with chicken, turkey, or pork.

Curry Sauce

This is admittedly an Anglicized version of this famous East Indian sauce. You can make it as delicate or as fiery as you wish by adjusting the amount of curry powder.

YOU WILL NEED:

condensed cream of chicken soup	butter (optional)
curry powder	apple (optional)
milk or light cream	onion (optional)
ginger or garlic powder (optional)	eggs
	shrimp, crab meat, or chicken

To 1 can condensed cream of chicken soup, add 1 flat tablespoon curry powder. Stir in ¼ to ½ can milk or light cream; ¼ teaspoon ginger or garlic powder may be added if desired. For an even better flavor you should lightly brown in 2 tablespoons butter 1 small apple, diced and peeled, and 1 small onion, chopped. Heat everything together and cook for 2 or 3 minutes.

AT SERVING TIME:
Add to this sauce quartered or halved hard-cooked eggs, shrimp, crab meat, or diced cooked chicken. Serve with rice and other curry accompaniments: chutney, salted almonds, India relish, grated coconut, chopped green pepper.

Diavolo Sauce

The Italians usually serve this piquant sauce with lobster. It is excellent, too, with grilled shrimp and very good to dress up leftover sliced beef, lamb, or pork.

YOU WILL NEED:

canned tomato sauce

vinegar

beef bouillon cube or beef
extract

cayenne or Tabasco sauce

mustard

Add to a cup of canned tomato sauce 4 tablespoons vinegar, 1 beef bouillon cube, dissolved in a little hot water, ½ teaspoon pepper, a dash of cayenne or a few drops of Tabasco sauce, ½ tablespoon prepared mustard. Mix well. Simmer about 10 minutes.

AT SERVING TIME:

Pass in a heated bowl or gravy boat or pour over and around baked or broiled lobster, grilled shrimp, or leftover sliced beef, lamb, or pork.

Estragon Sauce

The haunting flavor of tarragon added to canned beef gravy makes an interesting sauce to serve with meat or broiled chicken.

YOU WILL NEED:

canned beef gravy

tarragon vinegar

fresh or dried tarragon, or
parsley (optional)

To a can of beef gravy, add 1 tablespoon tarragon vinegar. Heat and simmer 3 or 4 minutes.

AT SERVING TIME:

Sprinkle with 1 tablespoon chopped fresh tarragon leaves or 1 teaspoon dried tarragon. If you have no tarragon, chopped parsley may be used.

Figaro Sauce

The idea of heating mayonnaise may seem startling, but it's very easy to do in a double boiler or in a small casserole or crock set

over hot but not boiling water. This heated mayonnaise forms
the basis for a quick version of a well-known classic sauce.

YOU WILL NEED:
mayonnaise   Worcestershire sauce
tomato ketchup   (optional)
parsley

To 1 cup mayonnaise add 1 or 2 tablespoons tomato ketchup, ½
tablespoon finely chopped parsley, and 1 tablespoon Worcester
shire sauce if desired. Warm in a small crock or casserole set
over hot water. Do not boil.

AT SERVING TIME:
Pass in a small warm bowl. This is particularly good with baked
fish.

Giblet Gravy

Ready in an instant. Our treatment gives it a dark, rich gloss and
a lively flavor.

YOU WILL NEED:
canned giblet gravy   hot pepper sauce
Kitchen Bouquet

To 1 can giblet gravy, add ½ teaspoon Kitchen Bouquet and 3
drops hot pepper sauce. Heat to bubbling point.

AT SERVING TIME:
Serve instantly with chicken or your Thanksgiving bird.

Golden Mushroom Sauce

The backbone of this delicious sauce is a condensed mushroom
soup, made with beef stock and flavored with sauterne wine.

YOU WILL NEED:
condensed golden   hot pepper sauce or
  mushroom soup   cayenne pepper
milk   nutmeg or mace
lemon juice

Blend together and heat a 10½-ounce can condensed golden mushroom soup with ¼ soup can milk. Add 1 teaspoon lemon juice, 3 drops hot pepper sauce or a few grains cayenne pepper, and a flicker of nutmeg or mace. Cook about 5 minutes, stirring occasionally. Makes about 1½ cups of sauce. Serves 4.

AT SERVING TIME:
Pour happily over hard-cooked eggs, steak, green beans, whole-kernel corn, mashed, baked, or boiled potatoes. And don't forget broiled fish.

Gloucester Sauce

This is one of the "cold English sauces" recommended by Escoffier himself to be served with cold meats. We suggest also that it makes an excellent dressing for egg or fish salads.

YOU WILL NEED:

mayonnaise made from olive oil	Worcestershire sauce
sour cream	dill, fennel, parsley, or chives
lemon juice	

To 1 cup mayonnaise, add 4 tablespoons sour cream. Stir well and add gradually 1½ tablespoons lemon juice and ½ teaspoon Worcestershire sauce.

AT SERVING TIME:
Place in a small bowl in the center of a platter on which you serve sliced cold cuts, or spread over the top of egg or fish salads. In either case, sprinkle the sauce lightly with chopped dill, fennel, parsley, or chives.

Mock Hollandaise Sauce

Hollandaise, the most impressive of sauces, terrifies inexperienced cooks—and many experienced ones. There are a number of ways to "mock" the lordly Hollandaise. This one made with prepared mayonnaise tastes and looks very good, but it is less expensive and far less hazardous.

YOU WILL NEED:

butter or margarine	cayenne (optional)
lemon juice	lemon peel (optional)
mayonnaise made with	
olive oil	

Pour about 1 inch of hot water into the bottom of a double boiler, set it on the stove over low heat. Put 6 tablespoons butter (¾ of a quarter-pound stick) into the top of a double boiler. Allow the butter to melt but under no circumstances to get foamy. Take the top pan off the fire. Stir in 1 tablespoon lemon juice, 2 tablespoons mayonnaise, a dash of salt, a few grains of cayenne pepper and, if desired, ¼ teaspoon grated lemon peel. Stir with the sauce still off the fire until smooth and well blended. Set over the hot water again for half a minute, just long enough to warm slightly. It is not necessary to serve Hollandaise piping hot. It is good when it is lukewarm.

AT SERVING TIME:
Pour over or pass separately with cooked asparagus, broccoli, cauliflower, or Frenched green beans, or use to make Eggs Benedict. Makes about ½ cup sauce—4 servings.

Sour Cream "Hollandaise"

Another ingenious way to approximate Hollandaise makes use of commercially soured cream—the kind you buy in cartons.

YOU WILL NEED:

sour cream	lemon juice
butter	cayenne

Warm ½ cup sour cream in the top of a double boiler but do not allow it to get hot. Stir into it 2 tablespoons softened butter combined with 2 tablespoons lemon juice. Season with a few grains of cayenne pepper, a little extra salt, if desired. This sauce may be made ahead of time. It need not be hot, only lukewarm, since it is served over hot vegetables, chicken, fish, or eggs.

AT SERVING TIME:
Use as a garnish for, or pass separately with, cooked asparagus, broccoli, cauliflower. Can also be used for Eggs Benedict. Makes about 1 cup sauce—serves 6 to 8.

Mint Sauce

Not only with the traditional roast leg of lamb but also with lamb chops, mint sauce is delightful. It is good, too, on a salad of Boston lettuce and sliced tomatoes—a boon to calorie counters.

YOU WILL NEED:
confectioners' sugar fresh or dried mint leaves
vinegar

Dissolve 1 tablespoon confectioners' sugar in ½ cup vinegar. If the vinegar is very strong dilute it with water. Pour over ¼ cup finely chopped mint leaves or about 2 tablespoons dried mint flakes. Let stand about 30 minutes in a warm place.

AT SERVING TIME:
Pass in a small pitcher with lamb.

Modern Mornay Sauce

Hundreds of epicurean dishes—fish, vegetables, eggs—call for Mornay Sauce, which is basically a cheese sauce and can be made with almost any kind of cheese.

YOU WILL NEED:
condensed cream of chicken milk or white wine
 soup   grated cheese

Strain a can of condensed cream of chicken soup to remove the bits of chicken and celery. Add ½ can milk or dry white wine, ½ cup grated cheese. A mixture of Parmesan and Swiss is particularly good. Cook over low heat or in the top of a double boiler until the cheese is melted and the sauce is thick and smooth. Continue cooking and stirring about a minute longer.

AT SERVING TIME:
Pour over or pass separately with cooked vegetables, fish or eggs.
Makes about 2 cups of sauce.

Quick Mousseline Sauce

YOU WILL NEED:
condensed cream of chicken   egg yolks
  soup   nutmeg or mace
white wine or water and
  lemon juice

To a can of condensed cream of chicken soup, add ½ can white
wine or ½ can water and 1 tablespoon lemon juice. Heat in the
top of a double boiler, stirring occasionally.

AT SERVING TIME:
Add to sauce 2 slightly beaten egg yolks diluted with a little of
the hot sauce. Season with a few grains of nutmeg or mace.

Sherry Newburg Sauce

The darling of the chafing dish! This sauce was originally composed to adorn lobster. It is equally good with shrimp or crab
meat.

YOU WILL NEED:
condensed cream of   egg
  mushroom soup   nutmeg and paprika
sherry   (optional)
milk or light cream
  (optional)

To a can of condensed cream of mushroom soup, add ¼ to ½
can dry sherry, or you may use equal parts of milk or cream and
sherry. Heat but do not boil.

AT SERVING TIME:
Add the beaten yolk of 1 egg or a whole egg slightly beaten and
dilute it with a little of the hot sauce. Season, if desired, with a
dash of nutmeg and a sprinkle of paprika.

Rarebit and Rarebit Sauce

This rarebit, which is also a sauce, is a very good one—so easy, so quick, so *sure!*

YOU WILL NEED:

processed American cheese   nutmeg or basil
beer, ale, or milk   cayenne (optional)
mustard

In the top of a double boiler over hot water, melt ½ pound (2 cups) processed American cheese, cut into small pieces. Add ½ cup beer or milk and stir until well blended. Season to suit your taste with ½ teaspoon of prepared or dry mustard, ¼ teaspoon dried basil or a few grains of nutmeg. A little cayenne pepper may be added if desired.

AT SERVING TIME:
Serve over cooked asparagus, broccoli, cauliflower, green beans, or lightly grilled tomatoes. Also good with fish and eggs. Makes about 2 cups of sauce.

Ravigote Sauce

Pickled pigs' feet or lambs' tongues in jars are among the less usual ready-to-serve meats. They are particularly delicious when served with this herb-flecked sauce.

YOU WILL NEED:

olive oil or salad oil   onion
vinegar   tarragon
capers   chives
parsley

Put into a small bowl 1 cup olive oil or salad oil, ⅓ cup vinegar, a little salt and pepper, 2 tablespoons capers, 1 tablespoon finely chopped parsley, 1 tablespoon very fine chopped onion, 1 teaspoon each chives and tarragon. If you have no fresh tarragon, 1 tablespoon of tarragon vinegar may be used but do not use all tarragon vinegar because the flavor is too strong. Mix thoroughly.

AT SERVING TIME:

Pass in a separate bowl or pour around sliced cold cuts such as tongue, meat loaf, etc. If you are serving canned pigs' feet or pickled lambs' tongues, a few tablespoons of liquor from the jar may be stirred into the sauce. Makes 1½ cups sauce.

Quick Sauce Robert

Using canned beef gravy, this piquant and interesting sauce is literally a matter of minutes.

YOU WILL NEED:

canned beef gravy	pickle
Kitchen Bouquet	cayenne
vinegar	green olives (optional)
shallot or onion	mustard (optional)
capers	

To a can of beef gravy, add ½ teaspoon Kitchen Bouquet to darken the color and brighten the flavor. Also add 1 tablespoon vinegar, 1 tablespoon finely chopped shallot or onion, 1 tablespoon capers, 1 tablespoon chopped pickle and a few grains of cayenne pepper. A half dozen chopped green olives and ½ teaspoon prepared mustard may be added if desired.

AT SERVING TIME:

Pass separately in a heated bowl or pour over beef, lamb, veal, or pork.

Salmi Sauce

A hot and savory sauce redolent of sherry or port—this delicious concoction is said to date back to the Middle Ages. It is particularly good with cubed leftover lamb, ham, or pork.

YOU WILL NEED:

canned beef gravy	sherry or port
currant jelly	parsley or chives (optional)
cayenne	

To a can of beef gravy, add ¼ glass currant jelly, a dash of cayenne. Heat and stir until jelly is melted.

AT SERVING TIME:
Add 2 tablespoons sherry or port. A little chopped parsley or chives may be used if desired.

Italian Spaghetti Sauce with Meat

There are a number of excellent tomato sauces with meat on the market. But even if you should have nothing on hand but a can of tomato soup and a ½ pound of hamburger, this sauce can be put together in a very few minutes.

YOU WILL NEED:

onion	olive oil, salad oil, or butter
garlic	condensed tomato soup
chopped beef	bay leaf

Brown 1 chopped medium-sized onion, 1 crushed clove garlic, and ½ pound chopped lean beef in 2 tablespoons olive oil, salad oil, or butter for about 8 minutes, or until the meat has lost its red color. Add 1 can condensed tomato soup, 1 bay leaf, ¼ can water. Simmer 15 minutes to ½ hour.

AT SERVING TIME:
Remove bay leaf. Taste and add extra salt and pepper if desired. Serve with spaghetti, macaroni, or rice.

Sauce Rouennaise

An unusual and delicious sauce to accompany roast duck. You may use the drippings from the duck or chicken in the sauce.

YOU WILL NEED:

canned giblet gravy	freeze-dried shallots or
red wine	instant minced onion
brandy or bourbon (optional)	

Add to a 10½-ounce can giblet gravy 1 cup red wine, 1 or 2 tablespoons brandy or bourbon (optional), and 1 teaspoon freeze-dried shallots or instant minced onion. Cook and stir quickly on top of the stove until reduced to half. Strain or not, as you wish.

AT SERVING TIME:
Serve in gravy boat.

Cheese Sauce Soubise

Pork or fish take to this sauce, but we also see it covering a mealy baked potato.

YOU WILL NEED:

canned cream of cheese soup	paprika
instant minced onion	milk
	parsley

To 1 can condensed cream of cheese soup, add 2 tablespoons instant minced onion, ½ teaspoon paprika, ¼ cup milk. Stir over low heat until smooth and creamy.

AT SERVING TIME:
Serve in sauce dish, sprinkled with finely chopped parsley.

Sauce Suprême

Suprême Sauce is what makes Chicken Suprême and glamorizes many other foods—such as eggs, fish, and vegetables.

YOU WILL NEED:

condensed cream of chicken soup	nutmeg
light cream or top milk	lemon juice
egg	

To 1 can of condensed cream of chicken soup, add ½ can light cream or top milk. Stir, warm, and strain out bits of chicken and rice. Just before serving stir in 1 or 2 slightly beaten egg yolks or whole egg. Season with a few grains of nutmeg and 2 teaspoons lemon juice.

AT SERVING TIME:
Pour the sauce over and around meat, poultry, or fish. When serving it with vegetables pour in a wide ribbon over the top of the vegetables and pass a separate bowl of sauce. Makes 2 cups sauce.

Sweet and Sour Sauce

This versatile sauce, made surprisingly from canned consommé and ginger snaps, does miraculous things for delicatessen meats such as sliced tongue, boiled ham, or sliced roast beef.

YOU WILL NEED:

consommé	brown sugar
vinegar	allspice
onion	bay leaf
raisins	cayenne
lemon	ginger snaps

Combine 1 can consommé, 1 can water, 4 tablespoons mild vinegar. Then add 1 small onion sliced thin, 4 tablespoons raisins, 1 small lemon sliced paper thin, 4 tablespoons brown sugar, ½ teaspoon whole allspice, a bay leaf, few grains of cayenne pepper. Simmer all together until lemon and onions are tender. Crumble 6 ginger snaps into the sauce. Stir until the sauce is smooth and slightly thickened. Do not strain.

AT SERVING TIME:
Arrange slices of tongue, ham, or beef in a heat-proof serving dish. Pour the sauce over the meat and heat for a minute or so. Garnish with parsley or water cress.

Tartar Sauce

To many people, fried fish, scallops, or oysters would be unthinkable without Tartar Sauce. This is a particularly easy and tasty version.

YOU WILL NEED:
    mayonnaise   onion or parsley (optional)
    India relish

Stir together ½ cup mayonnaise and ½ cup India relish; ½ tablespoon finely chopped onion or parsley may be added. Chill.

AT SERVING TIME:
It's a pretty thought to serve Tartar Sauce in lemon or lime shells as a garnish for a platter of fried fish.

Savory Tomato Sauce

Endless are the uses of this tasty tomato sauce made from a can of condensed tomato soup.

YOU WILL NEED:

condensed tomato soup	bay leaf
milk or water	parsley
beef bouillon cube or beef extract	cloves

To 1 can of condensed tomato soup, add ½ cup milk or water, 1 bouillon cube or ½ teaspoon beef extract, a bit of bay leaf, 1 tablespoon chopped fresh parsley, or 1 teaspoon dried parsley flakes, 4 cloves. Simmer a few minutes.

AT SERVING TIME:
Pass separately in a heated bowl or gravy boat or pour over left-over meats. Serve with fish or hard-cooked eggs, rice, noodles, macaroni, or spaghetti.

Quick Velouté Sauce

Endlessly useful for dozens of dishes, condensed cream of chicken soup provides an admirable short cut to this fine sauce.

YOU WILL NEED:

condensed cream of chicken   light cream
  soup   nutmeg (optional)

Combine 1 can condensed cream of chicken soup with ½ can light cream. Stir, heat in the top of the double boiler, stirring occasionally. Strain to remove any small pieces of chicken or vegetable. Season if desired with a few grains of nutmeg.

AT SERVING TIME:
Pour into a small heated bowl or gravy boat or pour over vegetables, fish, or chicken.

VARIATION: Suprême or Poulette Sauce
Just before serving, stir in 1 slightly beaten egg or 1 slightly beaten egg yolk diluted with a little of the hot sauce. Add ¾ teaspoon lemon juice. If desired, a 3-ounce can sliced and drained mushrooms may be added to the sauce.

Vinaigrette Sauce

For asparagus, broccoli, cauliflower, green beans, and also for fish, this simplest of sauces may be made from prepared French dressing or from oil and vinegar.

YOU WILL NEED:

French dressing   parsley or chives (optional)
India relish

To ½ cup bottled or homemade French dressing, non-creamy, add 3 tablespoons chopped India relish; 1 teaspoon finely chopped parsley and/or 1 teaspoon finely chopped chives may be added if desired. Stir well. Heat if you wish, or serve cold.

AT SERVING TIME:
Stir again just before serving to make sure that the ingredients are well blended. Pass separately or pour over vegetables, fish, or sliced meats such as tongue, ham, or lamb.

Vegetables

WITH A DIFFERENCE

STAND-BYS OF the hurried cook are canned and quick-frozen vegetables. Both can, when properly prepared, retain a great deal of the flavor, color, and vitamin value of garden-fresh vegetables. On the other hand, they can be, and very frequently are, ruined by carelessness—too much water, overcooking.

Once you were told to drain any canned vegetable, boil down the liquid, and then heat the vegetable. Unnecessary fuss! Put the entire contents (with a little of the liquid poured off, if you like) into a flameproof dish, preferably one attractive enough to go to the table. Do not cover—it ruins the color. Do not simmer—it ruins the texture. Bring to a full, rolling boil. Remove at once from heat and serve.

Or you might try the French technique of heating vegetables in butter. Melt butter or margarine in a heavy frying pan or saucepan, but do not brown. Place the vegetable in the butter. Toss with a fork until heated through.

Read labels for a wealth of essential information. They will tell you the style of the product, as well as the can weight, and, most times, how many cups it contains and how many servings you can expect from the can. It discloses other cooking information, too, such as whether a soup is ready to serve from the can, or whether the addition of liquid is required.

RECIPES

Asparagus Amandine
Baked Beans in Burgundy
Boston Baked Beans Gone to
  Heaven
Dilled Beans in Pimiento
  Cups
Persian Beets
Pickled Beets Flemish Style
Red Cabbage Amsterdam
Whole Cauliflower Allemande
Whole Cauliflower with
  Sauce Suprême and
  Walnuts
Hearts of Celery Mornay
Mock Purée of Chestnuts
Old Virginia's Corn Pudding
Eggplant Parmigiana
Mushrooms in Cream under
  Glass

Mushrooms in Dill Sauce
Creamed Onions au Celeri
French Fried Onions
Purée of Peas de Luxe
Broiled Franconia Potatoes
Dill-Buttered Potatoes
Potatoes Chantilly with
  Cheese
Sarah's Holiday Potatoes
Maple-Glazed Yams
Scalloped Sweet Potatoes with
  Apples
Sweet Potatoes Noisette
Sauerkraut Provençal with
  Red Wine
Tao Bean Sprouts
Spiced Scalloped Tomatoes
  with Herbs
Tomatoes Orégano

Asparagus Amandine

YOU WILL NEED:
  canned asparagus spears   almonds
  toast (optional)   lemon
  butter or margarine

Heat canned asparagus. Arrange on a heated serving dish or on
4 slices buttered toast. Meanwhile melt in a frying pan 4 tablespoons butter or margarine. Add 4 tablespoons slivered almonds.
Allow almonds to brown slightly in the butter.

AT SERVING TIME:
Pour butter and almonds over asparagus. Serve with lemon quarters. Serves 2 or 3.

Baked Beans in Burgundy

A casserole of baked beans that tastes like the cooked-all-day-long variety, but can be prepared in approximately 30 minutes.

YOU WILL NEED:

red burgundy wine
molasses
sweet Italian vermouth
soy sauce
Worcestershire sauce
bottled steak sauce
hot pepper sauce
dry mustard
chili powder

garlic salt
monosodium glutamate
rosemary
basil
marjoram
canned Boston baked beans
strips of Canadian bacon or
   beef salami

For 6 to 8 servings: Combine ½ cup red burgundy wine with ½ cup molasses, 2 tablespoons sweet Italian vermouth, 1 tablespoon each of soy sauce, Worcestershire sauce, and any good bottled steak sauce. Add 4 drops hot pepper sauce, ½ teaspoon dry mustard, ¼ teaspoon freshly ground black pepper, and pinches of chili powder, garlic salt, monosodium glutamate, rosemary, basil, and marjoram. Place in a small frying pan and cook, uncovered, till reduced to half the quantity (about 5 minutes).

Meanwhile, heat 3 large cans Boston baked beans, the pork-and-molasses type, on top of the stove to a sizzle, removing the pork to use later. Stir sauce into the beans gently, so that all the little beans are kin to the sauce. Pour into a casserole. Put pork on top of the beans and add a couple of strips of bacon. Canadian bacon is preferable for this top layer; beef salami is fine, too. Don't put a lid on the casserole, but place it in a preheated oven and let it sit there at 400° F. for 25 minutes, or until it develops a nice crust.

AT SERVING TIME:

Round out the meal with crusty rolls, or Boston brown bread if you're a traditionalist, a crisp garden salad, and a fruity dessert.

Boston Baked Beans Gone to Heaven

Several brands of baked beans with molasses are excellent. Only a little dressing up is needed to give them the appearance as well

as the flavor of those beans that are the pride of Boston. If you
have no bean pot serve them from a casserole.

YOU WILL NEED:

canned baked beans with	dry mustard
pork and molasses	dark molasses
onion	bacon or salt pork

Place 2 cans Boston baked beans (the kind that is made with
pork and molasses) in a bean pot or casserole along with 1
medium-sized whole onion, peeled, ½ teaspoon dry mustard, ½
cup dark molasses. Cover with sliced bacon or salt pork. Set in a
moderate oven, 350° F., and bake 30 to 40 minutes until the
beans are piping hot and bubbly and the bacon is crisp and
brown.

AT SERVING TIME:

Serve from bean pot along with sliced and heated canned Boston
brown bread, cole slaw, sliced tomatoes, and dill pickles. Serves 6.

Dilled Beans in Pimiento Cups

If dilled canned beans are not available, the regular type will
do very well.

YOU WILL NEED:

canned pimientos	oil and vinegar or French
canned dilled green beans	dressing
	fresh dill or parsley

Buy whole canned pimientos and open them out carefully into
cups. Set on a nest of lettuce leaves. Fill with canned dilled green
beans which have been chilled in a tart oil and vinegar or French
dressing. Sprinkle with chopped fresh dill, if available, or parsley.

AT SERVING TIME:

These colorful cups can also be used to rim a platter of fried or
broiled chicken or a proud roast of beef.

Persian Beets

Yogurt transforms a can of beets into a Near Eastern specialty.

YOU WILL NEED:
canned julienne beets   celery seed
grated lemon rind   honey
yogurt   parsley
lemon juice

In the top of a double boiler, combine 1 large can drained julienne beets, the grated rind of 1 lemon, ½ cup yogurt, 1 table-spoon lemon juice, 2 teaspoons celery seed, 1 teaspoon honey, ¼ teaspoon salt, ¼ teaspoon pepper. Heat but do not boil.

AT SERVING TIME:
Serve warm, generously sprinkled with chopped parsley.

Pickled Beets Flemish Style

From the old-time Flemish cooks come the tricks of seasoning which make this recipe unusual and unusually delicious.

YOU WILL NEED:
canned beets   brown sugar
vinegar   caraway seeds
bay leaf   parsley
allspice berries

Drain liquid from a 1-pound can of beets. Sliced, diced, julienne, or even tiny whole canned beets may be used. Heat ½ cup water with ½ cup vinegar, ½ bay leaf, 4 allspice berries, 1 tablespoon brown sugar, ½ teaspoon salt, dash of pepper. Let stand until well chilled.

AT SERVING TIME:
Sprinkle with caraway seeds and garnish with parsley. Serves 4 to 6.

Red Cabbage Amsterdam

Very popular in Holland is *roodekool,* which combines red cabbage and apples. This is the quick New World version.

YOU WILL NEED:

onion	nutmeg
bacon fat	cloves
canned red cabbage	lemon juice or vinegar
apple sauce	lemon

Brown a medium-sized chopped onion in 2 tablespoons bacon fat. Add to 1 16-ounce jar red cabbage along with 1 cup apple sauce, ¼ teaspoon nutmeg, 2 cloves. Cover, heat slowly over low fire until thoroughly hot and the flavors are well blended, stir occasionally. Taste and add extra salt, pepper, and a little lemon juice or vinegar if needed.

AT SERVING TIME:

Serve in heated dish, garnished with thin slices of lemon stuck with cloves and sprinkled, if desired, with a few gratings of nutmeg. Serves 4 to 6.

Whole Cauliflower Allemande

Since a whole cauliflower is so dramatic and since no one has as yet succeeded in canning or freezing the cauliflower in its entirety, you have no alternative but to cook it yourself. (Do not attempt to use the pressure cooker for this.)

YOU WILL NEED:

cauliflower	condensed cream of
lemon juice or white	mushroom soup
vinegar	grated Parmesan cheese
	paprika

Select a medium-sized cauliflower—the snowiest, most unblemished one you can find. Remove outer leaves. Cut off stalk. Soak 30 minutes head down in salted cold water. Cook head down in a deep pan of boiling water to which has been added 1 teaspoon of lemon juice or white vinegar. Do not cover the pan. A medium-sized cauliflower should cook in about 12 minutes. Overcooking makes it soft and mushy.

Drain the cauliflower. Place on a baking dish which can be used for serving. Cover with heated condensed cream of mushroom soup, undiluted. Sprinkle with ½ cup grated Parmesan cheese and a little paprika. Bake in a moderate oven, 350° F., until the cheese is melted and lightly browned.

AT SERVING TIME:
Bring to the table on its own baking dish. Garnish with water cress and sections of lemon lightly sprinkled with nutmeg.

VARIATION: Whole Cauliflower with Sauce Suprême and Walnuts

Cook cauliflower as above. Place on baking dish. Cover with Sauce Suprême (page 154). Top with buttered bread crumbs and walnut halves. (These can be secured in tins.) Bake in moderate oven, 350° F., until well heated and lightly browned.

Hearts of Celery Mornay

A delightfully different vegetable dish, made even more effortless because the celery hearts come in cans.

YOU WILL NEED:
canned hearts of celery   Mornay Sauce

Heat 2 1-pound cans hearts of celery. Drain thoroughly and divide each celery heart into three sections. Place in an ovenproof casserole. Prepare a recipe of Mornay Sauce (page 149). Pour the sauce over the celery hearts in casserole. Bake at 300° F. for 5 minutes or just long enough to glaze. Serves 6.

AT SERVING TIME:
Serve immediately from its own baking dish.

Mock Purée of Chestnuts

A real purée of chestnuts, made from scratch, is a delicacy the French serve proudly. However, a can of imported sweetened chestnut spread combined with mashed sweet potatoes is an inexpensive way to achieve a grand effect.

YOU WILL NEED:

canned sweetened chestnut
   spread
canned mashed sweet
   potatoes

Kitchen Bouquet
cayenne pepper
whipped cream

Stir ½ cup canned sweetened chestnut spread into 2 cups canned mashed sweet potatoes. Darken with ½ teaspoon Kitchen Bouquet. Add a few grains of cayenne pepper and salt to taste. Just before removing from the heat, add ½ cup of heavy cream, whipped.

AT SERVING TIME:
An inspired go-together with duck or Cornish game hen.

Old Virginia's Corn Pudding

There are sections of this country where it would be considered a sacrilege to serve fried chicken without this wonderful pudding. It is best when made with inexpensive canned cream-style corn.

YOU WILL NEED:

canned cream-style corn
milk
eggs

sugar
butter
onion or onion flakes

Combine a 1-pound can (about 2 cups) cream-style corn with 2 cups milk, 3 slightly beaten eggs, 2 teaspoons sugar, 1 tablespoon butter, 1 teaspoon salt, 1 tablespoon finely chopped onion or 1 teaspoon dried onion flakes. Bake in a buttered casserole in a slow oven, 325° F., about 40 minutes or until firm to the touch.

AT SERVING TIME:
Bring to the table in its own baking dish. Excellent with ham as well as chicken. Serves 6.

Eggplant Parmigiana

Parmigiana, of course, means Parmesan but it seems unfair to refer to this famous dish by any other than its Italian name. This recipe is authentic in every respect except that the tomato sauce comes out of a can.

YOU WILL NEED:

eggplant
olive oil
canned tomato sauce
basil (optional)
orégano (optional)

celery flakes (optional)
garlic or garlic extract
grated Parmesan cheese
mozzarella or Swiss cheese

Peel 1 large or 2 small eggplants and cut into thin slices. Brown in 1 cup olive oil and drain on paper. Into a buttered or oiled casserole place a layer of the fried eggplant. Cover with canned tomato sauce whose flavor has been heightened, if you wish, by the addition of basil, orégano, a few dried celery flakes and some crushed fresh garlic or garlic extract. Sprinkle with 3 tablespoons grated Parmesan cheese and cover with a layer of mozzarella or Swiss cheese sliced thin. Repeat. Top layer should be cheese. Bake in a hot oven, 400° F., for 15 minutes.

AT SERVING TIME:

Bring straight from the oven to the table and serve from the same dish in which it was baked. Serves 4.

Mushrooms in Cream under Glass

The French phrase for serving foods under glass is *sous cloche* or "under a bell," and you can get glass covers at specialty shops or department stores. However, heat-proof glass custard cups answer the purpose admirably and look very pretty too.

YOU WILL NEED:

canned whole mushrooms
butter
lemon juice
parsley

toast or English muffin
heavy cream or sour cream
brandy (optional)

Drain whole canned broiled-in-butter mushroom crowns, using 8 to 12 mushrooms to serve 2 people—depends on the size of the mushroom and the appetite. Heat mushrooms in 4 tablespoons butter with 1 tablespoon lemon juice, ½ teaspoon salt, few grains of pepper, 1 tablespoon chopped parsley. For each serving set a round piece of buttered toast or a halved and toasted English muffin on a heat-proof baking dish. Pile the mushroom caps neatly in a pyramid on top of the toast. Pour 4 tablespoons heavy cream (sweet or sour) over the mushrooms. Cover with glass bell or custard cup and bake in a moderate oven about 20 minutes. Cream will amalgamate deliciously with the toast and mushrooms.

AT SERVING TIME:

If you have classic bells leave them in place and bring the mushrooms to the table. If you are using custard cups remove them and dramatize the service by serving your mushrooms flambé: slightly warm 2 tablespoons brandy over a candle flame. Set alight and pour over mushrooms.

The flame lasts only a fraction of a minute but the effect is lovely and the flavor added by the brandy is considerable.

Mushrooms in Dill Sauce

In Germany they use the tiny yellow buttons from the Black Forest called "Pfifferlinge." These are imported now, and you can buy them here in cans. Or you may use American canned mushrooms.

YOU WILL NEED:

canned mushrooms	chopped dill or dried dill
canned beef gravy	weed
white wine (optional)	heavy cream

For 4 servings, you will need 2 large (6-ounce) cans of button mushrooms. Remove stems and slice in half. Heat and drain. Add the mushroom liquid to a 10½-ounce can beef gravy or, if you have no mushroom liquid, add ½ cup white wine, along with 2 tablespoons fresh, chopped dill or 1 tablespoon dried dill weed. Cook until reduced by half. Add ½ cup heavy cream and bring just to the boil. Add mushrooms.

AT SERVING TIME:
Serve either plain or on toast.

Creamed Onions au Celeri

A delicious creamed vegetable in seconds!

YOU WILL NEED:
canned cream of celery   thin cream
  soup   paprika
canned white onions   parsley

To a can of condensed, undiluted cream of celery soup, add 1 can white onions, drained, ½ cup thin cream, ½ teaspoon paprika. Heat gently.

AT SERVING TIME:
Sprinkle with chopped parsley.

French Fried Onions

With steak, grilled hamburgers, or liver, as a garnish for creamed dishes, or as an appetizer to serve between meals with cocktails or beer, nothing could be finer than French fried onions. Try the canned variety dressed up in this manner.

YOU WILL NEED:
canned French fried onions   cayenne (optional)
olive oil

Empty a can of French fried onions into a shallow oiled pan. Brush lightly with olive oil. Sprinkle with a few grains of cayenne or freshly ground black pepper. Heat in a moderate oven, 350° F., about 5 minutes.

AT SERVING TIME:
Serve very hot, preferably from the same pan in which they were heated.

Purée of Peas de Luxe

Since only the finest and freshest of green peas are used in the preparation of baby foods, they can be the basis for a specially delicate purée. Remember that one can provides only one adult portion.

YOU WILL NEED:

canned strained green peas   butter
   (baby-food type)   carrots or pimientos
heavy cream

To each can of strained green peas, add a tablespoon of butter and 1 or 2 tablespoons heavy cream, salt and freshly ground black pepper to taste. Heat, stirring constantly to prevent scorching, or use a small double boiler.

AT SERVING TIME:

Serve each portion in a small heated custard cup decorated with a ring of lightly cooked carrots or crossed strips of pimiento.

Broiled Franconia Potatoes

YOU WILL NEED:

canned small potatoes   Worcestershire sauce
butter   fine bread crumbs (optional)

Heat and drain a small buffet tin (about 1 cup) small potatoes. Brush with 2 tablespoons melted butter, which has been mixed with ½ teaspoon Worcestershire sauce. Roll in bread crumbs if desired. Set under the broiler until golden brown, turning once or twice to brown evenly.

AT SERVING TIME:

Serve with broiled meat or fish. The broiling, as a matter of fact, can be done at the same time as the meat is cooked but the potatoes should not be put under the heat until the meat is almost finished. Serves 2 or 3.

Dill-Buttered Potatoes

A clever and tantalizing twist on the indomitable potato, achieved by opening a can and adding a favorite herb.

YOU WILL NEED:

canned white potatoes   fresh dill, chives, or parsley
butter

Heat a can of little white potatoes, drain off liquid, and toss generously with melted butter, and flurries of fresh dill, chives, or parsley.

AT SERVING TIME:

If you want to experience spring in January, add a can of drained green beans, heated, to the potatoes.

Potatoes Chantilly with Cheese

Although the potato course rarely gets much attention at a dinner party this one most certainly will. It is a delicious combination of quick-frozen mashed potatoes, cream, and cheese.

YOU WILL NEED:

dehydrated or quick-frozen   heavy cream
  mashed potatoes   grated cheese
butter   nutmeg (optional)
milk

Prepare about 2 cups dehydrated or quick-frozen mashed potatoes, adding milk and butter according to package directions. Place in a shallow baking dish. Whip ½ cup heavy cream, fold in ¼ cup grated cheese. Season with salt, pepper, a few grains of nutmeg, if desired. Top the potatoes with the cream mixture and bake in a moderate oven, 350° F., until golden brown. If desired, the browning may be done under the broiler.

AT SERVING TIME:

Serve immediately from the baking dish. Serves 4.

Sarah's Holiday Potatoes

A new way with baking potatoes that brings out all the good potato taste.

YOU WILL NEED:

baking potatoes	paprika
butter	parsley
canned chicken broth	

Peel 3 large baking potatoes and slice thin. Heat 2 tablespoons butter in a heavy skillet and arrange the potatoes in layers, dotting each layer with a tablespoon of butter in dabs and sprinkling lightly with salt and pepper. Pour on 1 cup canned condensed, undiluted chicken broth. Cover the skillet and cook slowly until all the liquid is absorbed and the potatoes are soft. This should take about 20 minutes.

AT SERVING TIME:
Dust lightly with paprika, and sprinkle with parsley just before serving, which should be immediately.

Maple-Glazed Yams

Sweet potatoes laved with maple syrup—a divine go-together.

YOU WILL NEED:

canned sweet potatoes	butter
maple-flavored syrup	orange rind

Slice canned yams or sweet potatoes in halves, lengthwise. To the syrup or liquid in the can, add an equal amount of maple-flavored syrup and cook in a large skillet until the bubbles grow big. Add 2 or 3 tablespoons of butter and heat the potatoes in the syrup, turning several times till they take on a pretty glaze.

AT SERVING TIME:
Sprinkle with grated orange rind.

Scalloped Sweet Potatoes with Apples

YOU WILL NEED:

canned sweet potatoes   lemon and lemon juice
canned apple slices   mace, nutmeg, or allspice
brown sugar   lemon rind
butter

Cut 2 cups canned drained sweet potatoes into slices about ¼
of an inch thick. Arrange in layers in a buttered baking dish
along with an equal quantity of canned apple slices, also drained.
Sprinkle layers with ¼ cup dark brown sugar, 4 tablespoons
butter, 2 teaspoons lemon juice, ½ teaspoon nutmeg, mace, or
allspice. The top layer should be potatoes. Bake in a hot oven,
400° F., about 20 minutes or until thoroughly heated and
browned on top. If the casserole seems dry, pour over about ½
cup of the juice from the can of apples.

AT SERVING TIME:
Decorate the top with thin slivers of lemon rind. Particularly delicious with chicken in any form, ham, or pork. Serves 6.

Sweet Potatoes Noisette

Noisette is a French cordial flavored with hazelnuts. If you can't
find Noisette, you may use apricot brandy or almond liqueur,
sometimes known as orgeat.

YOU WILL NEED:

canned sweet potatoes   Noisette or apricot brandy
butter   or almond liqueur
hot pepper sauce   sliced toasted nuts

To 3 cups hot mashed canned sweet potatoes, add 3 tablespoons
softened butter, 2 drops hot pepper sauce, 3 tablespoons Noisette
liqueur. Stir in ¼ cup sliced toasted nuts, such as almonds,
Brazil nuts, or hazelnuts.

AT SERVING TIME:
Sprinkle with whole nuts to match or blend. Serves 6.

Sauerkraut Provençal with Red Wine

Canned sauerkraut is most versatile—it can be chilled, drained, and served raw in place of a salad or vegetable. However, one of the dressiest ways is French in origin.

YOU WILL NEED:

canned sauerkraut
onion
red wine
consommé or beef bouillon
    cube

sour cream (optional)
caraway or poppy seeds
    (optional)

Drain a 1-pound eleven-ounce can of sauerkraut. Add 1 thinly sliced onion, 1 cup red wine, ½ cup condensed canned consommé or ½ cup hot water in which 1 beef bouillon cube has been dissolved. Cover and cook slowly about 20 minutes. Do not drain.

AT SERVING TIME:

Since the juice is so delicious it is best to serve this sauerkraut in a deep sauce dish or saucer. Garnish, if you like, with sour cream and add a sprinkle of caraway, or poppy, seeds. Serves 4.

Tao Bean Sprouts

The Taoists of China have always been great vegetarians, and were among the first people of the world to emphasize nutrition.

YOU WILL NEED:

canned bean sprouts
butter or peanut oil

canned mushroom pieces
cashew nuts

Drain a 1-pound can of bean sprouts. Rinse in cold water. Heat a well-greased frying pan over high heat. Add a tablespoon of butter or peanut oil, a 4-ounce can mushroom pieces with their own liquid, and ¼ teaspoon salt. Stir and fry about 1 minute or until well heated. Add bean sprouts, cover, and cook 2 minutes longer. Sprinkle with freshly ground black pepper. Serve immediately.

AT SERVING TIME:

Scatter chopped cashews over the top before serving.

Spiced Scalloped Tomatoes with Herbs

The taste of old-fashioned favorites like this should not be tampered with. Although this recipe uses stewed tomatoes and packaged croutons, the flavor is traditional.

YOU WILL NEED:

plain or garlic-flavored	minced instant onion
croutons	brown sugar
canned stewed tomatoes	allspice

Butter a casserole and sprinkle with croutons. Pour in a No. 2½ can stewed tomatoes, 3 tablespoons instant onion, 2 tablespoons brown sugar, ½ teaspoon powdered allspice, salt and ground black pepper to taste. Cover with more croutons. Bake in hot oven (400° F.) until thoroughly heated all the way through and golden brown on top.

AT SERVING TIME:
Serve from baking dish. Makes 6 portions.

Tomatoes Orégano

YOU WILL NEED:

canned tomatoes	parsley
fine dried breadcrumbs	lemon juice
orégano	butter

Drain one can of No. 2½ tomatoes, arrange in a shallow buttered baking dish. Combine ½ cup fine dried breadcrumbs, ½ teaspoon orégano, ½ teaspoon salt, ¼ teaspoon pepper, 1 tablespoon chopped parsley, 1 tablespoon lemon juice, 3 tablespoons butter. Spread the mixture over the tomatoes and set low under the broiler until bubbly hot and delicately browned.

AT SERVING TIME:
This is a lovely accompaniment to a piping-hot casserole of macaroni and cheese!

Salads

HEARTY AND OTHERWISE

THE SALAD is the dream of the hurried gourmet, since preparation is reduced to a minimum and the most dramatic effects
can be secured with the least possible effort. There is one point,
however, at which you must not skimp or hurry and that is in the
careful washing of the greens. Formerly we were told that salad
greens should be washed as soon as they came from the garden or
market but now we are assured by the experts that it's best to
wash them as you need them. Salting the water is helpful and in
cold weather it is not necessary to freeze your hands—adding a
bit of warm water does no harm.

Careful drying with a clean soft towel or paper towel is just
about as important as thorough washing, for wet greens mean a
watery dressing. Salad greens should be crisp and well chilled.

So much for the mundane requirements of a good salad. The
rest is art. Fantasy and imagination play a large part in successful
salads but nowadays it is well to remember that the most effective
salads are casual. Ornate and overdecorated salads are no longer
smart.

RECIPES

The Classic Salad

To those who follow the French tradition, this is the only salad worthy of the name. Always it should be "tossed" at the table—the well-washed greens cut or torn into pieces and brought to the table in a large bowl. This bowl need not always be wooden. You can use china, glass, or pottery. But it should be *big*.

Fine vinegar and the best of oil are the heart and soul of a proper salad. Many sticklers insist that nothing but pure olive oil is permissible—and certainly the finest olive oil imparts a flavor that can be secured in no other way. However, some people prefer the flavor of dressing made of corn oil, peanut oil, or an oil that combines one of these and varying amounts of olive oil.

As to the vinegar, there is much difference of opinion. Some insist upon cider or wine vinegar; others prefer the sharp flavor of white vinegar. A large and ever widening group is devoted to tarragon and other herb-flavored vinegars. Even more numerous are those who combine a small amount of herbal vinegars with other types.

Without attempting to enter into the age-old controversies on whether oil and vinegar should be combined beforehand to make the dressing or whether oil and vinegar should be added first or last when a salad is dressed at the table, we offer directions reduced to ultimate simplicity.

Tossed Green Salad

Combine several different kinds of greens—romaine as well as iceberg lettuce, escarole, chicory, water cress. Whenever possible include the less usual types of greens—dandelion greens in season, corn salad, Boston lettuce, peppergrass, endive, and tender young leaves of spinach.

YOU WILL NEED:
garlic (optional)   olive oil
salad greens   vinegar or lemon juice

Rub a large salad bowl with a cut clove of garlic. Place in the bowl about 2 cups well-washed and dried, crisp and chilled salad greens.

AT SERVING TIME:
Sprinkle greens with ¾ teaspoon salt, a liberal sprinkling of freshly ground black pepper from the mill. Very slowly add 4 tablespoons olive oil tossing the greens lightly with fork and spoon until every leaf glistens. Then sprinkle with 1 tablespoon vinegar or lemon juice. Toss again—but not enough to wilt the salad. Taste a leaf and if necessary correct the seasoning. Serve immediately on chilled plates. Serves 3 to 4.

Austrian Sunday Salad

This hearty kidney-bean salad has its origin in Austria. This dressing is special, too, because of its "secret" ingredient: it keeps well for a long time in the refrigerator.

YOU WILL NEED:

For Salad:
lettuce
canned red kidney beans
onion
radishes
cucumber

For Dressing:
vinegar
water
garlic
dried parsley flakes
dry mustard
aromatic bitters
olive or safflower oil

Line a bowl with crisp, dry, leafy lettuces, preferably a combination of Boston and Bibb. Add a can of cooked red kidney beans, very well drained; 1 medium-sized red or sweet yellow onion, very thinly sliced, 8 or 10 radishes, 1 large peeled cucumber, also very thinly sliced.

Make ready in a small decanter or bottle a dressing prepared by pouring first into the bottle 1½ tablespoons vinegar and a tiny splotch (about a teaspoon) of water. Add 2 cloves garlic, finely crushed, 1 teaspoon dried parsley flakes, ½ teaspoon dry mustard, 2 drops aromatic bitters (this is very important), 1 teaspoon salt, ¼ teaspoon pepper, 1 cup safflower or olive oil. Shake thoroughly.

AT SERVING TIME:
Toss the salad just before serving, using a very small amount of the dressing—only enough to give a shiny coating, not a drop more!

California Pear and Palm Salad

An unusual mélange of fruits and vegetables topped by an extraordinary dressing thickened with crumbled soft white bread.

YOU WILL NEED:

For Salad:
lettuce
canned hearts of palm
carrots
canned pear halves
cucumbers

For Dressing:
walnuts
dehydrated horseradish
sugar
light cream
soft white bread crumbs
vinegar

On individual plates, arrange a couch of frilly lettuce. Top with disks of canned, chilled hearts of palm, small heaps of shredded carrots, canned drained pear halves, sliced cucumbers.

To make Walnut Dressing: Mix together ¼ cup finely chopped walnuts, 1 tablespoon dehydrated horseradish, 2 teaspoons sugar, ⅛ teaspoon salt, 1 cup light cream, 2 tablespoons soft white bread crumbs, 2 teaspoons vinegar or more to taste. Allow to mellow at least 20 minutes.

AT SERVING TIME:
Pass dressing in a chilled bowl so that everyone may serve himself.

Carrot Salad Italienne

The Italians serve this delectable dish either warm or cold, as a salad or a side dish. It's an attractive way to dress up canned carrots.

YOU WILL NEED:

canned carrots	garlic
olive oil	lettuce (optional)
wine vinegar	parsley (optional)

Heat 1 can carrots, drain, and while they are still hot, add 2 tablespoons olive oil, 1 tablespoon vinegar (red wine vinegar preferably), and 1 clove garlic. Season with salt and pepper. Cover and let stand at least half an hour.

AT SERVING TIME:
Serve either warm or cold, as a side dish or salad. If served as a salad, chill, place on lettuce leaves, and garnish with chopped parsley. Serves 4 to 6.

Chef's Salad

Practically anything in the way of meat, cheese, and salad greens can go into a chef's salad. It is basically a mixed green salad made hearty—and hence much more acceptable to men—by the addition of solid food usually cut into julienne strips.

YOU WILL NEED:

salad greens

Swiss cheese

boiled ham, salami or
  bologna

cooked chicken or tongue

egg

anchovies

chives or parsley (optional)

French dressing or oil and
  vinegar

mustard (optional)

To serve 4 put about 4 cups of crisp chilled salad greens into a garlic-rubbed bowl. Arrange on top of the greens in small heaps the following ingredients or any desired combination (everything should be in pieces shaped like match sticks): ¼ pound Swiss cheese, 1 cup boiled ham, salami, or bologna, 1 cup cooked chicken or tongue. Slice a hard-cooked egg and use that along with 8 anchovies to decorate the heaps. Sprinkle if desired with chopped chives or parsley.

AT SERVING TIME:

At the table add ½ cup French dressing or "dress" at the table in the French manner by slowly pouring on 6 tablespoons olive oil or salad oil, mix until the greens glisten, sprinkle with 2 tablespoons vinegar, season to taste with salt, freshly ground black pepper, a bit of mustard if desired. Serve immediately.

Chicken and Almond Mousse

YOU WILL NEED:

egg yolks

chicken bouillon cube

gelatin

canned, boned chicken

almonds

cayenne

heavy cream

celery or fennel

Beat slightly 3 egg yolks. Gradually and slowly add to them 1 cup hot chicken broth made from a bouillon cube. Cook this over hot water until mixture thickens. Add 1 tablespoon granulated gelatin soaked in 1 tablespoon cold water. Stir well until gelatin dissolves. Add a 6¼-ounce can boned chicken, flaked, and ½ cup salted almonds finely chopped. Season to taste with salt and a few grains of cayenne. Set in the refrigerator until mixture begins to thicken. Then fold in 1 cup heavy cream beaten until stiff. Turn into a mold and chill or into a bowl which can be brought to the table.

AT SERVING TIME:
Garnish with crisp leaves of celery or fennel, and celery or fennel sticks. Serve with small hot rolls. Serves 6.

VARIATION: Chicken Mousse with Sherry
Two tablespoons of sherry may be added to the mousse.

Chicken Salad with White Grapes

YOU WILL NEED:

cooked or canned chicken	heavy cream
lime, or lemon, juice	lettuce or escarole
mayonnaise or salad dressing	white grapes

Cut 2 cups chicken into pieces—not too small. Sprinkle with 3 tablespoons lime, or lemon, juice. Make a foamy salad dressing by adding to ¾ cup prepared mayonnaise or salad dressing, ½ cup heavy cream whipped.

Add half of this dressing to the chicken. Mix thoroughly. Pack into oiled bowl or 4 custard cups and allow to stand in the refrigerator until thoroughly chilled.

AT SERVING TIME:
Unmold on lettuce leaves on chilled individual plates or small platter. Cover salad with remaining dressing as if you were frosting a cake. Garnish with seedless white grapes. Serve with tiny hot cheese biscuits.

Crab Meat and Avocado Salad with Gloucester Sauce

This is a pretty—and delicious—main dish at lunch or supper.

YOU WILL NEED:
avocados   Gloucester Sauce (page 147)
canned crab meat   parsley or chives

Cut 2 medium-sized avocados in half crosswise. Scoop out and cut avocado into cubes. Combine with 2 cups cooked canned crab meat, which has been carefully picked over and separated into large flakes. Mix lightly with 1 cup Gloucester Sauce. Place mixture into avocado shells. Cover thickly with finely chopped parsley or chives. Serve immediately.

AT SERVING TIME:
Pass extra Gloucester Sauce in a small bowl if desired. Serves 4.

Crab Meat Ravigote

Canned crab meat from Japan or Alaska is particularly good. It's nice to have shell-shaped dishes—real crab shells or those of glass or plastic. But they aren't really necessary.

YOU WILL NEED:
canned crab meat   Ravigote Sauce (page 151)
French dressing   parsley
hard-cooked eggs

To 2 cups of canned crab meat, which has been carefully picked over and separated into large flakes, add 4 tablespoons highly seasoned French dressing and 2 finely chopped hard-cooked eggs. Mix thoroughly. Place in 4 shell-shaped dishes or lettuce cups. Pour Ravigote Sauce over each serving.

AT SERVING TIME:
Sprinkle liberally with finely chopped parsley, using about 1

tablespoon parsley on each portion. Serve 1 shell per person. Serves 4.

Dutch Bacon Salad

In the Pennsylvania Dutch country one is likely to be served a salad of young greens with a robust dressing primed with crisp bacon and its drippings.

YOU WILL NEED:

bacon	white vinegar
egg	water
sugar	lettuce, romaine, or dandelion greens

Cook 3 slices of bacon until crisp. Drain on paper towels and set aside. Let the drippings cool in the skillet. Meanwhile, beat together 1 egg and 3 tablespoons each of sugar, white vinegar, and water. Add to the bacon drippings and cook over low heat, stirring constantly until thickened. While still warm, pour over young lettuce, romaine, or dandelion greens.

AT SERVING TIME:
Add the crumbled bacon and serve immediately.

Four of Beans Salad

A veritable wealth of beans (4 different kinds) go into this salad. This recipe makes 2 quarts, but it's a worthwhile project, for it keeps getting better and better as it stands.

YOU WILL NEED:

sugar	canned wax beans
water	canned lima beans
vinegar	celery
canned kidney beans	onion
canned green beans	green pepper

Combine 2 cups sugar, 1 cup water, 2 teaspoons salt. Cook 10 minutes. Cool. Add 1 cup vinegar and 1 small can each of kidney, green, wax, and lima beans, all well drained. Cover and allow to stand in refrigerator as long as feasible, preferably overnight.

AT SERVING TIME:
Before serving, add 2 cups chopped celery; 1 large sweet onion, thinly sliced and separated into rings, 1 green pepper, diced. Salt and pepper to taste.

In-a-Minute Salad

A salad gathered from your kitchen shelf.

YOU WILL NEED:

canned potatoes	mayonnaise
garlic	dry mustard
onion	hard-cooked egg
canned green beans	

Drain an 8-ounce can of potatoes. (If potatoes are whole, slice them.) Combine in a garlic-rubbed bowl with 1/3 cup chopped onion and an 8-ounce can drained green beans. Stir in 1/3 cup mayonnaise seasoned with 1/2 teaspoon salt and 3/4 teaspoon dry mustard.

AT SERVING TIME:
Top with sliced hard-cooked eggs. Serves 4.

Molded Fruit Salad in Wine

Fruit-flavored gelatin desserts in which wine is substituted for part of the liquid offer quick wine jellies to be served as desserts. Various combinations may be used. We suggest below the flavors which combine most happily with different types of wines and various fruits.

YOU WILL NEED:

strawberry, raspberry, or cherry gelatin dessert	lettuce
red wine	creamed cottage cheese
canned drained fruit or fruit salad	sour cream
	sugar
	allspice

Make up a package of cherry, raspberry, or strawberry gelatin dessert according to package directions but use 1½ cups water and ½ cup red wine. Allow the gelatin to chill and thicken slightly. Then add 1 cup drained canned fruit or fruit salad. Raw apples, pears, or oranges may be combined with the canned fruit. The only type of fresh fruit you must not use is pineapple because it prevents gelatin from stiffening. Pour into a mold or bowl, place in refrigerator until firm.

AT SERVING TIME:

Unmold on bed of lettuce leaves covering chilled serving dish or platter. Pass separately a bowl of Mock Devonshire Cream made by combining 1 cup creamed cottage cheese with 1 cup sour cream, 1 teaspoon sugar, and few grains of allspice. Stir until very smooth. Serves 6.

Palace Court Salad

The Palace Court Salad, created by a chef of one of San Francisco's great hotels, is world-famous. A structured salad, it is unbelievably impressive with its dome of seafood or chicken set on a base of artichokes and sliced tomatoes which rests on a dais of shredded lettuce. The dais is gilded with chopped or sieved eggs, and the dome swathed in a rosy glow of dressing spangled with bits of green pepper.

YOU WILL NEED:

For Salad:	*For Dressing:*
iceberg lettuce	Thousand Island dressing
canned artichoke bottoms	hot pepper sauce
fresh tomatoes	sweet green bell pepper
hard-cooked eggs	
canned seafood or canned boned chicken	
mayonnaise	

For each person provide ½ cup finely shredded iceberg lettuce, crisp and chilled. Arrange on a cold salad plate, making a circle about 5 inches in diameter, 1 inch high. In the center set a large canned drained artichoke bottom. Cover artichokes with sliced tomatoes. Sprinkle and press around the edge of the dais a generous amount of hard-cooked eggs, chopped or sieved. You will need at least 1 egg for each portion of salad. Top with a mound (a custard cupful) of canned seafood (drained shrimp, crab meat, tuna, salmon) or canned boned chicken, mixed with mayonnaise, prechilled in its custard cup so that the salad when turned out will look more shapely.

AT SERVING TIME:

Cover lightly with Palace Salad dressing made by combining ½ cup Thousand Island dressing, 3 drops hot pepper sauce, 2 tablespoons finely chopped or freeze-dried sweet green bell peppers. Pass more dressing in a silver sauce boat or small bowl.

Tomato Aspic au Moment

Tomato aspic already jelled and ready to slice and serve comes in convenient cans. Since it is actually a pectin jelly rather than a gelatin product, the shape of the aspic does not depend upon chilling, so that you could take it right off the shelves, open the can, and serve. Chilling, however, does improve the flavor.

YOU WILL NEED:

canned tomato aspic   curry powder
lettuce or romaine   mayonnaise or sour cream
celery, fennel, or spring
  onions

Chill. Open both ends of the can and push the aspic onto a chilled plate. Cut into 4 or 6 slices. Garnish with lettuce or romaine, and crisp little circles of celery, fennel, or spring onions.

AT SERVING TIME:

Pass separately a bowl of curry-flavored mayonnaise or sour cream, made by adding ½ teaspoon curry powder to ½ cup dressing or sour cream. Serves 4 to 6.

VARIATION: Tomato and Cucumber Aspic in Cucumber Boats
Cut 2 medium-sized cucumbers in half lengthwise. Scoop out the center and cut into ½-inch cubes. Cut or break chilled canned tomato aspic into pieces. Combine with diced cucumber and place in cucumber shells. Garnish with parsley or water cress. Serves 4.

Sliced Tomatoes Basilica

The new sliced salad tomatoes, canned, are an excellent product and fill a long-felt need.

YOU WILL NEED:

canned sliced salad tomatoes	dried parsley flakes
vinegar	dried basil
olive oil	lettuce

To a 1-pound can sliced salad tomatoes, drained, add 1 table-spoon vinegar, 3 tablespoons olive oil, 1 teaspoon dried parsley flakes, and ½ teaspoon dried basil. Add salt and freshly ground pepper to taste. Mix gently. Cover and let stand in refrigerator at least a half hour.

AT SERVING TIME:
Serve portions on a chilled lettuce leaf, or nest of shredded lettuce. Makes 3 servings.

Sugared Tomatoes with Lemon Slices

YOU WILL NEED:

canned sliced salad tomatoes	granulated sugar
lemon	Bibb lettuce

Place tomatoes in a shallow chilled bowl. Cover with paper-thin slices of unpeeled lemon. Sprinkle with granulated sugar.

AT SERVING TIME:
Just before serving, arrange crisp leaves of Bibb lettuce around the dish.

Quick Breads

BISCUITS, WAFFLES, AND GRIDDLE CAKES

For BREAKFAST, lunch, or supper—with appetizers, soups, salads, main dishes—as a dessert or a dessert accompaniment, a hot bread adds interest and variety. Often it makes all the difference between a mere snack and a real meal.

In this chapter we have collected a number of suggestions for transforming bakeshop breads and rolls quickly and easily into hot breads with homemade fragrance and just-baked flavor.

The refrigerator section of your supermarket provides a wealth of biscuits and rolls. Buttermilk, flaky, Southern-style, baking powder biscuits. In rolls—crescent, cloverleaf, croissants, and you-name-it. All are ready to slip into your oven for perfect hot breads, or to transpose into any number of specialty breads. Even brioches, with a real Parisian look and taste, come packaged, already baked, at the bread stall.

In addition to many recipes describing new and interesting uses of mixes there are recipes that show how partially baked goods—brown 'n' serve breads, rolls, and cinnamon buns as well as quick-frozen waffles and canned griddle cake batters may be served in ways that are essentially new and exciting but which hark back to the days of long and lavish feasting.

Since various brands of mixes are packed in different-sized packages they often vary in proportions and ingredients. We have suggested in each case that the basic recipe on the package be followed for mixing and baking. Our recipes suggest additions and variations applicable to a large number of the most popular brands. We have also included a number of helpful tricks that do not generally find space on labels.

RECIPES

Herb Loaves
Ready-Baked Bread with Herbs
Boston Brown Bread
Quick Cheese Bread
Honey Loaf
Mexican Corn Bread
Bacon Buns
Butterscotch Rolls
Butterscotch Pecan Rolls
New-Fashioned Doughnuts
Onion Moons
Skillet Biscuits
Blueberry Squares
Date-Nut Muffins with Sherry
Honeyed Cinnamon Crisps

Salt Sticks
Hush Puppies
Louisiana Pain Perdu
Buttermilk Batter Cakes
Bacon Batter Cakes
Ham Batter Cakes
French Pancakes
Maple Pancakes
Oatmeal Griddle Cakes
Poor Knights (*Arme Ritters*)
Scots' Scones
Sure-Pop Popovers
Yorkshire Pudding
Quick Sally Lunns
Angel Sally
Nut Waffles
Wonders or Doughboys

Herb Loaves

A crusty French or Italian loaf of bread may be used in this fashion. But even better are the brown 'n' serve loaves which are partially baked and may be stored in the refrigerator for a couple of weeks or kept in the frozen-food locker for months. Bread heated and flavored in this fashion is a welcome change from the popular garlic bread.

YOU WILL NEED:
  brown 'n' serve French   dried or fresh chervil,
    bread   tarragon, or basil
  olive oil or butter

Brush loaf with olive oil or melted butter. Sprinkle over the top
dried or fresh herbs, rubbing them between the fingers in order
to release the oils. Bake in a hot oven, 450° F., about 10 minutes
or until lightly browned. These loaves need not be set on a pan
but can be cooked directly on the shelf of the oven. However, if
you use a pan, or cookie tin, it need not be greased.

AT SERVING TIME:
Bring the loaf whole and hot to the table, preferably in a basket
lined with a napkin.

VARIATION: Ready-Baked Bread with Herbs
A French or Italian loaf from the bakeshop may be brushed with
oil and sprinkled with herbs as above, but the oven should not
be hot, only about 325° F., and the time required should be cut
to about 5 minutes.

Boston Brown Bread

Boston brown bread is now available in tins. Generally it is or
should be served steamy hot, unless of course it is sliced thin for
sandwiches. On most tins of brown bread you will find directions
telling you to immerse the can in hot water. This method of
heating takes a long time, and what is more important, the hot
can is difficult to handle. The method suggested here is much
simpler.

YOU WILL NEED:
  canned Boston brown bread

Open a can of brown bread at both ends and push the bread out
of the can. Place in the top of a double boiler. Cover and heat
over boiling water.

AT SERVING TIME:

Bring to the table in one piece and slice about ½ inch thick; or slice in the kitchen and place in a bowl or basket lined with a napkin. Serve with Boston baked beans, of course, cole slaw, and apple pie for dessert. Serves 4.

Quick Cheese Bread

If Merlin himself set about to conjure up a miraculous loaf in minutes, he could hardly equal the success you will have with a couple of cans of refrigerated biscuits. This recipe makes 2 loaves.

YOU WILL NEED:

butter or margarine
refrigerated buttermilk
 biscuits

grated Cheddar cheese
chopped chives or parsley

Using 1 tablespoon butter or margarine, grease 2 9 × 5 × 3-inch loaf pans. Use 2 8-ounce packages refrigerated biscuits to fill each of the pans. Arrange 1 package (10 biscuits) standing up on their ends along each long side. Sprinkle each with 1 cup grated Cheddar cheese. Bake at 400° F. for 25 minutes or until breads are deep golden brown. Remove and cool on wire racks. Sprinkle each with a little chopped chives or parsley.

AT SERVING TIME:

Rounds out a salad meal, livens up tea time, provides a hearty hot bread for company or family meals.

Honey Loaf

YOU WILL NEED:

canned flaky refrigerated
 biscuits
honey

pecans
golden raisins
sweet butter

Lightly grease a 9 × 5 × 3-inch loaf pan. Separate 2 9½-ounce packages of flaky biscuits into 10 biscuits each. In saucepan, heat ½ cup honey, ⅓ cup chopped pecans, ⅓ cup golden raisins until just simmering. Line pan with 3 biscuits. Brush with a little honey mixture. Cut 3 biscuits in half lengthwise, and place ½ biscuit at each end and 2 along each side of loaf pan. Brush with more honey mixture. Fill pan by layering remaining biscuits, brushing each layer with honey. (Save a little for glaze after baking loaf.) Bake at 375° F. for 25 to 30 minutes, covering with foil to prevent overbrowning if necessary. Remove from pan and cool on wire rack. Brush top with remaining honey mixture.

AT SERVING TIME:

Serve with a crock of sweet butter and quantities of hot coffee.

Mexican Corn Bread

Corn bread with a difference—and a distinct south-of-the-border flavor.

YOU WILL NEED:

yellow cornmeal

all-purpose flour

sugar

baking powder

eggs

milk

cream-style canned corn

corn or peanut oil

grated American cheese

onion

canned jalepino peppers or sweet bell peppers

Sift together into a large bowl 2 cups yellow cornmeal, 1 cup all-purpose flour, 1 teaspoon salt, 2 tablespoons sugar, 3 teaspoons baking powder. Make a hole in the center of the mixture. Drop in 4 eggs, 1 cup milk. Mix as you would a muffin mixture —not hard or long. Then add 1 No. 303 can cream-style corn with the liquid, ½ cup corn or peanut oil, 1½ cups grated American cheese (may be sharp or mild, doesn't matter). Fold in also 1 cup finely chopped or grated onion and 4 or 5 canned jalepino peppers, drained and chopped fine. Instead of jalepino peppers, you may use 4 or 5 tablespoons sweet bell peppers.

Pour batter into 1 or 2 well-greased pans. Size or shape isn't crucial so long as you fill pans only half full. Bake in a moderately hot oven (375° F.) 20 to 25 minutes or until lightly gilded on top. The corn bread, when done, will shrink a little from the sides of the pan but it should still be quite moist in the center.

AT SERVING TIME:
Carefully transfer cake of corn bread to a wooden serving board, whisk to table, and cut into squares for serving.

Bacon Buns

YOU WILL NEED:

raw bacon   refrigerated biscuits

Sprinkle 2 tablespoons diced raw bacon over 1 package refrigerated biscuits just before baking.

AT SERVING TIME:
Absolutely delicious with creamy scrambled eggs.

Butterscotch Rolls

Partially baked brown 'n' serve rolls can be easily transformed into all manner of specialty breads. Sometime when you long for a touch of sweet and have nothing but plain rolls in the house, try this.

YOU WILL NEED:

butter or margarine   brown 'n' serve rolls
brown sugar

Soften and mix ½ cup butter or margarine with ¾ cup light brown sugar. Put half of the mixture in the bottom of a shallow pan. Place the rolls flat side down in the pan. Cover the top with the rest of the butter-sugar mixture. Bake in a hot oven, 400° F., 5 to 7 minutes. Remove rolls from pan immediately before syrup hardens.

AT SERVING TIME:
Serve warm with tea or coffee.

VARIATION: Butterscotch Pecan Rolls
Mix with the butter and sugar ¼ to ½ cup coarsely chopped pecans or walnuts.

New-Fashioned Doughnuts

With a can of refrigerated biscuits you can have doughnuts quick as a wink.

YOU WILL NEED:

| refrigerated biscuits | sugar |
| cooking oil | cinnamon |

Separate the biscuits in a 9½-ounce package of refrigerated biscuits. Using a small ¾-inch cutter, remove a doughnut hole from the center of each. In an electric skillet or saucepan pour 1½ inches cooking oil. Heat to 375° F. Fry doughnuts 4 or 5 minutes or until puffy and deep golden brown on both sides. (Turn halfway through cooking time to brown both sides.) In a paper or plastic bag combine ¼ cup sugar with ½ teaspoon cinnamon. Place doughnuts in bag and toss to coat with sugar mixture.

AT SERVING TIME:
Pile in a pyramid on a platter, to be eaten with bowls of fresh or canned fruit. Or you might omit the dusting of sugar and cinnamon and frost them with one of the many frosting mixes on the market (chocolate, etc.) .

Onion Moons

A can of refrigerated crescent rolls are transformed with onion flakes to baked rolls of distinction.

YOU WILL NEED:
    canned refrigerated crescent   dehydrated onion flakes
      rolls   paprika
    butter or margarine

Shape an 8-ounce package of refrigerated crescent rolls into individual crescents. Melt 1 tablespoon butter or margarine and stir in 2 tsp. dehydrated onion flakes. Brush crescents with mixture and bake at 375° F. for 10 to 12 minutes or until golden brown.

AT SERVING TIME:
Sprinkle with ½ teaspoon paprika and rush to table piping hot. Wonderful with fish! Makes 8 servings.

Skillet Biscuits

The wild and woolly West of our forefathers spawned the sourdough biscuits, which the ranch cook "baked" in a skillet. Today we use a can of buttermilk biscuits, but the results are amazingly similar—delicious little crusty biscuits!

YOU WILL NEED:
    canned buttermilk biscuits   butter
    shortening   honey or jam

For each package of 10 biscuits, put a tablespoon of shortening in a medium-hot skillet. Arrange the biscuits in one layer, cover, and cook about 10 minutes. Turn, adding another tablespoon of shortening, and cook another 5 minutes.

AT SERVING TIME:
Rush to the table, and provide plenty of butter and honey or jam.

Blueberry Squares

Sometimes the berries may cause a muffin to become a little
heavy or soggy, so we use a white cake mix, and place the berries
on top of the batter. The squares may be baked in muffin tins
but it is easier to use a square pan.

YOU WILL NEED:
white cake mix   sugar and cinnamon
blueberries   (optional)
                                         sweet butter

Make up a package of white cake mix according to directions.
Pour into a buttered square pan. Cover with ½ to 1 cup blueberries, either fresh, canned, or quick frozen. If canned or frozen
berries are used they should be well drained. Sprinkle very
lightly with 1 tablespoon sugar mixed with ½ teaspoon cinnamon, if desired.

AT SERVING TIME:
Bring to the table in the pan in which it was baked. Cut in
squares and serve warm with sweet butter.

Date-Nut Muffins with Sherry

YOU WILL NEED:
date-nut muffin mix   sour cream
milk   creamed cottage cheese
sherry or brandy   allspice
nutmeg

Follow package directions for date-nut muffins but substitute
for part of the milk ¼ cup sherry or brandy and add a few
grains of nutmeg. Bake in muffin tins according to directions.

AT SERVING TIME:
These muffins make a delicious dessert when served warm with
Mock Devonshire Cream, made by combining equal quantities
of sour cream and creamed cottage cheese, 1 teaspoon of sugar,
and few grains of allspice.

Honeyed Cinnamon Crisps

Packaged rye wafers take on zest with these trimmings.

YOU WILL NEED:

rye wafers	butter
honey	cinnamon

Set rye wafers on a cooky sheet, and place on each a teaspoon of honey, a dab of butter, and a sprinkle of cinnamon. Set under the broiler to heat and toast.

AT SERVING TIME:
Serve very hot—with tea, coffee, or chocolate.

Salt Sticks

YOU WILL NEED:

canned refrigerated biscuits	coarse salt
butter or margarine	sesame seeds

Separate canned biscuits and roll each into a 5-inch rope. Brush with 2 tablespoons melted butter or margarine. Sprinkle with 1 teaspoon coarse salt, and 1 teaspoon sesame seeds. Bake at 375° F. for 10 to 12 minutes or until golden brown.

AT SERVING TIME:
A delightful accompaniment for soups, salads, dips, or for the bread basket on a buffet.

Hush Puppies

Hush puppy mix is on the market. Add to the mix a little extra something in the way of seasoning, and you have an excellent quick crisp bread to serve with soups or salads or with cocktails.

YOU WILL NEED:
hush puppy mix   cayenne or Tabasco sauce
parsley

Make up mix according to package directions but add 2 tablespoons very finely chopped parsley and a few grains of cayenne
or 3 or 4 drops of Tabasco sauce. Bake on top of the stove on a
griddle or in the oven according to package directions.

AT SERVING TIME:
Serve hot as can be!

Louisiana Pain Perdu

Literally translated, *pain perdu* means "lost bread"—the bread
that would have been lost or wasted if a clever Creole cook had
not transformed it.

YOU WILL NEED:
eggs   butter
milk   sugar and cinnamon or
sherry (optional)   maple syrup, honey,
French bread   preserves, or marmalade

Beat together in a shallow bowl or deep soup plate 2 eggs, 1 cup
milk, ½ teaspoon salt, 1 tablespoon sherry, if desired. Soak in
milk and egg mixture 8 slices of crusty French bread cut about
½ inch thick. Bread should be soaked until soft but still shapely.
Brown on hot well-greased griddle or in butter in a frying pan,
browning first one side and then the other.

AT SERVING TIME:
Serve on heated plates sprinkled with sugar and cinnamon or
pass maple syrup, honey, preserves, or marmalade.

Buttermilk Batter Cakes

These are made with a ready-made batter, sealed under pressure
in a container with a valve which permits you to squirt out of

the can the exact amount you need for each cake—a great convenience for the small family or the lone-eater because the unused portion may be kept for several days in the refrigerator.

YOU WILL NEED:

canned buttermilk pancake
batter
melted butter

syrup, honey, or maple
sugar

Cakes may be baked on a heavy frying pan, a soapstone or an aluminum griddle. Test to be sure that the griddle or frying pan is hot enough for baking by dropping on the surface a bit of cold water. If it sputters and boils rapidly, the correct baking temperature has been reached. Usually it is not necessary to grease a griddle after an initial rubbing with unsalted fat or oil when it is new, but if you feel the need of greasing use a bit of bacon fat or a cut potato.

Pour 3 or 4 tablespoons of batter onto the griddle for a medium-sized cake. Direct the liquid to the center of the cake, and it will spread to the edges. Bake until the surface is dotted with tiny bubbles but not long enough for the cake to be dry on top. Turn once.

AT SERVING TIME:

Serve hot off the griddle on heated plates with melted butter and syrup, honey, or maple sugar.

VARIATIONS:

Bacon Batter Cakes

Sprinkle over the surface of each cake, before it is turned, 1 crisp slice of bacon coarsely crumbled.

Ham Batter Cakes

Cut boiled or baked ham into tiny cubes and sprinkle 2 tablespoons over each cake before turning.

French Pancakes

These are very different from griddle cakes—much thinner and of a different texture. Pancake mixes do not work very well for this type of cake, although you will find recipes listed on many packages. It is very simple to make the batter yourself, and incidentally, this is one place where you need not bother sifting the flour. Use it as it comes.

YOU WILL NEED:

all-purpose flour	salad oil
milk	sugar
eggs	cinnamon (optional)

Put ¾ cup flour and ½ teaspoon salt into a bowl. Make a well in the center and pour in 1 cup milk and 2 eggs. Stir and beat until perfectly smooth. Batter should be thin as coffee cream. If necessary, add a little extra milk. Heat a five-inch frying pan. Pour in a few *drops* of salad oil and tip so that the bottom of the pan glistens with a thin film of oil. Pour in 2 or 3 tablespoons batter—just enough to cover the pan thinly. Tilt so that mixture spreads evenly. Cook on one side. Turn and cook on the other side.

AT SERVING TIME:

Sprinkle with sugar or sugar and cinnamon. Roll up or fold in quarters and arrange on hot platter. Makes about 18 pancakes.

VARIATION: Maple Pancakes

Brush the pancakes with melted butter. Sprinkle with maple sugar. Roll and serve 2 or 3 per portion on a heated plate with a section of lemon which can be squeezed on the pancake.

Oatmeal Griddle Cakes

Although they are admittedly more time-consuming than merely pouring a portion of pancake mix from a box and adding milk, you will find these oatmeal griddle cakes worth the effort! Let these be your special treat for the family on extra special days.

YOU WILL NEED:

quick-cooking oatmeal	baking powder
milk	eggs
flour	butter or margarine

To 2 cups of quick-cooking oatmeal (uncooked), add 2 cups hot milk. Cook lightly. Meanwhile, sift together ½ cup flour, 2½ teaspoons baking powder, 1 teaspoon salt. Separate 2 eggs; beat the 2 yolks into the oats and milk mixture. Add 2 tablespoons melted butter or margarine and then stir in the dry ingredients. If batter seems too stiff to work (it is supposed to be stiffer than regular pancake batter), add ¼ to ½ cup milk. Beat the 2 egg whites stiff and fold into the mixture. Drop by tablespoons onto a hot greased griddle. When the surface is covered with bubbles, turn and brown on the other side. Oatmeal pancakes take longer to brown than other kinds. So don't get impatient. Don't turn them more than once. Makes 18 3-inch cakes.

AT SERVING TIME:
Here's a hint for keeping pancakes warm until all are ready to serve. Heat a slow oven. Set platter inside. As pancakes come off the griddle, slip onto platter, buttering each pancake as you go along. When all pancakes are cooked, divide them onto warm plates (which have also been stacked in oven), and rush to the table. That way the cook eats with the rest of the family. Provide an extra pitcher of melted butter, as well as maple syrup, honey, blueberry and strawberry preserves.

Poor Knights (Arme Ritters)

This is a German version of what we call French toast. As the name would imply, it is thrifty but aristocratic.

YOU WILL NEED:

stale bread	milk
jam, marmalade, or	almond or vanilla extract
preserves	butter
eggs	nutmeg

Spread 3 slices (¼ inch thick) stale white bread with jam, marmalade, or preserves. Top each with a slice of bread. Cut each sandwich in half diagonally. Do not remove crusts.

In a shallow dish or soup plate, beat 2 eggs with 1 cup milk, ½ teaspoon salt, ½ teasoon almond or vanilla extract. Soak sandwiches in mixture until softened but not mushy, turning them first on one side then on the other so that the bread will absorb all the egg and milk.

Brown first on one side then on the other in butter in a frying pan.

AT SERVING TIME:
Serve piping hot on warm plates and have on hand grated nutmeg so that each person may add a little nutmeg as desired.

Scots' Scones

Every family and every cookbook has a different recipe, and here's one of our favorites.

YOU WILL NEED:

all-purpose flour	**butter**
baking powder	**milk**
sugar	**egg**

Resift 2 cups all-purpose flour along with 1 teaspoon baking powder, 1 teaspoon sugar, ½ teaspoon salt. With a big fork, blend in 4 tablespoons butter until it looks like coarse sand. Add an egg beaten with ⅓ cup milk. Toss lightly until you get a dough. Divide into 3 parts and pat out into circles about ½ inch thick. Place on a buttered, lightly floured cookie sheet. Cut each circle into quarters with a knife. Brush with milk and bake in a hot oven (400° F.) about 15 minutes or until lightly browned.

AT SERVING TIME:
Serve hot, or split and toast.

Sure-Pop Popovers

Even without a mix, popovers are not at all difficult to make and they're so rewarding—if they pop! This recipe is considerably "speeded up": it eliminates the sifting of flour, the melting of shortening, and it adds for those who want further insurance a bit of baking powder.

YOU WILL NEED:

eggs
milk
salad oil
flour

baking powder (optional)
butter and jam, honey, or
preserves

Beat 2 eggs until light. Add 1 cup milk, 1 tablespoon salad oil (not olive oil). Beat together with a rotary egg beater. Add ⅞ cup all-purpose flour. Sifting is not necessary, but if you wish to sift the flour, use 1 cup flour measured after sifting. The reason for the difference is quite obvious for sifting aerates flour, makes it less bulky. With the flour add ¼ teaspoon salt, ¼ teaspoon baking powder, if you have it. Beat until smooth with the egg beater. The mixture should be heavy as whipping cream. If too thick, add a little more milk.

Heavy iron muffin pans are generally used for popovers but they are not necessary. You may use aluminum pans if you wish, or oven-proof custard cups. Grease thoroughly bottom and sides. Fill ½ full with mixture. Have the oven preheated to at least 500° F. When the popovers have popped, that is in about 15 minutes, turn down the oven to 400° F. and continue baking 10 to 15 minutes longer or until done. The crust should sound crackly-crisp when tapped with your finger nail, the inside staying pleasantly moist—almost doughy but not wet. To be really sure you must break one open.

AT SERVING TIME:

Serve hot with plenty of butter for breakfast with jam, honey, or preserves, with a luncheon salad, or a hearty supper soup. Makes 8 popovers.

VARIATION: Yorkshire Pudding

Use the popover batter, or popover mix, but bake in a 10-inch pan in which there must be fat—¼ inch deep hot beef drippings, bacon or sausage fat will do. Yorkshire pudding is best baked in a dish which can be brought to the table right from the oven. Cut in squares and serve with roast beef and gravy. By serving Yorkshire pudding you can transform sliced delicatessen beef and a can of beef gravy into an old-fashioned beef dinner.

Quick Sally Lunns

Who was Sally—where she lived or how her name happened to
be given to this popular Southern tea bread—we have never
discovered. Sally appears in many guises, in different regions of
the country. Risen Sally Lunn is made from a yeast dough, but
Quick Sally is made with baking powder.

YOU WILL NEED:

biscuit mix	sugar
milk	butter
eggs	

To 2 cups biscuit mix add ¾ cup milk, 3 eggs well beaten, ¼
cup sugar, and 2 tablespoons melted butter. Pour batter into
well-greased muffin tins and bake in a hot oven, 400° F., about
15 minutes.

AT SERVING TIME:
The old recipes say "run with Sally Lunn to the table," for this
tea bread must be served so hot that the butter melts into the
feathery bread instantly. Makes 12 Sally Lunns.

VARIATION: Angel Sally
Sally Lunn is often baked in an angel-cake pan or a ring mold.
The pans should be well greased with butter and the cake
baked at 350° F. about 40 minutes.

Nut Waffles

YOU WILL NEED:

quick-frozen waffles	honey, syrup, whipped
butter or margarine	cream, or vanilla ice
pecans, almonds, or walnuts	cream

Brush quick-frozen waffles with melted butter or margarine.
Sprinkle with coarsely chopped toasted pecans, almonds or walnuts. Set in a hot oven just long enough to heat thoroughly.

AT SERVING TIME:

Serve hot with honey or syrup or with whipped cream or vanilla ice cream as a dessert.

Wonders or Doughboys

YOU WILL NEED:

bread or hot roll mix
vegetable shortening or lard

sugar and cinnamon (optional)

Make up dough and allow to rise according to package directions for plain bread or rolls. Form dough into small balls about the size of a golf ball, or if you prefer, roll out dough 1/8 inch thick. Cut into strips and then into 2-inch squares or diamonds. Cover and let stand 10 or 15 minutes. Fry like doughnuts, dropping into deep hot fat, 375° F. (hot enough to brown an inch cube of bread in 40 seconds). Drain on paper towels.

AT SERVING TIME:

Serve hot as a bread, particularly with a hearty vegetable soup. Or shake in a paper bag with 1/2 cup sugar, 1 tablespoon cinnamon, and serve with coffee or tea in the afternoon.

14

~~~~~~~~~~~~~~~~~

Cakes, Pies, and Other Sweets

Mixes make child's play of baking. But one thing is certain, you must follow to the letter the directions on the package. Then, and only then, will you have perfect cakes, pies, cookies, and cupcakes—with a minimum of time, effort, and expense. Curiously enough, the novice often has better luck with mixes than the experienced baker, probably because she is less likely to improvise or use older and unsuitable methods.

Here are a few warnings and suggestions that will make baking with mixes easier, faster, surer—and more fun.

Do not sift any kind of mix. It is not necessary, for all ingredients have already been thoroughly combined in the manufacturing.

Do not undermix or overmix. If you have a hand beater, count your strokes. If you use an electric mixer, watch the second hand of your clock or use an egg timer.

All you need is paper to prepare your pans when baking a cake. Almost any kind of paper will do—waxed, brown, or plain white. No greasing is necessary. Cut a circle a little smaller than the bottom of the pan and be certain that the paper does not touch the edge of the pan or the cake will crack. For most cakes all that is needed is a small square of paper in the center of the pan. This is a good trick to remember when you're in a hurry.

Although there is some disagreement even among the experts about the necessity of preheating the oven, you are always on the safe side if you do light the oven about 10 minutes beforehand. An oven thermometer is almost a necessity, but if you have none, or if yours is untrustworthy, look in the glossary for old-fashioned ways in which to judge the heat of the oven. Opening the oven door lowers the oven temperature, so do this as little as possible.

Do not overbake either cakes, cookies, or pastries made from mixes. For a perfect cake, leave it in the oven the minimum time suggested on the package or maybe a few minutes less. If the cake shows just a sign of pulling away from the sides of the pan, it is done. Or place your finger lightly on the cake. If it makes no depression, the cake is done. Or insert a wire cake tester or a clean broom straw. If it comes out clean, the cake is done.

What you do to your cake after you take it from the oven is most important. Set the cake—pan and all—on a wire rack to cool for 5 to 10 minutes. The rack allows the air to get under the cake as well as around it. Loosen the cake around its edges. Turn upside down and peel off the paper carefully. Then turn right side up again on the rack to finish cooling. If a topping is to be baked on, place topping on hot cake. For a boiled or 4-minute frosting, cool cake about 30 minutes before frosting. Buttery frostings should be put on the cake when it is thoroughly cool, so that the heat of the cake will not melt the frosting.

A package of cake mix generally makes 2 8-inch layers. For a small half-size cake use half a package of mix. Mix in a small mixing bowl with half the amount of milk called for on the package. Beating and baking times remain the same.

Unless you are very sure of yourself and have had a great deal of experience not only in baking but in baking with mixes, it is wisest not to improvise too much on the basic ingredients: Do not add eggs unless your particular cake mix calls for them; do not use water instead of milk; do not vary the amounts of liquid. There are, however, a number of flavoring and glamorizing tricks that you can safely use. One to 3 teaspoons grated orange rind may be used. Buttermilk may be substituted for sweet milk in devil's food or chocolate cake mix. One-fourth to one-half teaspoon of extract (orange, lemon, almond, or peppermint) may be added to white or yellow cake. For pistachio flavor, use half and half vanilla and almond extracts. When spices are added, it is best not to use more than a teaspoon in all. Chopped nuts and/or chopped fruits are good in gingerbread, devil's food, chocolate, or spice cake mix, but be careful about adding too much of them to a white cake batter or they will sink to the bottom because this batter is usually thinner.

Pie baking has become child's play with the advent of canned pie fillings and frozen unbaked pie shells, available in frozen-food bins.

RECIPES

Applesauce Cake
Blazing Cake
Cherry Upside-Down Cake
Pineapple, Apricot, Peach, Loganberry Upside-Down Cake
Gâteau au Citron
Election Cake
Lady Baltimore Cake
Miracle Fruit Cake
Rigo Jancsi
Tropical Coconut Cake with Orange Coconut Frosting
Fluffy Uncooked Frosting
Pink Peppermint Frosting

Pistachio Frosting
Orange Frosting
Glazed Strawberry Tarts
Syrian Apple Dumplings
Tarte aux Pruneaux
Kentucky Bourbon Brownies
Miracle Coconut Macaroons
Apple Pie with Cheese
English Silk Pie
Lord Marlborough Pie
New Wave Mince and Pumpkin Pie
Peach Pizza
Crumb Pie Shell
Crumb Tart Shells

Applesauce Cake

A spice cake mix and canned applesauce make a quick modern version of this wonderful old-fashioned cake which can also be served warm as a pudding.

YOU WILL NEED:

spice cake mix
baking soda
powdered cloves
canned unsweetened apple-
    sauce

raisins and/or nuts
butter
flour
ready-whipped cream or
    sweetened sour cream

Make up a package of spice cake mix according to the package recipe. Add ½ teaspoon baking soda, ¼ teaspoon powdered cloves, 1 cup unsweetened applesauce, 1 cup raisins and/or nuts, cut into small pieces. Bake in 2 buttered and floured rectangular pans like bread pans. Baking time is slightly longer than cake without applesauce—about 40 minutes in a moderate oven, 350° F., or until done.

AT SERVING TIME:
Cut into slices about ½ inch thick. Serve cold or, if desired, cut in squares and serve warm with ready-whipped cream or slightly sweetened sour cream.

Blazing Cake

A blazing cake, incredibly dramatic, unbelievably easy.

YOU WILL NEED:

a ring of cake (lemon or orange chiffon, angel, or sponge)

canned cherry pie filling
rum

Buy or, if you're ambitious, make a ring of cake. Lemon or orange chiffon, angel, or sponge cake can be used. Cover the top with about a cup of canned cherry pie filling. At serving time, add to the rest of the can or jar 4 tablespoons rum. Heat and stir but do not allow to boil. Pour over and around the cake.

AT SERVING TIME:
At the table, in a small metal ramekin or mug, slightly warmed over a candle or on a hot tray, have another ¼ cup of rum. Get someone to extinguish the lights as you set a lighted match or taper to the liquor and pour it over the cake. After a second or two, let the lights come on again, cut the cake into wedges, and serve still flaming.

Cherry Upside-Down Cake

YOU WILL NEED:

canned pitted red sour
   cherries
butter or margarine

brown sugar
white cake mix
almond extract (optional)

Drain syrup from a 1-pound can of pitted red sour cherries and
save for sauce. Melt 4 tablespoons butter or margarine in a
heavy frying pan or a cake pan and add ½ cup brown sugar.
Place cherries in the pan close together. Pour on batter made
from a package of white cake mix. Bake at 350° F. about 25
minutes. Cool cake 5 minutes. Invert the pan on a plate and let
stand 1 minute before removing pan.

AT SERVING TIME:

At the table cut into squares and pass separately a sauce made by
cooking the syrup down to half the original quantity. A bit of
almond extract may be added to the syrup if desired.

VARIATION: Pineapple, Apricot, Peach, Loganberry
                      Upside-Down Cake

Any of the above fruits either canned or quick-frozen may be
used instead of cherries. They should be well drained. Pecans
may be placed on top of the butter-sugar mixture before the
fruit is added.

Gâteau au Citron

YOU WILL NEED:

chocolate or spice cake mix
citron peel or mixed
   candied fruits and peels
walnuts or other nut meats

confectioners' sugar
nut meats and candied
   cherries

Make up a package of chocolate or spice cake mix according to directions. Fold into the batter ½ cup diced candied citron peel or mixed candied fruits and peels, and ½ cup chopped walnuts or other nut meats. Bake according to package directions, preferably in a long narrow pan.

AT SERVING TIME:
Turn out on a platter. Dust lightly with confectioners' sugar and decorate with nut meats and candied cherries.

Election Cake

According to the Browns, learned commentators on culinary matters, the Connecticut Election Cake has always been dedicated to the feasting of both winners and losers. The recipe for this cake was invariably found "sandwiched between household accounts and directions for cough cures in old farm wives' note books." The cake is found under various names and with many different ingredients in many of our fifty states. Sometimes the recipe "was recognizable only by the fact that it was raised with yeast and had fruit in it." Here is an unorthodox version, prepared from a package of hot roll mix.

YOU WILL NEED:

hot roll mix	cinnamon
brandy or rum	nutmeg or mace
lemon	seedless raisins
	white frosting mix

Make up a package of hot roll mix according to package recipe for coffee cake. *But* for ½ cup of the liquid substitute ½ cup brandy or rum. Add to batter 1 teaspoon lemon juice, 1 teaspoon grated lemon rind, 1 teaspoon cinnamon, ½ teaspoon nutmeg or mace. When dough has risen to double its bulk, punch it down, and add 1 cup seedless raisins. Bake in greased bread tins according to package directions. When cold cover with white frosting made from a mix.

AT SERVING TIME:

Slice as you would bread and serve with coffee. In the old days this cake always ended the veal dinner, which was as essential to Election Day as turkey and pie for Thanksgiving.

Lady Baltimore Cake

One of the great glories of the table in Maryland and other parts of the South has been the Lady Baltimore Cake. A facsimile of this cake can be made from a package of white cake mix and the Fluffy Uncooked Frosting. Since Lady Baltimore has always been a queenly cake in size as well as delicacy, we suggest using 2 packages of white cake mix.

YOU WILL NEED:

white cake mix	pecans
almond extract	figs
rose flavoring (optional)	seeded raisins
Fluffy Uncooked Frosting	
(page 215)	

Make up 2 packages white cake mix according to directions. Add ½ teaspoon almond extract or 1 teaspoon rose flavoring. Bake in 3 8-inch round layer pans in a moderate oven, 375° F., 25 to 30 minutes or until done. Put together with Lady Baltimore Filling and top with Lady Baltimore Frosting.

Lady Baltimore Frosting and Filling

Double the recipe for Fluffy Uncooked Frosting. Save half the frosting for the top and sides of the cake and to the other half add ½ cup chopped pecan nuts, 3 dried figs cut into thin strips, ½ cup seeded raisins cut up, ½ teaspoon almond extract.

AT SERVING TIME:

This is a large cake which deserves your prettiest plate or platter and a garland of fresh blossoms and green leaves.

Miracle Fruit Cake

YOU WILL NEED:

spice cake mix
baking soda
sherry, rum, or brandy
 (optional)
pitted dates
seedless raisins

ready-to-use candied fruits
 and peels
egg white
maraschino cherries and/or
 nut meats

Make up a package of spice cake mix according to package directions adding ½ teaspoon baking soda. If desired, up to ¼ tablespoon sherry, rum, or brandy may be substituted for an equal quantity of liquid.

Combine 1 cup sliced pitted dates with ¾ cup seedless raisins, 1 cup ready-to-use diced candied fruits and peels.

Line a casserole with greased heavy waxed paper. Put in a layer of batter. Sprinkle with a layer of fruit, then batter, alternating fruit and batter till dish is ¾ full. The last layer should be batter. Bake in 375° F. oven about 1 hour or until done. Quick decoration: 15 minutes before the cake is done brush with a slightly beaten egg white; quickly arrange on the cake in a pattern bits of candied fruit, maraschino cherries, and/or nut meats. Return to the oven. Finish baking.

AT SERVING TIME:

A fruit cake may be brought to the table and served as well as stored in its own casserole. For a gala appearance, pin a napkin around the casserole and decorate with a spray of leaves. To serve fruit cake flambé, slightly warm ¼ cup brandy or rum, set ablaze and pour over the fruit cake. If possible, serve a little flame on each slice. If you store your fruit cake, pour a little brandy over it from time to time to keep it moist. Keep tightly covered in a cool place.

Rigo Jancsi

Rigo Jancsi (pronounced Yansee) is a two-inch layer of Bavarian cream between layers of chocolate cake with a chocolate frosting on the top. The original recipe made from scratch is a half day's chore, but we have a quick version contrived from a chocolate cake and a whipped dessert mix.

YOU WILL NEED:

frozen chocolate cake with
  a chocolate frosting
whipped vanilla-flavored
  dessert mix
almond extract
rum extract

butter
canned red sweet cherries
slivered almonds
powdered sugar
whipped cream

Cut a frozen chocolate cake with a chocolate frosting crosswise into two layers. Make up a 3¾-ounce package of whipped vanilla-flavored dessert mix—the kind you whip and chill—according to package directions, adding 1 teaspoon almond extract and 2 teaspoons rum extract with the water. Butter a shallow dish or pan. Line the bottom with a layer of cake. Spoon the pudding onto the cake. Scatter 1 large can red sweet cherries, drained well, on top of pudding. Cover with the second layer of cake. Allow to chill in the freezer at least 20 minutes or in the refrigerator at least an hour. Decorate with slivered almonds and sprinkle with powdered sugar and rosettes of sweetened whipped cream, if desired. Cut into rectangles with a slightly warmed knife. Serves 6 to 8.

AT SERVING TIME:

This is delicious served with strong black coffee, or, more elegantly, coffee laced with brandy.

Tropical Coconut Cake with Orange Coconut Frosting

YOU WILL NEED:

angel food cake
confectioners' sugar
lemon juice

orange juice
orange coloring
shredded coconut

Buy an angel food cake and spread with orange coconut frosting made without cooking.

Orange Coconut Frosting

Combine 3 cups sifted confectioners' sugar with a dash of salt, 1 tablespoon lemon juice, and enough orange juice to give a spreading consistency, about 3 to 4 tablespoons. Tint delicately with 3 drops orange coloring. Frost top and sides of cake and sprinkle thickly with 1½ cups shredded coconut while frosting is still soft. The moist southern-style coconut, which is packed in cans, is particularly good.

AT SERVING TIME:

This is most delicious when served together with orange sherbet. Cut cake at the table and pass the bowl of sherbet separately.

Fluffy Uncooked Frosting

This frosting has the look and flavor of real old-fashioned boiled frosting but there is no cooking involved—only a few minutes of beating.

YOU WILL NEED:

egg white	cream of tartar
sugar	vanilla

Combine 1 unbeaten egg white with ¾ cup sugar, ¼ teaspoon cream of tartar, and 1 teaspoon vanilla in a small deep bowl and mix well. Add ¼ cup boiling water and beat with a rotary egg beater or at the high speed of an electric mixer until the frosting will stand in stiff little peaks. This should take about 4 minutes. Makes 3 cups of frosting—enough to cover the top and sides of 2 8-inch layers. A cake with this frosting should be kept uncovered at room temperature. Don't put it in the refrigerator.

VARIATIONS:
Pink Peppermint Frosting

Use above recipe substituting for the vanilla ¼ teaspoon peppermint extract. Add a few drops of red pure-food coloring to tint delicately. Especially delicious on devil's food cake.

Pistachio Frosting

Use above recipe and decrease the vanilla to $\overline{1}/_2$ teaspoon. Add $1/_4$ teaspoon almond extract. If desired, tint a delicate green with pure-food coloring and garnish with pistachio nuts.

Orange Frosting

Use the above recipe but substitute for the boiling water $1/_4$ cup heated canned orange juice. Omit vanilla.

Glazed Strawberry Tarts

Many bakeshops will, if you ask them, make up for you either puff paste or piecrust shells for tarts. In some specialty food shops you can buy already baked tart shells. For this delicious dessert and many others, your own cracker-crumb crust may be used. The rest is wonderfully easy. You will note that a professional-looking glaze is given to the fruit by the simple expedient of melting bought currant jelly.

YOU WILL NEED:

tart shells	strawberries
ready-whipped cream	currant jelly

Into the bottom of 6 small or 4 large tart shells place a tablespoon of ready-whipped cream. On top of the cream, arrange large fresh or drained whole quick-frozen strawberries. Melt gently over a very low heat $1/_2$ cup currant jelly and pour carefully over the berries. Chill.

AT SERVING TIME:

Arrange tarts on a serving plate. Garnish with green leaves. A pint of fresh strawberries or a 12-ounce package of quick-frozen strawberries will make 6 tarts.

Syrian Apple Dumplings

A frozen, unbaked pie shell makes a marvelous, no-fuss casing for this delicious Syrian apple dessert.

YOU WILL NEED:

unbaked pie shell	allspice
canned sliced apples	cream and/or milk
sugar	cinnamon and nutmeg
butter	

Thaw a frozen, unbaked pie shell about 10 minutes. Down the center place a cup of drained canned sliced apples. Sprinkle with sugar, dot with butter, add a few grains of allspice. Fold to make a roll. Wet edges with cold water. Press together. Bake, seam side down, in a hot oven (450° F.) about 15 minutes or until browned.

AT SERVING TIME:

Cut into sections to serve 3 or 4. Pass a pitcher of warm cream (or milk or half-and-half) flavored with cinnamon and nutmeg.

Tarte aux Pruneaux

A royal purple plum tart, blessed with a whisper of kirsch, and put together in a twinkling.

YOU WILL NEED:

unbaked pie shell	cream
fine bread crumbs	egg
canned purple plums	kirsch or vanilla
sugar	cinnamon sugar

Sprinkle an unbaked pie shell with fine bread crumbs to keep juices from soaking in. Drain a 1-pound can of purple plums. Remove pits, cut in half, and arrange attractively, round side up, in the shell. Bake 15 minutes at 375° F. Meanwhile mix together ½ cup sugar, ½ cup cream, 1 egg, and 1 teaspoon kirsch or vanilla. Pour over fruit in pie shell and bake 10 to 15 minutes longer or until set.

AT SERVING TIME:

Sprinkle with cinnamon sugar.

Kentucky Bourbon Brownies

Oh, yes, there is a difference in brownies. Some are much drier than others. Some are sort of medium. Some seem a little more chocolatey. But the ones we really yearn for are the fudgey ones, and here's how to achieve them in a trice!

YOU WILL NEED:
> brownie mix   **canned black walnuts**
> semi-sweet chocolate bits   **bourbon**

Make up the package of brownie mix according to directions, adding a 6-ounce package of chocolate bits, ½ cup canned chopped black walnuts, and 2 tablespoons bourbon, substituted for that much liquid called for in mix. Bake according to directions.

AT SERVING TIME:
Take a bow and bake some more!

Miracle Coconut Macaroons

YOU WILL NEED:
> flake coconut   **egg**
> sugar   **almond extract**

Combine 1½ cups packaged flake coconut with ½ cup sugar. Mix well. Add 1 well-beaten egg and 1 teaspoon almond extract. Let stand about 5 minutes so that the ingredients will stick together. Drop by teaspoons on a greased cookie sheet and bake in a moderate oven, 350° F., about 15 minutes.

AT SERVING TIME:
Serve warm or cold with fruit or ice cream. Delightful when used to top a pudding such as Viennese Chocolate Mousse. Makes 1 dozen macaroons.

Apple Pie with Cheese

This is no place for a discussion of the immemorial rites and "rights" of making a proper American apple pie. Not only the great Henry Ward Beecher but many others have recorded their views on this topic. However, as an example of how tradition may work hand in hand with modern convenience, we suggest this recipe:

YOU WILL NEED:

apple pie
butter or margarine

American cheese
nutmeg

Buy the best apple pie you can find. Brush the top lightly with melted butter or margarine. Slice American cheese or buy the sliced variety. Cut the slices into strips about an inch wide and arrange on top of the pie like spokes of a wheel or in a lattice pattern. Sprinkle lightly with grated nutmeg, and set in a moderate oven, 350° F., about 10 minutes, or until the pie is warm and the cheese soft and lightly browned.

AT SERVING TIME:

The pie should be brought warm to the table and served with large cups of coffee.

English Silk Pie

One of the best, richest, and most voluptuous chocolate pies we've ever tasted, and the recipe is most unusual!

YOU WILL NEED:

butter
confectioners' sugar
eggs
vanilla

semisweet chocolate bits
graham cracker crust
whipped cream

Beat 1/3 cup butter with 6 tablespoons confectioners' sugar until smooth. Add 3 eggs, 1 at a time, beating after each addition. Stir in 1 teaspoon vanilla. Melt over hot water a 6-ounce package semisweet chocolate bits and add to butter-sugar mixture, beating briskly. Pour into a graham-cracker crust, ready-bought or made from packaged crumbs. Bake at 350° F. for 20 to 25 minutes or until slightly puffed and firm to touch. (It will sink back later.) Chill thoroughly.

AT SERVING TIME:
Decorate with swirls and poufs of whipped cream.

Lord Marlborough Pie

YOU WILL NEED:

custard pudding mix
Crumb Pie Shell (page
    221)

canned cubed apples
port wine or brandy
apple or crab apple jelly

Prepare custard pudding from a mix according to package directions. Cool slightly until custard is firm—about 15 minutes, stirring occasionally to keep smooth. Pour into 8-inch pie shell. Cover with canned well-drained cubed and ready-cooked apples (called pommettes). Sprinkle apples with 1 or 2 tablespoons port wine or brandy. Melt ½ cup apple or crab apple jelly and, when melted, spoon carefully over the apples. Chill immediately.

New Wave Mince and Pumpkin Pie

Since everyone always wants a little of both mince and pumpkin pie, the New Wave is a double feature, both in one shell and no baking on your part.

YOU WILL NEED:

a baked pumpkin pie
fruit juice, rum or brandy

canned mincemeat
marshmallows

For a crowd of 10 or 12, buy the largest pumpkin pie you can find. Add 2 or 3 tablespoons fruit juice, rum or brandy to 2 cups canned mincemeat and heat on top of the stove. Spread on top of the pumpkin pie. Make a ring and a center nosegay of marshmallows and set in the oven just long enough to melt and gild the marshmallows.

AT SERVING TIME:
Cut into small wedges, remembering it's a double pie. Best when served slightly warm.

Peach Pizza

Will fruit pizzas become our newest national dessert? They might, if this rich, bubbly, hot, golden disk of spicy sweetness makes the rounds. And it's so quick and easy to prepare. Peaches come from a can. The base is a biscuit or shortcake dough.

YOU WILL NEED:

sugar	canned sliced peaches
light cream (or milk and butter)	lemon juice
	cinnamon
packaged biscuit mix	nutmeg
butter	brown sugar
flour	whipped cream (optional)

Add 2 tablespoons sugar and ¾ cup light cream (or ½ milk and ¼ cup melted butter) to 2 cups packaged biscuit mix. Stir until just blended. Turn the dough out onto a board that has been well dusted with flour. Knead about 10 times. Pat or roll into a large circle about 13 inches in diameter and ease the disk onto a lightly greased and floured cookie sheet or pizza pan.

Meanwhile, drain 2 1-pound cans sliced peaches on paper towels. Cover the crust with peach slices, beginning at the outer edge and making a circular pattern. Dribble with 1 teaspoon lemon juice. Sprinkle with ¼ cup sugar mixed with 1 teaspoon cinnamon and ¼ teaspoon nutmeg. Top with crumble mixture made by combining 2 tablespoons firm butter with 4 tablespoons all-purpose flour and 4 tablespoons dark brown sugar. Fingers make the best tool for this. Bake in a hot oven (400° F.) about 20 minutes or until edges are golden brown and topping is bubbly.

AT SERVING TIME:

Serve warm, either plain or with whipped cream.

Crumb Pie Shell

Packaged bread crumbs or finely crushed graham crackers, gingersnaps, or zwiebacks may be used to make Crumb Pie Shell.

To an inexperienced cook or one who does not care to bother about pastry, this type of crust is most useful.

YOU WILL NEED:
fine crumbs   butter or margarine
sugar

To 1½ cups crumbs, add ¼ cup sugar, ½ cup melted butter or margarine. Save ½ cup of this mixture and use the rest to line a 9-inch piepan, patting it firmly against the bottom and the sides with the back of a spoon. Better still, do it with your fingers. Chill until firm in the refrigerator, or bake 8 minutes at 375° F. and then chill until you want to use it.

VARIATION: Crumb Tart Shells
Instead of using a piepan, line custard cups with crumbs, and firmly press them in. Bake or chill as above and use as the shell for any kind of tarts.

Desserts

PUDDINGS AND PUDDING SAUCES,

Soufflés, Frozen Desserts

A DRESSED-UP DESSERT goes a long way toward transforming a quick and simple meal into an occasion. Such desserts need not be fattening, and with all the help available at the grocery store and bakeshop even elaborate desserts are quick and easy.

On grocers' shelves today are dozens of mixes for puddings, pie fillings, ice creams, and sherbets; there are a multitude of canned and quick-frozen fruits, cakes, and cookies, ready-to-eat ice cream often in convenient storable cartons that fit into your ice trays, dessert sauces, ready-whipped and sweetened cream as well as a low calorie, high protein, quick-frozen topping, which looks and tastes quite a lot like whipped cream and is perfect for the calorie-counter.

One that is particularly useful is a custard flavor dessert mix. It contains no eggs, cooks in about 7 minutes, looks and tastes remarkably like old-fashioned baked custard. Many contain some arrowroot for finer texture and to prevent lumping. In addition to the usual flavors—vanilla, butterscotch, and chocolate—there is also caramel. Several pie fillings are equally fine for puddings: These include lemon, coconut, orange, and coconut-cream.

Instant pudding mixes are prepared with starch cooked under pressure at high temperatures. They make a finished pudding in only 30 seconds—need no cooking whatsoever and are merely beaten with cold milk. By increasing the amount of milk—using

1½ times as much as the recipe calls for—you can make creamy sauces from instant, as well as regular, pudding mixes. Since most of the puddings are on the sweet side it is usually unnecessary to add extra sugar, but do add plenty of pure, nonsynthetic flavor.

Almost all the dessert mixes have one drawback in common—artificial flavoring. In the recipes that follow, this taste of synthetic vanillin is generally masked by the addition of pure extract, spices, wine, brandy, or rum.

Always follow exactly the directions on the package. You will be admonished to stir the pudding constantly. Do it faithfully and keep stirring for about half a minute after the custard or pudding is removed from the heat. Allow cooked puddings to cool at room temperature for a few minutes before placing them in the refrigerator. Sudden changes from hot to cold may cause them to become watery.

RECIPES

Apple Pan Dowdy
Apple Snow with Cinnamon Sauce
Frozen Pain du Pomme Glacé
Apricot Bavarian
Baked Alaska (Baked Ice Cream)
Light Blancmange
Butterscotch Blancmange
Mocha Blancmange
Carolina Trifle
Chocolate Ice Cream Roll
Christmas Wreath Pudding Flambé
Coeur à la Crème
Easy Crêpes Suzette

Italian Monte Bianco
Instant Cherry Cobbler
Lemon Ice-Box Cake
Orange Omelet au Rhum
Peach Soufflé Glacé
Pears with Eggnog Sauce
Pineapple Crunch Pudding
Glamorous Rice Pudding
Miracle Chocolate Soufflé
Viennese Chocolate Mousse
Berries Jubilee with Ice Cream
Strawberry Flummery
Strawberries Romanoff
Tipsy Parson
Whiskey Fudge Balls

Apple Pan Dowdy

In this version of the old-time apple pan dowdy, three short-cut foods are combined.

YOU WILL NEED:

butter

canned sliced apples

molasses or brown sugar

nutmeg

cinnamon

white cake mix

whipped cream or ready-
   whipped cream

In the bottom of a buttered baking dish, arrange 2 cups canned apple slices drained. Sprinkle with ¼ cup molasses or brown sugar and ¼ teaspoon each nutmeg, cinnamon, and salt.

Make up a package of white cake mix according to directions. Pour batter over apples. Bake in a moderate oven, 350° F., 20 to 25 minutes or until cake is done.

AT SERVING TIME:

Bring to the table in its own baking dish. Cut into squares and serve with sweetened whipped cream or ready-whipped cream. Serves 6.

Apple Snow with Cinnamon Sauce

An old-fashioned pudding, an old-fashioned sauce—both made without *any* cooking.

YOU WILL NEED:

egg whites

canned applesauce

lemon juice

green food coloring
   (optional)

instant pudding mix

milk

cinnamon

Beat 3 egg whites until stiff enough to stand in peaks after the beater is withdrawn. Fold in 2 cups canned applesauce. Flavor with 2 tablespoons lemon juice—a little more if you think it is needed. A drop or two or green pure-food coloring may be added, if desired. The applesauce should be very, very cold and so should the sauce.

Cinnamon Sauce

Make up a package of instant pudding mix—the kind that requires only beating, no cooking. Follow the package directions but increase the amount of milk by 1 cup and add ¾ teaspoon cinnamon—enough to give the sauce a spicy flavor.

AT SERVING TIME:
Serve within a half hour after making the pudding. It is prettiest when piled in the center of a shallow glass or china serving bowl with the sauce poured around the edge and additional sauce passed in a pitcher or bowl. Serves 6.

Frozen Pain du Pomme Glacé

In the old, opulent days Rector's restaurant in New York City served a number of desserts frozen in layers. They were known as *pains,* or loaves. These still look and taste wildly elaborate, although nowadays, with canned pie fillings and bought ice cream, it takes only a matter of moments to make them.

YOU WILL NEED:
vanilla ice cream   cinnamon
canned apple pie filling   canned chocolate sauce

Into the bottom of a refrigerator tray, place a ½-inch layer of vanilla ice cream. Spread with 1 cup canned apple pie filling, slightly crushed and flavored with ¼ teaspoon cinnamon. Cover with another layer of vanilla ice cream. Refreeze.

AT SERVING TIME:
Cut into squares or rectangles and serve with canned·chocolate sauce, hot or cold.

VARIATIONS:
Cherry, peach, apricot, and pineapple pie fillings may be used in the same way. For blueberry, add a dash of lemon juice. Try

nutmeg, instead of cinnamon, with cherry and apricot. Put a sprinkling of sherry or kirsch over the pineapple. Vary your sauces and ice creams, too. Chocolate ice cream, for example, with cherry pie filling is superb!

Apricot Bavarian

We present the easiest Bavarian ever. The secret is in beating the egg whites with the gelatin mixture, instead of separately as in the old-fashioned way.

YOU WILL NEED:

sugar	canned apricot halves
unflavored gelatin	egg white
canned apricot nectar	heavy cream
canned lemon juice	canned whole apricots

In a double boiler, mix 1/2 cup sugar, 1 envelope (1 tablespoon) unflavored gelatin, dash salt. Add a 12-ounce can (1½ cups) apricot nectar. Heat and stir over hot water until gelatin melts. Remove from heat and pour into a small mixing bowl. Add 3 tablespoons lemon juice and a 1-pound can apricot halves, drained thoroughly, and either rubbed through a sieve or whirred in a blender for a couple of seconds. Now stir in one unbeaten egg white. Place mixture in refrigerator. When the mixture has chilled till partially set (about 1½ hours), whip (with electric mixer) till it's light and fluffy and soft peaks have formed. In a separate bowl, whip 1/2 cup of heavy cream. Fold the whipped cream into the gelatin mixture and pour into a 1-quart melon mold, scraping out bowl with rubber spatula. Chill till firm (2 to 3 hours).

AT SERVING TIME:
Unmold onto chilled platter and decorate at each end with a cluster of 3 whole apricots and sprigs of water cress.

Baked Alaska (Baked Ice Cream)

Formerly Baked Alaska was a dessert never attempted by the home cook but left to the restaurant—and the fancy restaurant chef. Today it is no trick to make. Remember only one thing—ice cream that goes into the oven must be carefully and completely insulated.

YOU WILL NEED:

sponge cake   confectioners' sugar
ice cream   cream of tartar (optional)
egg whites

The trick is to protect the ice cream from the oven heat. This is done by means of a board, paper, and most important of all a thick layer of meringue. Cover a small board with brown paper cut to fit. On top of the paper place a layer of cake. Set 1 quart ice cream, which must be very hard frozen, on top of the cake. Cover cake and ice cream *completely* with a meringue made from 6 stiffly beaten egg whites to which has been gradually added 6 flat tablespoons confectioners' sugar and, if you have it, 1/4 teaspoon cream of tartar. *There must be no holes in the meringue.* Bake in a hot oven, 400° F., 4 or 5 minutes just long enough for the meringue to take on a golden tinge around the peaks.

AT SERVING TIME:

Lift the board onto a platter and hide the edges of the board with a garland of green leaves. Slice about an inch thick. Serves 8.

Light Blancmange

The cookbooks of long ago called for "clarified isinglass" or "Irish moss" for the making of this pudding. Today we put it together with vanilla pudding mix.

YOU WILL NEED:

vanilla pudding mix   grated lemon rind
milk   egg whites (optional)
sherry or Madeira   canned peaches or apricots

Make up a package of vanilla pudding mix according to directions but use only 1¾ cups milk. Remove from the stove. Add

¼ cup Madeira or sherry, 1 tablespoon grated lemon rind. Fold in stiffly beaten whites of 2 eggs for a very light and delicate pudding. Pour into a mold that has been previously rinsed in cold water. Chill several hours.

AT SERVING TIME:
Turn out on a plate or tray. Decorate with canned drained sliced peaches or apricots.

VARIATIONS:

Butterscotch Blancmange

Use butterscotch pudding mix and instead of lemon rind use grated orange rind.

Mocha Blancmange

Use chocolate pudding mix and add to the milk 2 teaspoons instant coffee. Decorate the mold with whipped cream instead of fruit.

Carolina Trifle

There is no set recipe for this famous English dish. Much depends on the resources of the household at the moment.

YOU WILL NEED:

lady fingers or sponge cake	whipped or ready-whipped
jam	cream
sherry, Madeira, or port	egg white
almonds	cinnamon
grated lemon rind (optional)	candied cherries, kumquats,
custard or vanilla pudding	or jelly
mix	

Split lady fingers or use thin small slices of sponge cake. Spread with jam and arrange in the bottom of a glass bowl. Sprinkle with sherry (Madeira or port may be used). Then add 3 or 4 tablespoons canned shredded almonds and 1 tablespoon grated lemon rind if desired. Over all pour custard made according to package directions from custard-flavored mix or vanilla pudding mix. Let stand in the refrigerator several hours or, better still, overnight.

AT SERVING TIME:

Garnish with 1 cup sweetened whipped cream or ready-whipped cream to which has been added 1 stiffly beaten egg white, ¼ teaspoon cinnamon. Garnish with candied cherries, drained preserved kumquats, or bits of bright jelly or preserves. Serves 8 to 10.

Chocolate Ice Cream Roll

A delicious chocolate ice cream roll is available in the frozen-food bins of even the least pretentious stores and delicatessens. Serve with a dressed-up prepared chocolate sauce—no one could ask for a finer dessert.

YOU WILL NEED:

quick-frozen chocolate ice cream roll
prepared chocolate sauce

sherry or sherry and brandy
nuts

The chocolate roll itself needs no preparation. Just place it on an attractive dish, preferably one deep enough for the sauce to be poured around it. For sauce—heat gently in the top of a double boiler 1 cup prepared chocolate sauce with 1 tablespoon sherry or ½ tablespoon sherry and ½ tablespoon brandy.

AT SERVING TIME:

Sprinkle slivered canned almonds or other chopped nuts over the roll. Pistachio nuts are particularly attractive. Slice at the table. Additional sauce may be passed in a small pitcher or bowl. For a larger group set two or more rolls end to end and cover the separation with a piping of ready-whipped cream.

Christmas Wreath Pudding Flambé

Far more beautiful than a plain pudding for a holiday meal is a fruit cake heated in the top of a double boiler until fragrant and steamy, then served afire. This idea dates back many centuries to the days when Christmas and New Year's fruit cakes were "censed" for luck. Most effective for this purpose are the fruit cakes which are baked in a ring mold. There are several good brands.

YOU WILL NEED:

fruit cake   brandy or rum
candied citron or   hard sauce
   maraschino cherries

Steam fruit cake in top of a double boiler or in a covered pan set over hot water until thoroughly heated.

AT SERVING TIME:

Place on a heated platter or tray. Arrange around the edge strips of candied citron and maraschino cherries to form a berried wreath. In the inner circle of the ring, place a small custard cup or crock with ¼ cup slightly warmed brandy or rum. Set the brandy ablaze and bring flaming to the table. Serve in slices with a bit of the burning brandy spooned over the portions. Pass separately hard sauce which can be bought in jars and is much better if slightly thinned with a little added rum, brandy, or fruit juice.

Coeur à la Crème

This is one of the classic desserts of spring in France. The original method requires something like a gallon of whole unpasteurized milk and a good many hours of souring and draining. Our reasonable facsimile is made from ordinary cream cheese.

YOU WILL NEED:

cream cheese   strawberries, raspberries, or
light cream   preserves
confectioners' sugar
   (optional)

To a 3-ounce package of cream cheese, add 2 tablespoons light cream, just enough to give the cheese a thick spreadable consistency. Mash the cheese well with a fork and blend thoroughly. Add a few grains of salt and, if desired, 1 teaspoon confectioners' sugar. Line a heart-shaped basket or a heart-shaped mold with a square of wet cheesecloth and press the cheese into it, folding the cloth over the top. Chill in the refrigerator several hours or overnight. Turn out on a dish (the cheesecloth corners make it particularly easy to do this). Remove the cloth of course.

AT SERVING TIME:
Surround with sliced sugared strawberries, raspberries, fresh or quick-frozen red-currant jam, or any other preserve which pleases you. One 3-ounce package of cheese makes dessert for 1 or 2, depending on appetite.

Easy Crêpes Suzette

Flaming Crêpes Suzette are one of the most dramatic of desserts. They are practical for the company dinner because the pancakes can be made several hours ahead of time and simply reheated in the orange-flavored brandied sauce. Classic recipes for the sauce include a variety of liqueurs. Here, orange marmalade takes the place of orange rind, orange juice, orange-flavored liqueur, and sugar.

YOU WILL NEED:

French pancakes (page 199)	brandy, curaçao, or Grand
butter	Marnier
orange marmalade	lemon juice (optional)

Make batter and fry pancakes as for French pancakes, using the smallest frying pan you can find—about 3 to 4 inches in diameter. Fold pancakes into quarters. If done ahead of time, place pancakes on a plate or a biscuit sheet so that they do not touch each other. Cover with a piece of waxed paper.

To make the sauce melt ½ cup butter (sweet butter is best but not absolutely necessary). Stir in ½ cup shredded orange marmalade.

AT SERVING TIME:
Heat the pancakes in a shallow frying pan, special Suzette pan or heat-proof platter over a flame at the table, turning them in the sauce. Add ½ cup brandy and set fire to the brandy. Curaçao

or Grand Marnier may be used instead of brandy. Serve flaming on heated plates, 2 or 3 to a person. A few drops of lemon juice is usually sprinkled over each portion as it is served, but this is not absolutely necessary. If the flame dies down or is not high enough to suit you, pour on a little more brandy. This amount should make about 18 pancakes.

Italian Monte Bianco

Monte Bianco, Mont Blanc, or White Mountain—whichever name you use—is a classic Continental dessert that will be a source of pride to you when you serve it. The purée of chestnuts can be bought in cans at quality grocery stores and is worth keeping on hand for those times when you want a quick and glamorous dessert.

YOU WILL NEED:

canned puréed chestnuts	ready-whipped cream
sweetened whipped cream	meringues (optional)
golden rum, vanilla extract, kirsch, or maraschino liqueur	

Combine equal quantities sweetened whipped cream and canned purée of chestnuts. Flavor to taste with 1 or 2 tablespoons of golden rum, vanilla extract, kirsch, or maraschino liqueur. Add flavoring bit by bit to make certain that it does not overpower the taste of the chestnuts.

AT SERVING TIME:

Pile lightly in a pyramid on a serving dish. Decorate with ready-whipped cream so that it will look like a snow-capped mountain. If you like, you may buy from the bakeshop already-baked meringues and set these in a circle around the mountain. Meringues usually come in pairs—get three pairs—set halves around pyramid. One cup or an 8-ounce can of chestnuts should make 6 servings, for it is very rich.

Instant Cherry Cobbler

YOU WILL NEED:

canned cherry pie filling	refrigerated biscuits
dark corn syrup	sugar
butter or margarine	nutmeg
vanilla extract	cream

In a well-greased 9-inch pie plate, combine a 1-pound 5-ounce can of cherry pie filling with 2 tablespoons dark corn syrup, 1 tablespoon butter or margarine, and ½ teaspoon pure vanilla extract. Place in 350° F. oven for 10 minutes. Meanwhile, separate an 8-ounce package refrigerated biscuits, and place them on an ungreased cookie sheet. Brush with 2 tablespoons melted butter or margarine; sprinkle with a mixture of 2 tablespoons sugar and ½ teaspoon nutmeg. Bake according to package instructions. Place biscuits in individual bowls, pour filling over.

AT SERVING TIME:

Serve warm with cream. Serves 6.

Lemon Ice-Box Cake

An ice-box cake is ideal for a company dinner or a buffet supper because it takes no last-minute preparation. This one made from lady fingers and a lemon pie mix is always good after a heavy dinner because the flavor is delicate and light.

YOU WILL NEED:

butter	eggs
lady fingers	whipped cream
canned lemon pie filling	ready-whipped cream

Brush the inside of a large mold or bowl with melted butter. Line with 30 lady fingers. If they come in pairs, separate and use 30 halves, placing the rounded side against the bowl.

Into a can of lemon pie filling, fold in lightly ½ cup cream whipped. Place in center of mold. Cover with plate or waxed paper and chill 12 hours or longer.

AT SERVING TIME:
Loosen edges of mold with a knife blade. Place serving plate over mold. Turn upside down. Remove plate. Garnish pudding with swirls of ready-whipped cream. Serves 6 to 8.

Orange Omelet au Rhum

Very like a soufflé is a puffy omelet cooked on top of the stove, made with concentrated quick-frozen orange juice flamed with rum, sprinkled with powdered sugar, and containing a surprise of orange slices. This is an inspired solution to the problem of nothing-in-the-house-for-dessert.

YOU WILL NEED:

eggs	canned mandarin orange
concentrated quick-frozen	sections
orange juice	powdered sugar
butter	rum

Beat separately the yolks and whites of 4 eggs. The yolks should be beaten until thick and daffodil-colored—the whites until stiff. To the yolks add ½ teaspoon salt, tablespoon concentrated (undiluted) quick-frozen orange juice. Gently fold in the stiffly beaten whites. Heat an omelet pan or heatproof serving dish. Butter the sides as well as the bottom. Ladle half the egg mixture into the pan, cover with small can mandarin orange sections, drained. Add rest of omelet mixture. Cook slowly, do not lift the edges as for a regular French omelet. As soon as the omelet is puffy and around the edge a delicate brown, place in 375° F. oven or 3 inches away from the broiler in order to brown the top. To judge whether the omelet is sufficiently cooked, touch it with your finger. If the finger stays clean it is done.

AT SERVING TIME:
You need not fold this type of omelet but merely sprinkle with powdered sugar. Slightly warm 4 tablespoons rum, set a match

to the rum and pour blazing around the omelet. Serve immediately. Serves 4 to 6.

Peach Soufflé Glacé

A suave, chilled, orange-flavored soufflé, blessed with peaches. Very elegant.

YOU WILL NEED:

unflavored gelatin	almond extract
eggs	heavy cream
orange juice	canned sliced peaches
sugar	macaroons
grated orange rind	chopped nuts
vanilla extract	

Sprinkle 1 envelope unflavored gelatin over ¼ cup cold water. Separate 4 eggs. Mix the yolks with ½ cup orange juice and ½ teaspoon salt. Add ½ cup sugar. Cook in the top of a double boiler over boiling water, stirring constantly, for 4 to 5 minutes, or until thick and custardy. Stir in the gelatin, 1 teaspoon grated orange rind, and ½ teaspoon each vanilla and almond extract. Cool. Meanwhile, beat 4 egg whites until stiff. Beat 1 cup heavy cream. Pile on top of the egg whites. Gently stir in the orange mixture. Put a layer of canned sliced peaches, drained, in a 2-quart bowl or soufflé dish. Add ½ of orange mixture. Repeat layer of peach slices. Add remaining orange mixture. Chill until firm.

AT SERVING TIME:
Decorate with sliced peaches and crushed macaroons, and sprinkle chopped nuts over all. Serves 8.

Pears with Eggnog Sauce

Bottled eggnog with or without spirits is available in all parts of the country—especially during the holiday season. It makes a simple dessert unusual and delicious.

YOU WILL NEED:

bottled eggnog	egg whites
sherry, rum or brandy	canned pears
(optional)	nutmeg (optional)

Flavor bottled eggnog with sherry, rum, or brandy as desired. Gently fold 2 stiffly-beaten egg whites into 2 cups eggnog.

AT SERVING TIME:

Drain canned pears. Place in dessert dishes or sherbet glasses rounded side up and pour eggnog sauce over. Sprinkle with grated nutmeg. Serves 6 to 8.

Pineapple Crunch Pudding

No one is quite sure who first dreamed up this extraordinary invention, using a cake mix that has not been stirred up into a batter.

YOU WILL NEED:

butter-pecan cake mix	pecans
butter or margarine	ice cream or whipped cream
canned pineapple pie filling	

In a large bowl, toss a 13½-ounce package butter-pecan cake mix with ¼ cup melted butter or margarine. In a buttered 9 × 9 × 2-inch baking dish, combine 2 1-pound 5-ounce cans pineapple pie filling with 1 cup broken pecans. Top with butter-pecan cake mix. Bake at 375° F. for 30 minutes or until deep golden brown.

AT SERVING TIME:

Serve with ice cream or whipped cream. Serves 8.

Glamorous Rice Pudding

A prepared rice pudding takes on elegance when shaped in a mold and surrounded with big luscious quick-frozen or canned loganberries. Inexpensive and unusual!

YOU WILL NEED:
   canned rice pudding   canned or quick-frozen
   butter   loganberries

Brush with melted butter, a mold that holds 1 pint. Fill with canned or prepared rice pudding. Place in the refrigerator and chill several hours or overnight.

AT SERVING TIME:
Unmold on a shallow but not absolutely flat serving dish. This is done easily if you loosen the edges with a knife. Place the plate on top of the mold and turn the whole thing upside down, shaking gently to release the pudding. Garnish with quick-frozen or canned loganberries. If quick-frozen berries are used, they should be almost but not entirely thawed—a little iciness improves the shape as well as the taste. If canned, pour off about half the liquid or else you will have too much juice. Serves 6.

Miracle Chocolate Soufflé

A package of chocolate tapioca pudding mix can be transformed into soufflé. The tapioca helps to keep the soufflé high without interfering with its delicacy—the grains do not show or alter the taste. This recipe suggests a way to make the soufflé rise high in the center in the manner of the French restaurants. Really wonderful!

YOU WILL NEED:
   chocolate tapioca pudding   eggs
      mix   sherry or brandy (optional)
   milk   confectioners' sugar

Make up a package of chocolate tapioca pudding mix and milk according to directions. Add, 1 at a time, 6 egg yolks, beating well after each addition. Then fold in lightly 6 stiffly beaten egg whites. Flavor with 4 tablespoons sherry or 1 tablespoon brandy, if desired.

To bake, pour mixture into unbuttered straight-sided baking dish that can come to the table. Pottery is preferred. Fill 7/8 full and make a deep cut all around the soufflé mixture, an inch from the edge. Set in a very hot oven, 425° F., and bake 15 to 20 minutes. This method makes a soufflé with a crusty top and leaves the center soft enough to serve as a sauce.

AT SERVING TIME:
Shake a little confectioners' sugar over the top of the soufflé to give it a professional touch and serve instantly. Serves 6.

Viennese Chocolate Mousse

YOU WILL NEED:

instant coffee
semisweet chocolate pieces
eggs
vanilla or almond extract,
  rum, or brandy

macaroon (optional)
whipped cream (optional)
crème de cacao (optional)

In a bowl, put 2 tablespoons water, ½ teaspoon instant coffee, a 6-ounce package of semisweet chocolate pieces. Place the bowl over hot water and stir until chocolate mixture is melted and blended. Add ¼ teaspoon salt. Beat 4 egg yolks until thick and lemon colored. Add 1 teaspoon vanilla or almond extract or 2 teaspoons rum or brandy. Fold in lightly the whites of 4 eggs beaten until very stiff. Spoon into 6 tiny demitasse cups or small sherry or cocktail glasses. Chill.

AT SERVING TIME:
For the true Viennese touch, top each portion with a small macaroon and pass a bowl of whipped cream well flavored with whatever flavoring was used in the pudding or, best of all, with crème de cacao liqueur using 1 tablespoon liqueur to 1 cup whipped cream. Since this dessert is very rich it should serve 6.

Berries Jubilee with Ice Cream

Any dinner no matter how simple takes on distinction when it comes with a flambé dessert. Cherries Jubilee are exceedingly

well known—almost too well known to be exciting. Either fresh
or quick-frozen strawberries or raspberries, however, may be
used in the same fashion.

YOU WILL NEED:

lemon   brandy
concentrated quick-frozen   vanilla ice cream, lemon or
   orange juice   orange sherbet
strawberries or raspberries

Cut a peel from 1 lemon and leave it curled cork-screw style.
Place in a shallow pan—a chafing dish if convenient. Add 2
tablespoons quick-frozen orange juice, undiluted. Heat gently
about 3 minutes pressing the peel to get all the flavor. Add 1
pint fresh or quick-frozen whole strawberries or raspberries and
toss berries around in the hot juice. Pour on ¼ cup brandy.
Warm and light with a match.

AT SERVING TIME:

Do all this at the table if you can and serve the flaming berries
over vanilla ice cream, lemon or orange sherbet.

Strawberry Flummery

A flummery was once a kind of sweet porridge but now denotes
a mixture of lightly stewed fruits or berries combined with slices
of white bread, either *au naturel* or baked together.

YOU WILL NEED:

sliced white bread   canned strawberry pie
butter or margarine   filling
                                         whipped cream (optional)

Butter 8 slices of bread on both sides and fit into a 9-inch pie
plate. Add a 1-pound 5-ounce can strawberry pie filling. Top
with bread circles or squares, buttered on both sides. Bake at
425° F. for 20 minutes or until bread is golden brown.

AT SERVING TIME:

Serve with whipped cream, if desired. Serves 6.

Strawberries Romanoff

In strawberry season all over the world the most famous restaurants feature—each with its own variation—this classic combination of fine strawberries, orange juice, curaçao, and cream. To achieve the most dramatic effect arrange the makings on a tray and put the dessert together at the table.

YOU WILL NEED:

fresh or whole frozen
   strawberries
orange juice

vanilla ice cream
curaçao

Arrange on a tray an attractive bowlful of strawberries. If you use quick-frozen berries, have them almost but not completely thawed. To 1 pint berries add 1 cup orange juice. Also have on hand a bowl of vanilla ice cream—about a pint—and a bottle of curaçao. Provide yourself also with a fork and a large spoon for serving.

AT SERVING TIME:

Stir and soften vanilla ice cream with a fork. Add ¼ cup curaçao (Cointreau, Grand Marnier, or brandy may be used). Stir into the ice cream. Serve strawberries on chilled plates and top each portion with a couple of spoonfuls of the liqueur-flavored ice cream. Serves 6.

Tipsy Parson

This combination of sponge cake and wine-flavored sauce dates back to the English colonists. It is called tipsy because of the wine in the sauce—parson because it was so often served when the preacher came to Sunday dinner.

YOU WILL NEED:

sponge cake layers
currant, grape, or apple
   jelly
canned almonds

vanilla-flavored pudding
   mix
sherry or Madeira wine

Buy from the grocery store 2 sponge cake layers, the kind that are usually sold for shortcake. Place currant, grape, or apple jelly between the layers. Sprinkle the jelly liberally with canned shredded almonds. Place the top layer over the jelly. Spread the top of the cake with a thin layer of jelly and sprinkle with almonds.

Tipsy Sauce

Prepare the sauce from a package of vanilla-flavored pudding mix by using 1½ as much liquid as required for a regular pudding. Cook according to package directions. Add ½ cup sherry or Madeira. Stir and chill.

AT SERVING TIME:
Cut cake into regular servings and pass chilled sauce in a separate bowl. 6 to 8 servings.

Whiskey Fudge Balls

A package of chocolate fudge frosting mix, a touch of spirits, and you have a sophisticated, adults-only candy that also makes a delightful gift.

YOU WILL NEED:

butter or margarine	chopped pecans
bourbon whiskey	dry cocoa
dry chocolate fudge frosting mix	

Melt 2 tablespoons butter or margarine with 1 tablespoon water and 2 tablespoons bourbon whiskey in the top of a double boiler. Blend smoothly a 14-ounce package of dry chocolate fudge frosting mix. Heat over rapidly boiling water 5 minutes, stirring occasionally. Mix in ½ cup chopped pecan nuts. Cool. Form into balls.

AT SERVING TIME:
Roll each ball in cocoa. Makes 3 dozen.

🌿 16 🌿

~~~~~~~~~~~~~~~~~~~~~~~~

Fruits

TO END THE MEAL

WHEN IN DOUBT, serve fruit. Fresh, quick-frozen, or canned—raw or cooked—plain or glamorized in any number of tempting ways— fruit is almost everybody's favorite dessert. So many different kinds of fruits and berries in so many different guises are now available, quick frozen or canned—it is sad to confine your attention entirely to old favorites. Have you, for instance, heard of the many forms in which the apple is being packed—in slices for pies and puddings, cubed and sweetened for compotes, in the form of applesauce sweetened or unsweetened—baked apples, too, in cans or quick frozen? Now all year round you can have your favorite fresh berry desserts with quick-frozen strawberries, blackberries, blueberries, boysenberries, cherries, loganberries, and youngberries, too. Be sure to include them in your menu plans.

And when you serve the stand-bys—canned peaches, pears, cherries, and pineapple—present them imaginatively. A touch of vanilla or almond extract added to the syrup, a little brandy or wine—a frosty sauce made of whipped vanilla ice cream. All these can lend variety. Be wary though; do not overpower the delicate flavor of fruit with too much flavoring or trimming. The recipes that follow pursue a judicious middle course.

RECIPES

Apple Croûtes	Baked Peaches Italienne
Baked Apples Garni	Baked Stuffed Peaches with
Baked Apples with Orange	Macaroons
Baked Apples Porcupine	Pickled Peaches New Style
Cerises au Claret	Pineapple Paraguay
Honeydew Melon in the	Pineapple Royale
English Fashion	Pears of Paris
Stewed Figs à la Glace	Medieval Pears
Grapefruit Tía Maria	Coconut Compote
Mandarins à la Mexico	Exotic Compote
Peach Ambrosia	Hot Fruit Compote

Apple Croûtes

Baked apples can be bought either canned or quick frozen. Generally there are 3 or 4 apples in a can or carton. There are a number of ways to dress up these apples to make them look and taste homemade.

YOU WILL NEED:

sliced white bread or	currant jelly
English muffins	vanilla or almond extract
butter or margarine	heavy cream or sour cream
baked apples	

In butter or margarine brown 6 slices of thin white bread from which the crusts have been removed. Or toast lightly and butter generously 6 halves of English muffins. Cut down through the center 3 canned baked apples. Set cut side down on the bread. Melt ½ cup currant jelly and add ½ teaspoon vanilla or almond extract. Spoon carefully over the apples. Allow to stand long enough for the jelly to thicken—about half an hour or less in the refrigerator.

AT SERVING TIME:

Serve with plain cream, whipped cream, or slightly sweetened sour cream. (Whole baked apples may be used but they make rather a large dessert—too much for most people.) Serves 6.

Baked Apples Garni

YOU WILL NEED:

baked apples	cinnamon
butter	lemon juice
red cinnamon drops or red	lemon peel (optional)
pure-food coloring	

Place apples in a buttered heat-proof glass pie plate or other shallow serving dish. Drop into the center of each apple 2 or 3 red cinnamon candies or lacking these, add to the syrup from the apples a few drops of red pure-food coloring and sprinkle apples with cinnamon and a few drops of lemon juice, using about ½ teaspoon on each apple. A twist of lemon peel may be put in the center of the apples, too, or laid over the top. Pour about ½ inch of apple liquid into the bottom of the baking dish. Cover and allow to heat in a hot oven, 400° F., about 10 minutes or until warm.

AT SERVING TIME:

These are most delicious when served warm with a pitcher of plain heavy cream. However you may use whipped cream if you like. Serves 3 or 4.

VARIATIONS:

Baked Apples with Orange

Into the center of each apple, place 1 teaspoon undiluted quick-frozen concentrated orange juice.

Baked Apples Porcupine

Set 4 well-drained baked apples in the baking dish. Cover each apple completely with a stiff meringue made by beating the whites of 2 eggs with 2 tablespoons sugar. Meringue may be flavored with ½ teaspoon vanilla. Stick almond halves all over the meringue porcupine fashion. Sprinkle lightly with granulated sugar. Place in a moderate oven, 350° F., 5 minutes. Then increase the heat to 400° F. and bake 5 minutes longer or until delicately brown. *Do not put any liquid in the bottom of the pan.*

Cerises au Claret

YOU WILL NEED:

canned sweet cherries	red currant jelly
cinnamon	ladyfingers or macaroons
claret	

Drain juice from a 1-pound 14-ounce can sweet cherries. Add to the juice a stick of cinnamon or ½ teaspoon powdered cinnamon, and a cup of claret. Cook until about ⅓ of the liquid has boiled away. Then add 8 tablespoons currant jelly. Put the cherries back into the juice. Chill very well.

AT SERVING TIME:
Serve from a cold glass bowl, with lady fingers or macaroons. Will serve 8.

Honeydew Melon in the English Fashion

A delicious first course for a Sunday brunch or luncheon.

YOU WILL NEED:

honeydew melon	granulated or superfine
canned kumquats or	sugar
mandarin orange sections	lime juice
powdered ginger	

Cut a honeydew melon into wedges about an inch wide. Remove seeds and peel. Lay on a clear glass plate, seed side up, like the petals of a flower. In the center place a cluster of drained canned kumquats or mandarin orange sections. Sprinkle the melon very lightly with powdered ginger.

AT SERVING TIME:

Pass what is known in England as castor sugar, which we know better in the United States as granulated, or if you like, super-fine, and pass a small chilled pitcher of lime juice, mixed with a bit of the syrup from the kumquats or oranges, to spark the melon.

Stewed Figs à la Glace

Canned figs deserve to be a lot more popular. They're particularly good with a pep-up of liquor or a bit of candied ginger.

YOU WILL NEED:

canned figs	rum or brandy
vanilla ice cream	

Thoroughly chill canned figs.

AT SERVING TIME:

Place a scoop of vanilla ice cream into individual dessert dishes, sherbet glasses, or champagne glasses of the saucer type. On top of the ice cream carefully place 2 or 3 figs together with a little of the syrup. Add a teaspoon of rum or brandy to each portion.

Grapefruit Tía María

A delightful fruit cup, quickly prepared and highly individual.

YOU WILL NEED:

canned grapefruit sections	coffee beans (optional)
coffee liqueur	

Drain a chilled 1-pound can grapefruit sections, saving juice. Arrange in 4 individual stemmed champagne glasses. Into each glass pour a bit of the juice and 2 tablespoons coffee liqueur. Return to refrigerator and chill for an hour, long enough to absorb the flavor.

AT SERVING TIME:
Drop a couple of coffee beans on top of each serving as a garnish, if desired. Serves 4.

Mandarins à la Mexico

YOU WILL NEED:

canned mandarin orange sections	golden rum
grated orange peel	fresh or dried mint leaves

Turn the canned mandarin orange sections and their juice into a serving dish. Sprinkle generously with orange peel, either freshly grated or dried. Sprinkle lightly with golden rum. Cover and let stand at room temperature for about an hour or longer, so that the rum and orange flavors become deliciously blended.

AT SERVING TIME:
Sprinkle with fresh mint leaves. Or, lacking fresh mint leaves, use a scattering of dried mint leaves and add them before the mellowing.

Peach Ambrosia

The traditional ambrosia of the South is made of oranges, but this delightful variant uses canned or quick-frozen sliced peaches.

YOU WILL NEED:

canned or quick-frozen sliced peaches	lemon juice
shredded coconut	sherry or white port

Drain canned peaches or quick-frozen sliced peaches. Save the juice. Arrange in a glass bowl suitable for serving. Alternate layers of peaches and shredded coconut. To 2 cups peaches, use about 1 cup shredded coconut. Add to the juice of the peaches 1 tablespoon lemon juice and 2 tablespoons sherry or white port. Sprinkle over peaches and coconut.

AT SERVING TIME:
This dessert may be served as soon as it is made, an advantage over the old-fashioned ambrosia which had to stand for several hours at least in order to blend the flavors. Makes 4 servings.

VARIATION:
One cup sliced bananas, oranges, or diced pineapple may be added to the peaches. Increase coconut to 1½ cups. Serves 6.

Baked Peaches Italienne

Pesche ripiene they are called in Italy. There, of course, they are always made with fresh, large peaches which are not too ripe. But our own canned peach halves make an excellent substitute.

YOU WILL NEED:

canned peach halves	lady fingers
nuts	white wine
almond extract	white or brown sugar
grated lemon or orange rind	

Drain a large can of peach halves. Place 6 on a buttered baking pan, preferably one that can come to the table. Make the stuffing for the peaches by mashing together 2 peach halves, ½ cup finely chopped toasted almonds or other nuts, ½ teaspoon almond extract, a bit of grated lemon or orange rind (about 1 teaspoon), and 4 lady fingers cut into very fine pieces. If the mixture is not moist enough to hold together, add a couple of teaspoons of peach syrup from the can. Form into balls about the size of a peach seed. Place in the peaches and cover with other peach halves so that the peaches look whole. Pour over them ¼ cup white wine. Sprinkle with ¼ cup white or brown sugar. Bake in a moderate oven about 10 minutes or until the sugar has formed a pretty crust.

AT SERVING TIME:
Serve warm or cold. 6 servings.

VARIATION: Baked Stuffed Peaches with Macaroons
In the above recipe use 8 macaroons instead of lady fingers and omit the almond extract.

Pickled Peaches New Style

A bowl of spiced peaches goes well with almost any meat dish. Great with curry. Or you can serve them with cream cheese as dessert.

YOU WILL NEED:

canned peach halves	mixed pickling spices
whole cloves	vinegar

Drain a large can of halved peaches and save the juice. Stud each peach half with a whole clove and lay in saucepan. Mix 1 tablespoon pickling spices and 1 tablespoon vinegar in juice and pour over peaches. Heat to boiling; cook gently 3 minutes. Let stand off heat to mellow, the longer the better.

AT SERVING TIME:
Serve warm or chilled.

Pineapple Paraguay

This is a very simple idea, but the flavor is extraordinary.

YOU WILL NEED:
canned pineapple chunks   rum
cinnamon sugar

Drain canned pineapple chunks, sprinkle with cinnamon sugar and allow to stand at least 20 minutes.

AT SERVING TIME:
Add a few drops of rum if you must gild the lily.

Pineapple Royale

For a party nothing could be more impressive than this Escoffier dessert. You must choose a pretty pineapple with a well-shaped topknot of leaves.

YOU WILL NEED:
large pineapple with leaves   canned peach halves
canned or quick-frozen fruit   large strawberries or
  salad or cocktail   blueberries
kirsch, brandy, Cointreau,
  or Grand Marnier

Cut off the top of the pineapple with the bunch of leaves and set aside in a safe place. Scoop out the pineapple, leaving a wall about half an inch thick all around and at the bottom. Cut fresh pineapple into small pieces and combine with 1 can (or 1 package frozen) fruit cocktail or fruit salad, drained. (The pieces of fruit are larger in fruit salad.) Sprinkle with 2 tablespoons kirsch, brandy, Cointreau, or Grand Marnier. Place fruit back into the pineapple. Set the top in place and if you wish to follow the great tradition surround the base of the pineapple with canned peach halves and large fresh or quick-frozen strawberries or blueberries.

AT SERVING TIME:
Decorate with shiny green leaves. (Violet or rose leaves are particularly appropriate.) If desired, a little liquor such as is used to flavor the fruits may be sprinkled lightly over the canned

peaches. A slight frosting of confectioners' sugar over leaves and fruit is effective. (For looks only.) The number of servings depends upon the size of the cans and the number of fruits used.

Pears of Paris

So simple to make, so delicious to serve. Just a can of pears, some apricot jam and a little spirit.

YOU WILL NEED:

canned pear halves	apricot jam
rum, kirsch, or Madeira	grapes
wine	vanilla ice cream

Cover canned pear halves with an apricot sauce made by adding 2 tablespoons rum, kirsch, or Madeira wine to 1 cup finely mashed apricot jam.

AT SERVING TIME:

Surround with halved, seeded grapes, preferably muscat, and top with a scoop of vanilla ice cream.

Medieval Pears

"Wardonys in Syrup" is the ancient name, and you are told to "caste on a potte, and boyle hem till hey ben tender." Well and good—then! But today "wardonys" are known as pears, and we just open a can, flavor the syrup with spices and red wine, and have a delicious, refreshing dessert to end our meal.

YOU WILL NEED:

canned pear halves	fresh or powdered ginger
red wine	saffron
cinnamon stick	

Drain a No. 2½ can of pear halves. Measure the liquid and add an equal quantity of red wine. Add a small stick of cinnamon; a half-inch knob of green ginger, peeled, or ¼ teaspoon powdered ginger; ¼ teaspoon saffron. Boil down quickly until reduced to half. Pour over the pears. Cover and allow to cool in their own liquid.

AT SERVING TIME:
Serve warmish or chilled.

Coconut Compote

A delightful variation on ambrosia!

YOU WILL NEED:

canned pineapple chunks	fresh bananas
canned mandarin orange sections	canned coconut
	Cointreau

Thoroughly chill a can of pineapple chunks and mandarin orange sections. Combine at the last minute with bananas cut into thick slices and add a generous amount of coconut, preferably the moist Southern style.

AT SERVING TIME:
Add a dash of Cointreau and serve in your prettiest bowl.

Exotic Compote

With canned mangoes, papayas, and other tropical fruits widely available in supermarkets across the country, it is beautifully simple to serve this exotic compote when you want a light, refreshing dessert to end a heavier meal.

YOU WILL NEED:

canned papaya chunks	fresh lime
canned mango slices	sherry
canned pineapple chunks	sugar

Drain and save the juices from a 15-ounce can papaya chunks, a 15-ounce can mango slices, and a 13½-ounce can pineapple chunks. Add to juices 1 small lime, sliced. Cook down to half. Add 2 tablespoons of sherry and sugar to taste. Pour over fruits.

AT SERVING TIME:
Serve fruit and syrup hot or cold in an attractive compote dish.
Makes 6 servings.

Hot Fruit Compote

A combination of leftover canned fruits or several small picnic-
size cans of fruits make the most interesting hot compotes. Particularly good combinations are apricots, pears, sour cherries or
greengage plums, sweet black cherries and peaches or pineapple,
purple plums or prunes and canned mandarin orange sections.

YOU WILL NEED:

canned fruits	pure-food coloring
sherry, port, brandy, rum,	(optional)
or Grand Marnier or	cookies and/or ice cream
vanilla or almond extract	

Heat together fruits and juices. Flavor to taste with sherry, port,
brandy, rum, or Grand Marnier. Or if you wish, omit liquor
and simply add to the fruits a little vanilla extract, or a few
drops of almond extract—not enough, however, to overpower
the fruit flavors. If the syrup looks pallid, add a few drops of
pure-food coloring.

AT SERVING TIME:
Serve warm or chilled with cookies and/or ice cream.

Time-Saving Beverages

Iₙₛₜₐₙₜ ₜₑₐ, coffee, and chocolate are certainly here to stay. So convenient and economical—in many busy households they have already become indispensable. Suggested in this chapter are a number of ways for serving instant beverages to the best advantage.

A number of party drinks—punches and nogs—are included. Each is a short-cut recipe using either canned, bottled, or quick-frozen fruit juices or, in some cases, sherbet or ice cream bought or made from a mix.

One point cannot be overemphasized: Hot drinks should be hot, hot, hot. Whenever possible, demitasse cups should be heated. This is not difficult. You can put them into an oven set at *not more than 200° F.*

Cold drinks must be cold, cold, cold. If you are giving a party, you may find yourself faced with an ice-cube shortage. You can, of course, freeze ice cubes ahead of time emptying and saving the cubes in bowls in the refrigerator until needed, but there is an easier way. In cities and in medium-sized towns you will find listed in the classified section of your telephone directory one or more ice companies who will deliver to you in cartons—at no great expense—any quantity of ice cubes as well as shaved or finely crushed ice so necessary for juleps, frozen daiquiris, cobblers, and the like. They can also send you large chunks of ice for your punch bowl.

On the subject of punch bowl ice, those of you who are fortunate to have a large freezing compartment in your refrigerator or a deep-freeze will find it a simple matter to make your own ice blocks by freezing water in a bowl, mold, or deep pan. If you wish, you may decorate the ice by placing in the water to be frozen flowers, leaves, or fruits. Imagine the drama provided by a bunch of grapes frozen into a block of ice!

RECIPES

Instant Demitasse
Demitasse with Cinnamon
  Stick
Café Royale
Instant Espresso
Viennese Coffee
Coffee Cobbler
Café Diable
Coffee Fiesta
Coffee Louise
Flaming Irish Coffee
Old-Fashioned Boiled Coffee

Frosted Mocha
Frosted Mocha with Rum
Ice-Saving Iced Tea
Iced Tea Angostura
Flaming Tea Bowl
Tea Punch
Holiday Nog
Hot Orange Toddy
Peach Champagne
Quick Fish House Punch
Wassail
Wassail for the Young

Instant Demitasse

Some connoisseurs still object to instant coffee but because it is so easy, so quick, and so economical to use its use is becoming more and more widespread. There are a number of ways by which one may add a full body and a stronger flavor to an instant demitasse.

YOU WILL NEED:
  instant coffee

By using standard measurements—a measuring cup and a measuring spoon, you can be assured of uniform quality in your demitasse. For instance, you make 6 servings pour 2 *measuring cups* of actively boiling water on 2 level *measuring* tablespoons of instant coffee. Stir to assure brew of even strength. To make 12 servings use 4 measuring cups of water and 4 level measuring tablespoons of instant coffee.

Prize Hint: Add instant coffee to *cold* water. Bring to a boil and boil for 30 seconds. Amazing—the difference.

AT SERVING TIME:

According to tradition, the demitasse is generally served in the living room after dinner, but since most of us do not have special dining rooms nowadays, many hostesses prefer to bring the demitasse to the table and serve it along with the dessert. To keep the coffee piping hot, it is convenient to set the coffee pot over a candle-warmer. These are available at most department store houseware counters now and are quite inexpensive. The candle flame is not hot enough to harm even a thin china coffee pot.

VARIATION: Demitasse with Cinnamon Stick

Into each demitasse cup, place a stick of cinnamon which is to be used as a stirrer. The cinnamon stick looks attractive and adds a delicate flavor to the coffee.

Café Royale

This is a simple trick which will most certainly add a gala note to any occasion. Serve demitasse in the usual fashion and provide rum, brandy, or Grand Marnier. Each person flames his own coffee in this way: The coffee spoon is dipped into the coffee to be warmed. Then the spoon is rested on the rim of the coffee cup. A lump of sugar goes into the spoon, and over the sugar is poured a little liquor. If the liquor is slightly warmed beforehand, you are certain to have a good blaze. Set a match to the liquor. Let it flame up for a minute or so, and then drop the flaming sugar into the cup. For those who do not like sugar in their coffee, the liquor may be flamed in the spoon without sugar. This ceremony is most effective if the room is darkened.

Instant Espresso

Espresso devotees can now have their strong, delicious brew instantly— from a jar—which is a time-saver in that guests may have as many cups as they like without the hostess's having to re-brew, as is usual with the classic espresso pot. Have ready a large teapot of boiling water. Measure a demitasse spoon, heaping, of instant espresso, into a demitasse cup, fill with boiling water. Provide small disks of lemon peel (do not cut into the white part) to squeeze, first over the coffee to release the oil, then to drop into the cup for added flavor.

Let us mention in passing that if you do prefer to brew your espresso from ground coffee, it is no longer necessary to have a regular espresso pot. It can be brewed in your electric coffee maker or in an ordinary percolator or dripolator. Use one level-to-rounded tablespoon for each demitasse cup of water.

Viennese Coffee

It is traditional in Vienna and throughout the Austrian Tyrol to serve strong hot coffee topped with whipped cream, not only after dinner but at any time during the day. Make up instant demitasse for 6. In an attractive chilled bowl, pass ready-whipped cream delicately flavored, if desired, with a little brandy or liqueur. Instead of whipped cream, vanilla ice cream may be passed in the bowl. This should be softened with a fork and flavored with brandy, rum, or liqueur. Use a tablespoon of liqueur to a cup of cream or ice cream.

Coffee Cobbler

In Europe many wines and liqueurs are served in small glasses over shaved or finely crushed ice. This is an attractive way to serve demitasse on a warm summer evening. Fill sherry or cocktail glasses with very finely crushed or shaved ice. Pour over the ice instant demitasse. Top with a swirl of ready-whipped cream and decorate with a bit of glazed fruit. Serve with short straws, which are made by cutting ordinary ice cream soda straws into 2 or 3 pieces.

Café Diable

Special pans, burners, and ladles are available for making and serving this most dramatic of after-dinner coffees, but it can be done and very effectively with any chafing dish.

YOU WILL NEED:

brandy
orange and lemon peel
lump sugar
cloves

cinnamon stick
Instant Demitassee (page 256)

Heat but do not boil in a chafing dish or Café Diable pot 1½ cups brandy along with the thin outer peel of ½ orange and ½ lemon, 8 lumps of sugar, 4 cloves, a stick of cinnamon. Warm a small ladle by holding a match under it or hold it over the candle flame. Dip up about 2 tablespoons of the spice-brandy mixture and place 2 sugar lumps in the ladle. Set fire to the sugar. Lower the blazing spiced brandy into the bowl, which will blaze up in its turn, and while it is blazing pour in 2 measuring cups instant demitasse.

AT SERVING TIME:

All the above should, of course, be done with some ceremony at the dinner table in a darkened room. Ladle the Café Diable into tiny coffee cups after the flame has died down. 8 to 10 servings.

Coffee Fiesta

To a mug or cup of hot coffee, add 1 tablespoon canned, ready-to-spread, chocolate frosting. Add a fluff of whipped cream or topping.

Coffee Louise

When brewing coffee (instant or otherwise), add a small piece of vanilla bean or a few drops of vanilla extract.

Flaming Irish Coffee

Bless the Irish for giving us Irish coffee—and it becomes even more elegant when it is served flaming.

YOU WILL NEED:
Irish whisky   strong, hot black coffee
lump sugar

Heat a silver bowl and ladle by rinsing with very hot water. Pour in 1 cup of Irish whisky. Add 4 lumps sugar. Fill after-dinner cups with strong, very hot black coffee, ¾ to the top. Dip up a ladleful of the Irish whisky. Add 2 more lumps of sugar. Warm by holding it over a candle flame. Then ignite. Fill each cup to the brim with the flaming whisky.

AT SERVING TIME:
Don't worry about the remaining whisky in the bowl. Everyone will have seconds.

Old-Fashioned Boiled Coffee

Long years ago country cooks made coffee with a whole egg, shell and all, and steeped it for 5 minutes in an enamel-lined coffeepot, or just any old enamel-lined pan.

YOU WILL NEED:
ground coffee   egg

To make 8 cups of the very best coffee, pour 6 measuring cupfuls of cold water into an enamel-lined coffeepot or pan. Meanwhile, break 1 large raw egg and throw it, shell and all, into a bowl along with 9 heaping tablespoons of regular or percolator grind coffee and a couple of tablespoons of cold water. Stir. When the water boils, dump in the coffee mixture and stir until the coffee "stops trying to boil over." Allow to steep at least 5 minutes in a warm place.

AT SERVING TIME:
Pour through a strainer if you're not using a coffeepot equipped with same.

Frosted Mocha

One of the most delicious summertime beverages imaginable is put together from ready-to-serve products—requires no cooking whatsoever.

YOU WILL NEED:

canned chocolate syrup	vanilla ice cream or ready-
quick-frozen coffee	whipped cream
concentrate	nutmeg or cinnamon
milk	

Put into a bowl or into a cocktail shaker 5 tablespoons chocolate syrup, 3 teaspoons quick-frozen coffee concentrate, and 1½ cups milk. Beat with a rotary egg beater or shake in cocktail shaker. Fill 3 or 4 tall glasses with ice cubes. Pour the mixture over the ice. Top with a spoonful of vanilla ice cream or ready-whipped cream.

AT SERVING TIME:
Serve immediately with a few gratings of nutmeg or a dash of cinnamon over the top. Serves 3 or 4.

VARIATION: Frosted Mocha with Rum

If desired, a jigger of rum may be poured into the bottom of each glass. In this case the drink should be stirred with a long-handled spoon, and the cream or ice cream may be omitted.

Ice-Saving Iced Tea

During the iced-tea season, it is always difficult to keep a sufficient supply of ice cubes on hand, especially when your refrigerator space is not unlimited. Here are two helpful suggestions.

YOU WILL NEED:

loose tea or tea balls	cloves (optional)
boiling water	powdered sugar or sugar
mint	syrup
lemon, lime, or orange	

Tea intended for icing should be made double strength: Use 1 or 2 teaspoons tea or at least 1 tea ball for each glass. To make 6 servings, pour a small amount of boiling water—about 1 cup— over 6 to 12 teaspoons tea or 6 tea balls. Cover and allow to steep about 5 minutes. Strain into a pitcher and add 3 cups cold water.

AT SERVING TIME:

Fill tall glasses with ice cubes. Pour tea over ice. Garnish with mint sprigs and sections of lemon, lime, or orange, stuck with cloves if desired. Pass powdered sugar or sugar syrup in a small pitcher.

VARIATION: Iced Tea Angostura

A couple of drops of angostura bitters, such as are used for old-fashioned cocktails, will add an interesting flavor and color to iced tea.

Flaming Tea Bowl

On a cold winter evening after skiing or just walking, nothing could be more appropriate than this hot and spicy drink. It has the further virtue of being inexpensive and very easy.

YOU WILL NEED:

hot tea	golden rum
lemon	cinnamon sticks (optional)
honey	

To a quart of hot tea made from your very best tea add 1 lemon, thinly sliced, and 4 teaspoons honey. Stir well.

AT SERVING TIME:

Bring punch to the table in a chafing dish or a casserole which will fit over a candle-warmer so that it will keep blazing hot. Warm separately but do not boil 1 cup golden rum. Set rum ablaze with a match. Pour into the hot tea and ladle into cups or mugs. If you have them you may put cinnamon sticks in the cups for stirrers. Makes 6 to 8 servings.

Tea Punch

Quick-frozen concentrated lemonade takes all the work and fuss out of the making of a party punch. This one is decorated in the Continental fashion with thin strips of cucumber rind. In the watermelon season, green watermelon rind may be substituted for the cucumber. When borage grows in the garden, this may be used, either with or instead of the cucumber peel, because it has a cucumber-like flavor and fragrance.

YOU WILL NEED:

hot tea	white wine
quick-frozen lemonade con-	cucumber rind
centrate	borage (optional)

To a quart of hot tea, add 1 can quick-frozen concentrated lemonade, 3 cups white table wine, and 3 strips cucumber rind. Cover and let stand about 5 minutes. Don't let cucumber rind stay in too long for it may give a bitter flavor to the drink.

AT SERVING TIME:

Place a block of ice in a punch bowl—or any large and attractive mixing bowl will do. Pour the punch mixture over the ice. Stir 2 or 3 times to chill and ladle into small cups or glasses. How much punch you should make for a party depends, of course, on the kind of party and the kind of guests. Usually, however, you can count upon 2 to 4 cups per person, which means that a quart will serve 4. This recipe should serve 8.

Holiday Nog

Instead of going to all the bother of beating egg yolks, egg whites, and cream for an eggnog party, try this very simple and most delicious recipe made with ice cream from the corner store.

YOU WILL NEED:
vanilla ice cream   milk
rye or bourbon whiskey   grated nutmeg
golden rum

Place 1 pint vanilla ice cream in a bowl. Pour over it 2 cups rye whiskey or bourbon whiskey, 1 cup golden rum, 1 cup milk. Beat with a rotary egg beater until the ice cream is almost melted and the nog is foamy.

AT SERVING TIME:
Ladle into small punch cups and sprinkle with grated nutmeg. Serves 6.

Hot Orange Toddy

YOU WILL NEED:
canned frozen orange juice   rum (optional)
brown sugar

Dilute a 4-ounce can frozen orange juice according to directions. Add 4 teaspoons brown sugar. Bring just to a boil. Remove from heat and add 3/4 cup rum if desired. Can also be served without rum.

AT SERVING TIME:
Serve in small mugs or goblets.

Peach Champagne

This might be considered a drink or a dessert—it may be served as either. Special tall footed glasses are available in Europe for serving it, but any commodious wide-mouthed wine or beer goblet may be used.

YOU WILL NEED:

fresh and juicy small peaches or canned whole peaches plain or brandied	brandy or peach brandy (optional) champagne

Prick a small juicy peach all over with a fork to release the juices (or use a canned whole peach or a brandied whole peach). Place in a large glass. Add a tablespoon of brandy or peach brandy, if desired.

AT SERVING TIME:
Pour in enough very well chilled champagne to fill the glass just about half full. Provide teaspoons so that the peach can be eaten after the champagne has been consumed. One quart of champagne serves 6.

Quick Fish House Punch

Probably the most famous as well as one of the most potent punches in all the world was invented by America's oldest cooking and eating club called the State in Schuylkill. Their Fish House Punch is served in a special Lowestoft china bowl which was presented to the club in 1812. We have not tampered with the ancient recipe except to substitute bottled lemon juice for the fresh squeezed variety, and bottled sugar syrup instead of the loaf sugar. The only ingredient that might not be available is

peach brandy. Peach liqueur or cordial may be used in its stead
and in that case a little less sugar is needed.

YOU WILL NEED:

sugar syrup	water
lemon juice	peach brandy or peach
golden rum	liqueur (optional)
brandy	block of ice

Combine in a large bowl 1 cup sugar syrup, 3 cups bottled lemon
juice, 2 bottles golden rum (or 1 bottle Jamaica rum and 1
bottle golden rum), 1 bottle brandy, 2 quarts water, ½ cup
peach brandy or peach liqueur. If peach liqueur is used cut
down the amount of sugar syrup to ¾ cup. If desired, the peach
liqueur may be omitted entirely. Stir well and allow to "ripen"
in a cool place for 2 or 3 hours.

AT SERVING TIME:

Place a large block of ice in the bowl. Stir until liquid is chilled.
Ladle into punch cups or glasses. Since this punch is very strong,
this amount should be ample for 20 persons.

Wassail

On Christmas Eve, New Year's Eve, or Twelfth Night, the
wassail bowl is traditional, for

> When midnight bells are tolled, let's gather 'round the Wassail
>   Bowl.
> Let the wealthy and great roll in splendor and state
> I envy them not I declare it
> I eat my own lamb, my own chicken and ham
> I shear my own fleece and I wear it.

So goes the inscription on a lordly eighteenth-century wassail
bowl of the same era as this recipe, which we have adapted for
modern living.

YOU WILL NEED:

canned baked apples	nutmeg
bottled apple juice	lemon rind
vanilla extract	honey or brown sugar
cinnamon stick	(optional)
cloves	brandy or apple jack

Warm 12 canned baked apples in the oven, providing 1 for each guest. To 3 quarts apple juice add 1 teaspoon vanilla, stick of cinnamon, 2 teaspoons whole cloves, a whole nutmeg cracked or ½ teaspoon nutmeg, and a little thin lemon rind. Also if desired, add 2 tablespoons honey or brown sugar. Simmer for a few minutes. Pour while hot into punch bowl.

AT SERVING TIME:
Place a baked apple in each mug. Pour on 1 or 2 jiggers (3 tablespoons) of brandy or apple jack that has been slightly warmed. Set aflame and ladle the spiced apple juice over the apple. Serve with a spoon. Serves 12.

VARIATION: Wassail for the Young
Even without brandy or apple jack, Wassail can be a very festive drink. Simply omit liquor.

🌿 18 🌿

Can-Opener Parties

AMERICA TODAY is probably the most "entertaining" civilization in all the world and in all history. But our entertainment is our own. We specialize in help-yourself parties. Most of our finest party menus require comparatively little effort. They are simple and easy to achieve. Generally our party dishes can be cooked ahead of time; and most of them—at least most of those featured in this chapter—will wait obligingly, retaining their good looks and good taste not only for minutes and hours, but even for days in the refrigerator or weeks in the freezer.

The menus in this chapter rely more or less upon processed foods—canned, frozen, or dehydrated. In order to be truly successful they also require some sort of keep-warm equipment. There are innumerable warming devices on the market, ranging all the way from candles or alcohol lamps to electric chafing dishes, and best of all, electrically heated, thermostatically controlled warming trays.

All the recipes in this section are designed to serve a party of twelve. All of them have something extra-special in the way of flavor, drama, and enticement. In many of them wines or beer or spirits are used, not only because they add so much to the taste, but also because it has been discovered by great chefs that foods so flavored tend to improve and mellow rather than deteriorate as they stand.

RECIPES

Aspic of Beef à la Mode
Blanquette de Veau
Brunswick Stew
Carbonnade of Beef
Cassoulet of Beans
Chicken Curry
Chicken Tetrazzini
Fruited Breast of Chicken
Filet of Sole with Vermouth
Hungarian Beef Paprika

Hunter's Stew
Lazy-Luscious Lasagna
Old Charleston Chicken and
    Oyster Fricassee
Pasta with Clams Bianco
Shrimps Armenonville
Soul Food for New Year's
Pimiento Pilaf Presentation
Sukiyaki, Chain-Store Style
Trout in Champagne

Aspic of Beef à la Mode

For a buffet supper in summertime nothing could be more appealing than this simple-as-can-be version of one of the most delightful of Parisian specialties.

YOU WILL NEED:

roast beef or leftover pot
    roast
fresh or dried tarragon
carrots
green and black olives

unflavored gelatin
canned consommé
tarragon vinegar
Tabasco sauce

You may start with cold roast beef from the delicatessen, or you could use leftover pot roast cut in slices about 1/4 inch thick. Arrange 16 slices of beef, overlapping slightly, in a shallow serving dish or a deep platter. Sprinkle with 2 tablespoons of fresh tarragon or 1 tablespoon dried tarragon. Garnish attractively with very thin slices of carrots and green and black olives.

Now make an aspic by softening 4 envelopes of unflavored gelatin in 1 cup cold water. Heat 2 cans consommé. Add the

softened gelatin and stir until dissolved. Flavor with 2 tablespoons tarragon vinegar and 3 or 4 drops of Tabasco sauce. Cool
until the aspic mixture is syrupy. This will take about 30 minutes
in the refrigerator or about 10 minutes in the freezing compartment; but be sure to time yourself if you use the freezer, because
the aspic will get grainy if it is kept too long in the freezing compartment.

Pour aspic over the beef slices, being careful not to disarrange
the decoration. Chill until set. This will take about 2 hours in
the refrigerator.

AT SERVING TIME:
Serve with heated crusty bread. Provide one hot vegetable and
a salad. Serves 12.

Blanquette de Veau

This is one of the treasures of French cuisine, a dish with a delicate flavor and a silky smooth sauce. This recipe makes enough
to serve 12 people. If there isn't a large party in the offing, you
might make up the same quantity—some to eat at once and two
or three portions to put into the freezer.

YOU WILL NEED:

veal	onions
cream of chicken soup	canned mushrooms
dry white table wine	egg yolks

Have 6 pounds of boneless veal cut into 1-inch cubes. Put the
veal cubes into a large kettle with 3 cans of condensed cream of
chicken soup and 3 cups very dry white wine, like California
Riesling. Add 1½ cups water and 3 medium-sized onions thinly
sliced. Cover and cook slowly for 1 hour. Five minutes before the
hour is up, add three 6-ounce cans of button mushrooms, sliced
or whole.

AT SERVING TIME:
Place 3 slightly beaten egg yolks in a warm serving dish; slowly
add the sauce from the kettle, stirring constantly. Then put the

meat into the sauce. Keep warm but do not allow to boil after the eggs are in or the sauce will curdle.

Serve with rice and a tossed green salad.

In spring at violet time, you might want to serve a Parisian salad of fresh young greens and wild violets.

Brunswick Stew

You can buy an excellent Virginia-made Brunswick stew in cans, but it is not widely distributed. Luckily, however, you can make one almost as fast by combining several products that are universally available.

A Brunswick stew is one of the many traditional dishes that it is difficult to classify. Some call it a stew; others call it soup. Some people prefer the meat in very small pieces; others, in bigger chunks. Some like it hot with Worcestershire sauce and Tabasco. Others like it mild or winey. In this recipe you have room to express your own preferences. This recipe should provide sustenance for 12.

YOU WILL NEED:

canned beef stew
canned chicken fricassee
canned tomatoes
canned succotash
sherry and/or Worcester-
   shire sauce

Tabasco sauce (optional)
canned consommé or
   chicken broth (optional)
packaged bread crumbs
   (optional)

Heat together 3 cans each of the following: beef stew, chicken fricassee, tomatoes, succotash. Let simmer 5 minutes.

As for seasoning: In the Carolinas they would add 1½ cups sherry and about a tablespoon of Worcestershire. In Georgia there would be no sherry but maybe 3 tablespoons of Worcestershire. In Virginia they might use the sherry and instead of Worcestershire several dashes of Tabasco sauce.

If you want a more liquid dish, add canned consommé or chicken broth. If you would rather have a thick stew, add about ½ cup packaged bread crumbs.

AT SERVING TIME:
Ladle into deep hot plates or shallow bowls. Serve with squares of hot corn pone or corn sticks and plenty of cole slaw.

Carbonnade of Beef

Originally this dish came from Belgium. Essentially it is a beef stew, but it is made with beer.

YOU WILL NEED:

beef from rump	brown sugar
flour	tomato sauce
bacon fat or butter	celery flakes
malt vinegar	parsley flakes
beer	bay leaf
canned onion soup	thyme
(without cheese)	canned consommé (if
canned carrots	necessary)

Order 5 pounds of beef cut from the rump. Ask the butcher to slice the meat ½ inch thick. And when you get home, pound it thinner and cut the slices into 2-inch squares.

Shake the meat in a plastic bag along with ½ cup flour. After the meat has been well floured, brown the pieces in ½ cup bacon fat or butter. Remove the meat from the pan and add to the rich brown glaze that the meat has left 3 tablespoons malt vinegar, 2 cups beer, 3 cans onion soup (the kind that does not contain cheese), 1 can sliced carrots, 2 teaspoons brown sugar, ½ cup tomato sauce, 2 teaspoons dehydrated celery flakes, 2 teaspoons parsley flakes, 1 bay leaf, ½ teaspoon dried thyme. Bring to a boil, then lower the heat and simmer about 5 minutes.

Now place the meat and the gravy in layers in a casserole that can come to the table. The gravy should cover the meat. If you haven't enough gravy, add condensed canned consommé. Cover the dish tightly with its own lid or aluminum foil and cook about 1 hour or until the meat is very tender.

AT SERVING TIME:
Bring to the table in its own baking dish and serve with fluffy boiled potatoes or, if you prefer, with rice, hominy grits, or polenta. Beer, of course, is the ideal accompaniment, and dill pickles have an especial affinity. Serves 12.

Cassoulet of Beans

In almost every country in the world you will find interesting bean dishes. Among the most noted are the various cassoulets of France. In the old days such dishes required days of preparation, soaking, simmering, baking. Now all that is necessary is to combine canned beans with different kinds of meat. The popular baked beans in tomato sauce give an authentic look and flavor. Or those smoky beans known as "Campside" may be used.

We think that a cassoulet is more interesting if the meat is in good-sized pieces. If, however, your party is to be a buffet, you can of course use cubes of pork instead of pork chops. Leftover meats can be used, but they should be browned very lightly.

YOU WILL NEED:

pork chops or cooked, diced pork	powdered ginger
bacon or other drippings	tomato-sauced beans
onion	red or white table wine or
garlic	dry vermouth or sherry
rosemary	packaged bread crumbs
	parsley

Brown 12 small pork chops or 4 pounds of cooked, diced pork in bacon fat or drippings. Place in a well-buttered casserole along with a large onion cut into quarters and 2 cloves garlic that have been put through the press or ½ teaspoon instant garlic. Sprinkle both sides of the browned meat with salt, pepper, a little rosemary, and a touch of powdered ginger.

Open 4 cans (1 pound 5 ounces each, about 10 cups) tomato-sauced beans. Arrange in the buttered baking dish with pork chops. The chops should be half hidden, half showing.

Pour on 1 to 2 cups red or white table wine or dry vermouth or ½ cup sherry. Sprinkle with packaged bread crumbs. This recipe is particularly good if put together the day before, refrigerated overnight, and put in oven before the party.

About 2 hours before the party, place the refrigerated cassoulet in a moderately hot oven 375° F. for 1 hour or until bubbling hot and golden brown.

AT SERVING TIME:

Sprinkle generously with fresh parsley. Serve with heated crusty rolls and a green salad. Serves 12.

Chicken Curry

A magnificent curry, rich with chicken, seems a perfect dish for large gatherings, since it is "fork food"—that is, no silverware is needed except a fork. It makes a charming buffet, too, surrounded by bowls of rice and appropriate curry accompaniments.

YOU WILL NEED:

canned chicken à la king	catsup
onion or onion flakes	shredded coconut
canned whole button	mustard
mushrooms	Worcestershire sauce
garlic	ginger
curry powder	

To 6 cans chicken à la king, add 3 chopped onions gently fried, or 3 tablespoons toasted onion flakes; 2 3-ounce cans button mushrooms; 3 cloves garlic, crushed; 3 tablespoons curry powder; 3 tablespoons catsup; 3 tablespoons coconut; a little salt; ¼ teaspoon dry mustard; 1 tablespoon Worcestershire sauce; and ½ teaspoon powdered ginger. Stir well. Bring to a boil. Remove from flame, cover, and allow to stand in a warm place 10 to 20 minutes.

AT SERVING TIME:
Heat but do not boil. Serve with boiled rice and appropriate curry accompaniments, such as chutney, chopped hard-cooked egg, shredded coconut, whole pickled peaches, watermelon pickle, chopped cashew nuts.

Chicken Tetrazzini

This delightful combination has the advantage of being very simple and easy to prepare—and economical, too. Can be baked in individual casseroles or in a large shallow baking dish, whichever is most convenient.

YOU WILL NEED:

thin spaghetti or vermicelli	white wine (optional)
butter or olive oil	Cheddar cheese
onion	canned boned chicken
garlic	pimientos
condensed cream of	parsley
mushroom soup	paprika

Cook 1 pound thin spaghetti or vermicelli in boiling salted water until just tender but not soft. Drain and mix thoroughly with a little melted butter or olive oil.

Cook ½ cup chopped onion and 1 clove garlic (crushed) in 2 tablespoons butter or olive oil until tender. Blend in 4 cans condensed cream of mushroom soup and 2 cups water or 1 cup water and 1 cup dry white wine. Stir until smooth. Add 2 cups (½ pound) shredded sharp Cheddar cheese (preferably not processed). Save remaining cheese to use later. Cook over low heat until cheese is melted. Stir occasionally. Fold in 4 (6-ounce) cans of boned chicken, diced or broken into pieces; add ¼ cup drained chopped canned pimientos and ¼ cup chopped fresh parsley or 2 tablespoons parsley flakes.

Butter baking dish lavishly. Place the cooked spaghetti on the bottom of the baking dish. Cover with the chicken mixture, sprinkle with 2 cups grated cheese, and fleck lightly with paprika. Bake in hot oven, 425° F., until the sauce bubbles and the top browns: about 20 minutes for a large casserole, or 10 minutes if you use individual casseroles.

AT SERVING TIME:
Serve in the original baking dish garnished with bouquets of parsley. A wonderfully good and complete meal when served with assorted relishes. Serves 12.

Fruited Breast of Chicken

A glorious fruited chicken, somewhat Oriental in appearance, easily prepared hours ahead of time. If you like, however, it can be ready to serve in half an hour, or you can turn the oven lower and cook it longer.

YOU WILL NEED:

chicken breasts or small frying chickens	canned pineapple chunks
fresh lime or lemon juice	canned pineapple juice
garlic powder	soy sauce
eggs	marmalade
flour	powdered ginger
milk	lemon juice
peanut oil	brown sugar
white pepper	cornstarch
canned mandarin orange slices	fresh green peppers
	fresh tomatoes

Remove the bones from 6 chicken breasts and cut in halves lengthwise to make 12 portions. Or you could cut 3 small frying chickens into quarters. Rub all over with fresh lime or lemon juice and sprinkle lightly with garlic powder. Dip each piece into a batter made by smoothly blending together 2 eggs, 1½ cups flour, 1½ cups milk, 1½ tablespoons peanut oil, 1½ teaspoons salt, ½ teaspoon white pepper. Drop a few pieces at a time into hot oil deep enough to cover, and fry until crisp and lightly browned. Remove, drain on paper towels, and keep warm. Place in an attractive shallow baking dish. Meanwhile drain (saving liquid) 2 small cans mandarin orange sections, 2 medium cans pineapple chunks. Arrange fruit over chicken.

Prepare sauce by boiling together for 2 or 3 minutes 4 cups canned pineapple juice, 1 cup each of the liquids drained from the oranges and pineapple, 4 tablespoons soy sauce, 2 tablespoons marmalade (orange or ginger), 1½ teaspoons powdered ginger, 3 tablespoons each lemon juice and brown sugar, 3 tablespoons cornstarch. Bring to a boil. Cook 1 or 2 minutes, or until clear and slightly thickened. Pour over and around the chicken. Bake in a hot oven (400° F.) about 15 minutes. Arrange around the edges of the dish 3 large green peppers and 3 tomatoes, cut in chunks. Baste with sauce and bake about 5 minutes longer, or until chicken is beautifully tender and vegetables are richly glazed.

AT SERVING TIME:

Serve with a chilled soup; rice, combined with grated orange rind and sliced water chestnuts, cooked in orange juice instead of water; refrigerated crescent rolls; a cool lime sherbet, and Kentucky Bourbon Brownies (see page 218).

Filet of Sole with Vermouth

This is an elegant Friday feast, wonderfully easy to do.

In this dish the vermouth is the same kind that you use for making a dry Martini. It imparts to the dish not only the quality of a dry white wine and a brandy but also the flavor of many delicate herbs.

YOU WILL NEED:

frozen fillets of flounder or red perch	instant onion
	dry vermouth
butter	packaged bread crumbs
white pepper	chives or parsley

Thaw 3 packages frozen fillets of flounder or red perch just enough to separate them. Cut crosswise in halves. Place in a well-buttered shallow baking dish and sprinkle with 3 teaspoons salt, ¾ teaspoon white pepper, and 1 teaspoon instant onion. Combine 2 cups dry vermouth with 1 cup water and pour over the fish. Cover with 1 cup packaged bread crumbs; dot with 3 tablespoons butter.

Bake in a moderate oven (350° F.) for 25 minutes or until the fish is cooked and the top lightly brown.

AT SERVING TIME:
Strew generously with chopped chives or parsley, and serve with new potatoes boiled in their jackets, peas or asparagus, and a cucumber and tomato salad. Serves 12.

Hungarian Beef Paprika

This is an unusually savory goulash. Made with canned onion soup in a pressure cooker, it is practically workless and ever so swift.

YOU WILL NEED:

butter or chicken fat	capers
beef for stew	bay leaves
flour	parsley flakes
canned onion soup	dry sherry
Hungarian paprika	broad noodles
vinegar	poppy seeds, almonds, or
caraway seeds	bread crumbs
fresh or dried marjoram	

Heat 3 tablespoons butter or chicken fat in a heavy kettle, a Dutch oven, or a big pressure cooker.

Have ready 6 pounds of beef for stew cut into inch cubes. Put the meat into a bag with a cup of flour and shake until the meat is evenly covered. Brown in hot fat, turning occasionally.

Add 3 cans condensed onion soup, the kind that does not have cheese in it. (To be sure, look at the list of ingredients on the label.) Add 3 tablespoons sweet Hungarian paprika. The better and fresher the paprika, the better the stew. Add also 3 tablespoons vinegar, 3 tablespoons caraway seeds, 1 tablespoon dried marjoram or twice that amount of fresh marjoram, 2 tablespoons capers, 3 bay leaves, a couple of tablespoons of parsley flakes and 1 cup dry sherry.

Cook in a pressure cooker at 15 pounds pressure 15 minutes. Allow to cool, open the cooker, remove bay leaves. Or you may cover the kettle and cook at a slow simmer about 2 hours or until the meat is tender.

AT SERVING TIME:
Serve with broad noodles well buttered and sprinkled with poppy seeds, almonds, or bread crumbs. Canned or quick-frozen Italian green beans make a delightful accompaniment. Serves 12.

Hunter's Stew

Now that quick-frozen rabbits, cut up for stew, are available at any time of the year in all sections of the country via the frozen food bins, even the hunter who comes home empty-handed can celebrate. Or if you like, you may substitute beef for rabbit. For a party of 12, home from the hills and hungry, these proportions should be ample.

YOU WILL NEED:

canned sauerkraut	dehydrated onion soup
canned sliced mushrooms	canned beef gravy
bacon	sugar
frozen rabbit (or beef stew meat)	whiskey

Drain 2 cans sauerkraut; add 2 (6-ounce) cans sliced mushrooms complete with their liquid. Cover and simmer gently about 20 minutes. While they are simmering, cut 6 strips of bacon into small pieces and fry in a heavy frying pan. Remove the bacon from the pan and add 4 pounds cut-up rabbit or beef stew meat and brown in the bacon fat.

To the browned meat add the sauerkraut and mushrooms along with 1 package dehydrated onion soup, 2 cans beef gravy, 1 cup hot water, 1 tablespoon sugar, bacon bits, ½ cup bourbon (any good whiskey will do). Place in a large casserole; cover and bake in a slow oven, 325° F., about 2 hours or until the meat is tender.

Many of the older recipes for this type of stew suggest that it should be set aside in a cool place for 24 hours to mellow.

AT SERVING TIME:
Reheat. Serve with potatoes boiled in their jackets or baked stuffed potatoes. Regular baked potatoes are good, too, but they are not recommended for a party for they need to be served the instant they are ready. Baked stuffed potatoes, on the other hand, can be kept on the buffet table for a good long time and can even be frozen and reheated.

Whole small tomatoes are often served as an accompaniment to a hunter's stew, and all kinds of raw vegetables are also appropriate.

Instead of French bread, you might brush a loaf of caraway-seeded rye bread with butter and heat in aluminum foil in the oven.

Lazy-Luscious Lasagna

No one, not even an Italian connoisseur, would ever guess that any corners are cut in the preparation of this specialty. Classical recipes call for the widest kind of ribbon pasta with many layers of sauce, several kinds of cheese, chopped meats, and meatballs. But here we use quick-frozen lasagna. When combined with cottage cheese or Italian ricotta 1 package quick-frozen lasagna can be counted on to serve 2 guests generously. This recipe serves 12.

YOU WILL NEED:

garlic

olive oil

canned marinara sauce

creamed cottage cheese **or**
  ricotta

quick-frozen lasagna

Parmesan cheese

Rub a large shallow baking dish or pan (which can come to the table) with a cut clove of garlic and brush with olive oil. Open 2 cans of marinara sauce. Cover bottom of baking dish or pan with marinara sauce and save a little for the top. Then spread a layer of creamed cottage cheese or ricotta about 1 inch thick. You will need about 2 pounds of ricotta or 4 of the usual containers of creamed cottage cheese for this. On top of the cottage cheese or ricotta place 6 packaged quick-frozen lasagna and spread the rest of the marinara sauce. Bake in a moderate oven (350° F.) for about 30 minutes or until the sauce bubbles.

AT SERVING TIME:

Sprinkle generously with 2 cups Parmesan cheese and serve with a salad of hearts of escarole or dandelion greens.

To complete the meal, have a large platter of antipasto made up of celery, salami, radishes, olives, canned pickled Italian peppers, pickled eggplant (which is called caponata), canned pimientos, sardines, anchovies, and tuna fish sprinkled with capers. For dessert: fresh fruit or berries, and/or raspberry, lemon, or orange sherbet.

Old Charleston Chicken and Oyster Fricassee

If you wish you could, of course, omit the oysters and you would still have one of the most interesting chicken fricassees that anyone has ever tasted.

YOU WILL NEED:

canned chicken fricassee   canned broiled-in-butter
nutmeg   mushrooms
anchovy paste   lemons
pale dry sherry   capers
egg yolks   toasted almonds
oysters

To serve 12 generously, use 6 cans chicken fricassee. Add ¾ tea-spoon nutmeg, 2 teaspoons anchovy paste, and 1 cup pale dry sherry. Cover and heat, but do not boil or the chicken will fall apart and become shreddy.

In a bowl, beat 3 egg yolks lightly; add to the egg yolks a little of the sauce from the chicken, stirring until smooth. Then little by little add more of the hot sauce to the egg mixture and finally turn the mixture into the kettle.

Heat 3 dozen fresh or frozen oysters in their own juice until the edges begin to curl—about 2 minutes. Combine with the oysters 3 cans sliced broiled-in-butter mushrooms drained, ½ cup lemon juice, 3 tablespoons capers.

Put everything together and heat but, once again, do not boil. Keep hot over hot water in a warming oven set about 180° F. or on an electric hot tray set at low heat.

AT SERVING TIME:

Garnish with the thinnest possible slivers of lemon peel and toasted almonds. Serve with rice.

Pasta with Clams Bianco

For those who have true appreciation of the full glories of Italian pastas, *in bianco* represents the zenith. It is a white sauce guiltless of flour or any thickening and guiltless also of tomato.

All sorts and shapes of pasta may be used in this recipe—exceedingly thin spaghetti, vermicelli, linguini, or fettucini, all of which are of varying thicknesses.

You can also add drama and interest to the dish by using pasta in the shape of shells or quills, bow knots, wheels or corkscrews. (Not only Italian shops but even supermarkets now carry a wide variety of shapes and sizes.)

Count on 4 pounds of pasta for 12 people and you'll *surely* have enough. A giant-size kettle or two large ones are required.

YOU WILL NEED:

garlic	parsley
olive oil	pasta
canned minced clams	

Crush or finely mince 6 cloves of garlic and cook them in 1½ cups olive oil. Add liquid from 6 10½-ounce cans of minced clams and save the clams to add later. Add ½ cup chopped fresh parsley, 1 tablespoon salt, and ½ teaspoon pepper. Simmer sauce for 10 minutes. Then add clams and simmer exactly 2 minutes —no longer.

About 15 minutes before serving time, cook 4 pounds of pasta according to package directions. Be sure not to overcook. Each type of pasta requires a different cooking time.

AT SERVING TIME:

Drain the water from the pasta. Add the sauce, mixing it gently but well. Turn onto well-heated platters or bowls and serve immediately.

Serve with a green salad made up of escarole, cooked cauliflower flowerlets, black olives, cut-up celery, and tomatoes, mixed with a dressing of olive oil and lemon.

Shrimps Armenonville

One of the most beautiful restaurants in the world is the Café Armenonville set in the fairylike gardens off the Bois de Boulogne in Paris. It was here that we got their original recipe for their renowned chafing-dish specialty. Years later we evolved a quick version made with canned quick-frozen cream of shrimp soup and quick-frozen shrimp. Canned shrimp could be used, but at the present writing they are not as good as the frozen. The best of frozen shrimp are individually quick-frozen and will rattle when you shake the package. This type is all deveined and shelled, too.

YOU WILL NEED:

quick-frozen cream of   pale dry sherry
   shrimp soup   Tabasco sauce
milk   nutmeg
curry powder or paste   quick-frozen shrimp
prepared mustard   eggs
Worcestershire sauce

To make 12 generous servings, use 4 cans quick-frozen cream of shrimp soup and 2 soup cans of milk. Heat along with 2 tablespoons curry powder or paste, 1 tablespoon prepared mustard, 1 tablespoon Worcestershire sauce, ¾ cup pale dry sherry, a few drops of Tabasco sauce, and ¼ teaspoon nutmeg. When the sauce is thoroughly hot but not boiling, add 4 packages of quick-frozen shrimp. Bring to a boil and cook slowly until the shrimps are pinkish and done. This will take only about 2 minutes. Remove from the stove.

Beat 2 whole eggs or 4 egg yolks slightly along with 2 tablespoons sherry. Stir a couple of spoonsfuls of the hot sauce from the shrimp into the eggs and then turn the whole thing into the sauce. Keep hot but do not boil.

AT SERVING TIME:

Present in a chafing dish along with heated wild rice or parsleyed rice and canned stewed tomatoes sprinkled with garlic-flavored croutons. (You can buy croutons in jars, too.)

Soul Food for New Year's

An institution among Southerners for generations, Soul Food has been recently "discovered," taken up, become a rage! Especially on New Year's Day you must have "collards, or other such greens, to bring green folding money; black-eyed peas for coins; and pork for luck."

YOU WILL NEED:

bacon or salt pork   canned black-eyed peas
celery   hot pepper sauce (optional)
onions

Dice ½ pound bacon or salt pork and fry till crisp. Add 2 stalks celery and 2 small onions, finely diced. Cook until onion is soft. Then add 6 1-pound cans black-eyed peas. Heat. Season with plenty of freshly ground black pepper, or a healthy sprinkle of hot pepper sauce.

AT SERVING TIME:
Serve with the "collards or other such greens" mentioned above, rice with the peas, baked ham from a can. Provide a cruet of vinegar to pass with the cooked frozen collards, mustard greens, or leaf spinach. Also sweet potatoes, hot corn bread, sliced tomato and scallion salad, and Ambrosia for dessert. Real Southern Soul Food!

Pimiento Pilaf Presentation

Here's a party dish that requires very little effort, yet the effect is exciting. A huge mound of delicious pilaf, surrounded at its base by your own choice of meats, seafood, or chicken.

YOU WILL NEED:

rice	onion
butter or margarine	canned pimientos
canned chicken broth	parsley
lemon juice	salted almonds
celery	

Sauté 2 cups regular long-grain rice in 4 tablespoons butter or margarine until rice is pale gold and transparent. Add 8 cups chicken broth, and 2 tablespoons lemon juice. Bring to a boil. Cover tightly. Turn flame down very low and cook 14 minutes, or until liquid is absorbed. Fluff with a fork. Meanwhile, melt in a heavy fry pan ¼ cup butter or margarine. Add ¾ cup thinly sliced celery, 2 medium onions, finely chopped, and ¼ cup diced canned pimientos. Cook gently until onions and celery are tender. Then, with 2 forks, toss the mixture into the hot rice. Add salt (if needed) and freshly ground pepper to taste. Sprinkle generously with chopped parsley.

AT SERVING TIME:

Heap pilaf in the center of a large platter and sprinkle with coarsely chopped salted almonds. At its base, lay individual pieces of golden broiled chicken, cubes or thin slices of canned ham, heated slices of canned tongue, broiled lobster tails, dribbled with melted butter, or any other favorite meats your fancy suggests.

Sukiyaki, Chain-Store Style

This special party dish is *not* one that waits. An adaptation from the Japanese, it uses only products available at any grocery store.

Quick and dramatic, sukiyaki should be prepared at the table in full view of your admiring guests—not at all difficult to do in this day of supremely portable electric units and electric skillets.

YOU WILL NEED:

beef suet or peanut oil	chicken broth or consommé
Bermuda onions	frozen chip steaks or fresh
celery	rump steak
canned sliced mushrooms	soy sauce
frozen leaf spinach	sugar
canned bean sprouts	steamed rice
spring onions	raw eggs (optional)

Arrange all the ingredients attractively on one or two large platters.

Rub a heated frying pan with pieces of beef suet, using about 4 pieces 1 by 2 inches, and after you have rubbed the pan leave the suet in the pan. Or, in place of suet, use 3 tablespoons peanut oil. Add 3 large sliced Bermuda onions; cook till onions are golden. Now add 3 cups thinly sliced celery, three drained 6-ounce cans sliced mushrooms, 3 packages frozen leaf spinach, 6 cups drained canned bean sprouts (three 16-ounce cans), and 3 bunches spring onions with 3 inches of tops left on (cut these into 1-inch pieces). Cook only until vegetables are thoroughly heated, about 3 minutes.

Now add 1 can (1⅓ cup) condensed chicken broth or consommé. There should be just enough liquid to cover bottom of pan. Over the top of the vegetables place 3 packages (about 3 dozen) very thin quick-frozen chip steaks or 3 pounds rump steak sliced paper thin. Cover and allow to steam about 5 minutes. Then add ¾ cup soy sauce. Sprinkle with 3 tablespoons sugar and simmer until the vegetables are done but still on the crisp side. A little more broth or soy sauce may be added, if you wish.

AT SERVING TIME (which means immediately):
Spoon the sukiyaki onto steamed rice. For interesting authenticity, provide each guest with a tiny bowl in which there is a raw egg. Each person breaks the egg and dips morsels of his sukiyaki into the egg. It gives a delicious flavor. Have on hand extra soy sauce for those who want it. A light beer is an excellent accompaniment.

Always there must be tea. Try Japanese tea if you can get it, Chinese tea, or any green tea.

Trout in Champagne

As prepared in Paris this dish is an intricate work of art. There, the trout is skinned and boned but the head and tail are left on. Often the fish are stuffed with chopped trout. But we have simplified the method enormously without altering the essential character of the dish. The sauce, even though it is made with canned cream of mushroom soup, is still rich with butter and eggs ineffably blessed with champagne. Quick-frozen trout from Iceland are available in many parts of the United States, but if your shop is out of trout, you may use fillets of any other delicate fish like flounder or perch.

YOU WILL NEED:

trout or fillets	champagne
canned whole mushrooms	condensed cream of
carrots	mushroom soup
shallots	egg yolks
garlic	lemon juice
onion or instant onion	cayenne pepper or Tabasco
bay leaf	sauce
thyme	

Provide 1 small trout or 1 small whole fillet for each person. For 12, place a dozen fish or fillets in a long shallow baking dish which has been lavishly buttered.

Drain three 4-ounce cans of whole mushroom caps and place them around the fish, along with 3 thinly sliced carrots, 1/2 dozen shallots put through a garlic press, 2 cloves of garlic also put through the press, and 1 medium-size onion finely chopped or 1 tablespoon instant onion. Add 1 bay leaf and sprinkle lightly with the merest pinch of thyme and a little salt and pepper. Moisten with 2 cups champagne. Cover the dish with a lid or with buttered aluminum foil and set in a moderate oven, 350° F., 20 to 30 minutes.

When the fish is opaque and flakes off easily at the touch of the fork, remove it from the oven. Drain or dip the juices out of the baking dish and combine with 1 cup champagne, 1 can condensed cream of mushroom soup, 4 slightly beaten egg yolks, and 3 tablespoons lemon juice. Do the combining off the stove. Then place the sauce over low heat and heat slowly while beating continuously until the sauce is well combined and very smooth. Be careful not to allow the sauce to boil. Add a mere mite of cayenne pepper or a couple of drops of Tabasco sauce.

AT SERVING TIME:
Place the fish on a large warm platter, pour the sauce over it, and arrange the mushrooms around the edge.

How to Open ...

As any vaudevillian will tell you, the opener is crucial. First step toward becoming an impresario with a can opener is obviously getting the contents out of the can, the jar, or the bottle. Even in this day of technological miracles this process can range from easy and instantaneous to annoying, exasperating, and sometimes, impossible.

Have you ever tried to cope with an imported ham? A sardine can that has lost its key? Jars with twist-off tops that refuse to twist off? Lids that will not flip? If you have ever had your temper frayed as you wrestled with a blunt old-fashioned can opener or your fingers snagged on jagged edges, you must certainly realize that in order to savor fully the ease and convenience of can-opener living you must consider the opener.

It pays to put some thought into choosing a can opener. The most expensive is not necessarily the best, nor is the cheapest always a bargain. Never buy a can opener unless you have an opportunity to try it first. A good can opener should be easy to use. It should not require too much pressure to puncture the can, and the opener should not be difficult to turn. The cut should be smooth, never jagged. Blades should be easy to clean and easy to keep clean. There is probably no more germ-laden area in the kitchen than a wall-type can opener that has become crusted with food particles. When a can opener cannot be immersed in water it should be cleaned with a brush and detergent.

Good-quality hard steel is necessary for a can opener that is to be given constant use, for if the steel is not as hard as the can the blades become blunt and dulled. For occasional use a light, inexpensive, well-designed can opener will prove useful. For constant service it is usually better to pay more and get one that is durable and sturdy.

Every home should have at least one can opener that is equipped with a magnet that automatically lifts and holds the lid. The magnet not only will protect your fingers, but it will also keep the sterile contents of the can from becoming contaminated. This feature is especially important when you are opening baby foods, especially fruits that are served without additional heating.

PARADE OF OPENERS

Just as there are dozens of receptacles, dozens of different kinds of cans, jars and bottles, all sorts of different shapes and different closures, there are also dozens of tools for opening.

For the can there are openers that range in size from 1½ inches to 15 inches. There are some that are gilded and so small that they can hang from a charm bracelet or a watch fob. Many are attached to the wall. Quite a few plug into electricity. At least one electric can opener is portable—or, at least, portable to the length of the cord.

In addition to equipment designed specifically to open cans, there are numerous devices that flip up lids, take off tops, puncture beer cans, and whirl surely, neatly, and swiftly around a vacuum can.

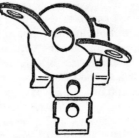

Small but mighty is a self-adjusting disc cutter. The flexible disc cutter adjusts automatically to any variations in the thickness of the rim, opens cans of all sizes and shapes. Operates with only one hand.

The littlest can opener is only 1½ inches long. Originally designed by the military for K rations, it is constructed on a simple but sound engineering principle. The blade folds back so that it can be carried in the pocket or purse. Ideal for the traveler, it is available at shops that sell sporting equipment.

For all jars and bottles with screw tops, this opener is indispensable. It adjusts to lids from 1 to 3 inches in diameter.

Cap removers come in all sizes and in all types of metal from giveaways of plated steel to "gifts" of brass, copper, silver, and even gold. It's wise to have plenty of them in the kitchen, also at the dining table, the drink-mixing center, and in the picnic hamper.

For the well-appointed table you should have an attractive beer and fruit juice opener. These come with many different kinds of handles—plastic, wood, even silver and gold.

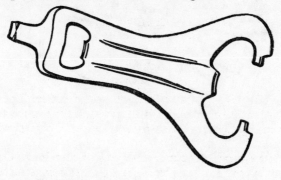

Utility combination can opener will open not only cans but also bottles. Punches cans and pulls corks.

This plier-type hand can opener is a de luxe version of a sturdy and highly versatile opener first developed for civil defense. With

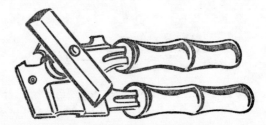

Tahitian wood handles, it is particularly handy as well as beautiful. Will not split, burn, stain, can be put in the automatic dishwasher.

The can opener on the wall has been called the hub of the home in America. The best of them have excellent features including one-hand operation; a grease-sealed cutting wheel; powerful, long-lasting magnet to lift lids and hold tight; heavy plating of chrome or copper; enamel that is baked and will not chip; and cutting surfaces that are super-honed to keep their edges for a long time.

With such automatic can openers, lids are completely severed,

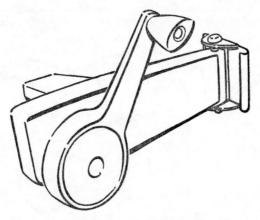

leaving a clean smooth edge. A built-in click tells you when to stop turning the handle after the lid is served. A quarter turn backward releases the can.

Extremely useful in kitchens where there is no space to attach a wall bracket is an opener attached to a bracket, which stands on a table top.

Another table-top can opener, also for kitchens with limited wall space, comes equipped with a large and ever-clinging vacuum cup that will hold fast to any nonporous horizontal surface. Can be set up or put away in seconds.

Several companies that make blenders and mixers also have can-opening attachments.

Outstanding in this group is a portable electric can opener that has many fine features. It is compact, easy to handle, easy to

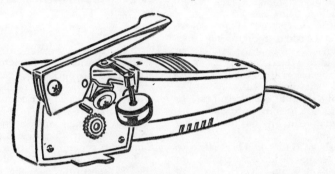

clean; it has a folding magnetic lid lifter and is so light and small that it fits in the palm of your hand. It can be mounted on the wall or kept on the shelf. A six-foot cord makes it easy to use wherever you stand.

Most of the new electric can openers are now designed to open any odd-sized as well as standard can, and many come equipped with knife sharpeners.

Glossary

~~~~~~~~~~~~~~~~~~~~~~

Ac'cent. Brand name for a popular product containing monosodium glutamate. (See Monosodium Glutamate.)

American Cheese. White American Cheddar contains no coloring, but the usual yellow or golden type generally is artificially colored. Cheddar increases in sharpness with age. The young, mild cheese is best for slicing. Older ripened cheese becomes crumbly but has a finer flavor.

Anchovy (Fillets). There are two types of anchovies, Spanish (or Italian) and Norwegian (or Swedish). The former are the true anchovies, while the second are made from tiny fish called sprat.

Anchovy Paste. Comes in tubes and is made of finely crushed or ground anchovies. Used in canapés and salad dressing.

Anise. Sweet, spicy, licoricelike flavor; anise flavoring or seeds are used in baked goods, pickles, and candy.

Apple Brandy or Apple Jack. A true brandy distilled from apple cider. In France it is known as Calvados.

Asbestos Pad. A piece of asbestos material usually sold with a metal rim and handle. Can be obtained at most five-and-ten-cent stores, hardware or department stores. Useful for slow simmering or warming of foods at low heat. Baking dishes and Pyrex pans may safely be placed on asbestos pads over burners at low heat.

Baking Powder. A leavening agent used in quick breads: (1) tartrate type made of cream of tartar, tartaric acid, bicarbonate of soda, and starch; (2) phosphate type made with calcium, acid phosphate; (3) a combination type, generally referred to as double acting. It is not advisable to substitute one for another.

Basil or Sweet Basil. An annual herb of the mint family. Fresh or dried, the savory leaves are used in spaghetti sauces or in tomato dishes.

Bay Leaves. Aromatic leaves of the laurel tree, dried and used for flavoring pot roasts, stews, pickles, vinegar, soups, and fish —especially good with any tomato mixture.

Benedictine. A sweet liqueur, often served instead of dessert; very good over ice cream.

Blue or Bleu Cheese. A Roquefort-type cheese made in this country, Denmark, or Argentina. In the United States, blue cheese is made with the same type of mold as French Roquefort, but generally of cow's milk rather than ewe's milk.

Camembert. A famous French cheese with a soft, mottled rind, which can be eaten. The inside is soft and creamy. Good American Camembert is now being made.

Can Sizes. Approximate contents in the most popular sizes of cans and jars. *6 oz.:* contains ¾ cup, used generally for mushrooms, instant foods, tomato paste, tomato sauce, and meat spreads. *8 oz.:* contains about 1 cup, used for fruits, vegetables, fish products, boned cooked chicken, specialties.* *Picnic Can:* contains approximately 10½ oz., about 1¼ cups, used for condensed soups, some fruits, vegetables, meat and fish products, and specialties.* *No. 303:* commonly called the 1-pound can, contains approximately 14 to 17 oz., 1¾ to 2 cups, used for fruits, vegetables, meat products, ready-to-serve soups, pork and beans, baked beans, cranberry sauce, and specialties.* *No. 2:* contains 1 lb. 4 oz., or 2½ cups, used for juices, ready-to-serve soups, and specialties.* *No. 2½:* contains 1 lb. 13 oz., or 3½ cups, used for fruits, some vegetables. *46 oz.:* contains 3 lbs. 3 ozs., or 5¾ cups, used for fruit and vegetable juices, pork and beans, condensed soup for restaurant, hotel, and institutional use. *No. 10:* a very large can containing 6½ to 7¼ lbs., or 12 to 13 cups, used mainly by hotels, restaurants, and institutions, in which fruits, vegetables, baked beans, soups, and other specialties * are packed. If you want these cans for a large gathering, any grocer can order them for you.

* Usually a food combination such as macaroni, spaghetti, Spanish-style rice, Mexican-type foods, Chinese foods, tomato aspic, etc.

Catsup. Popular condiment sauce containing tomatoes, vinegar, spices.

Caviar. Any fish roe preserved by salting is a caviar, but the word was originally applied only to sturgeon roe. An economical caviar is prepared commercially from the roe of the whitefish.

Caviar (red). The roe of salmon.

Cayenne Pepper. Similar to red pepper, but made from small red pods of tropical peppers. It is dull red and very hot, and is used for catsups, relishes, fish, stews.

Celery Salt. Made by grinding celery seeds and salt together. Good with fish, boiled or fried eggs, potato salad, salad dressings, tomato dishes, and Irish stew.

Celery Seed. Seeds of celery used for flavoring.

Chablis. A white table wine.

Chafing Dish. Usually consists of two pans that fit into each other —a hot-water pan on the bottom and a "blazer," which is the top or cooking pan. When hot water is placed underneath the "blazer," foods can be kept warm for a long time. Most chafing dishes are equipped with a heating element—alcohol lamp, Sterno, or electric.

Chapon. The heel of a loaf of French bread or crusty roll into which a peeled halved clove of garlic has been pressed (may be held in place with a toothpick). This is usually tossed with a salad to impart a garlic flavor.

Chartreuse (yellow or green). Famous liqueur made only by monks in the French Alps.

Cheddar. (See American Cheese.)

Cheese (How to Keep). Cut portions of cheese can be kept moist if they are wrapped in a cloth, dampened in a weak salt solution, about 1 tablespoon of salt to 1 pint of water.

Chervil. A parsleylike herb with a flavor reminiscent of parsley and basil. Can be bought dried.

Chili Powder. Main ingredient is chili pepper. Mexican pod peppers are ground and blended with various spices. It is used for making chili con carne and as a seasoning.

Chili Sauce. A condiment made of tomatoes, green peppers, and onions, with some sweetening spices and vinegar. Useful in salad dressings, sauces, stews, or casserole dishes.

Chives. One of the most useful of cooking herbs. Chives belong to the onion family, have very thin, threadlike green stems which are cut into fine bits and used in cooking and as a garnish.

Chutney. An East Indian relish, made of sliced mango, ginger, raw sugar, spices, and herbs. American versions combine chopped dry fruits. Home-type chutneys are made from apples or pears, chopped beets, horseradish, or pickle. Chutney is served with curried dishes.

Citron. The fruit of the citron tree usually put up in two forms; "glacé," which means covered with a light coat of sugar; and "drained," which has all surplus sugar removed. Glacéed citron is usually diced, ready to use.

Cointreau. Clear, pale, orange-flavored liqueur. It imparts a subtle flavor to many desserts.

Coloring. (See Vegetable Coloring.)

Coriander. Small, light brown seeds used in making curry powder and in cakes, also for flavoring pickles, sausages, and mixed green salads.

Cottage Cheese. A soft, unripened, fresh cheese with a white color and a mild taste. Highly perishable. Does not freeze well.

Cream Cheese. A soft, unripened cheese akin to cottage cheese, but of a finer texture, made from cow's milk enriched with cream.

Crème de Cacao. A cordial that has a strong sweet mocha flavor; excellent for flavoring whipped cream or frozen desserts.

Crème de Menthe. A green, rose, or white mint-flavored liqueur.

Cumin. Seeds something like caraway, used in making curry powder and seasoning sausages, rice dishes, soups, cheese, and canapés.

Curaçao. A cordial made of orange peel and spices.

Curry Powder. A mixture of herbs and spices. The various brands differ somewhat in proportion of ingredients.

Dill. Seeds of an herb of the parsley family. Widely used for pickling. Good for flavoring sauerkraut, salads, and soups.

Dubonnet. A French wine fortified with herbs and flowers. There are two kinds, regular red Dubonnet and white or blond Dubonnet, which is used as a flavoring for chicken and fish dishes.

Edam Cheese. A hard, Dutch-type cheese, often packed in a ball shape. Outside of Holland it has a bright red paraffin coating.

Endive. A salad green mostly imported from Belgium served either raw or cooked.

English Muffins. A raised yeast muffin which must be split and toasted before it is served.

Escarole. A lettucelike salad green with a delicious, bitter tang.

Extracts. Made, in most instances, from the essential oils of the items that give the extracts their names. These oils are generally dissolved with alcohol. The oil gives the extract its flavor. When the juices of fresh fruit, such as pineapples, raspberries, and strawberries are used, the flavor may be fortified. Such fortified extracts must be labeled "imitation."

Fennel. The feathery leaves of this plant are used as a flavoring or garnish. The fleshy bulb, which has an anise flavor, is cut into sections and served like celery.

Fillets. Strips of meat or fish. Fish fillets are usually cut off the backbone. The skin is removed and there are few, if any, bones. A filet mignon is the eye of a sirloin steak, usually cut into individual slices.

Fines Herbes. A combination of herbs, usually parsley, water cress, chives, tarragon, chervil. Any two or three of these may be used in equal proportions to make a dish "aux fines herbes."

Finnan Haddie. Lightly smoked haddock. Available loose in dry form, but for timesaving it is best to buy it in cans or jars, for this type of finnan haddie can usually be used immediately without soaking or cooking.

Finnochio. The Italian name for fennel.

Flags. For the International Cheese Board see page 27. Can be secured from stationery stores or from the United Nations Information Office, UN Secretariat, New York. A complete set of paper flags for all the United Nations sells for about one dollar.

French Bread. A long, crusty loaf, the longest and thinnest of which are often known as flutes. Rolls made of the same dough are generally referred to as French, club, or hard rolls.

Garlic. A bulb that is divided into sections, popularly known as cloves or buds. Instead of fresh garlic, you may use garlic essence, powder, or salt. Since most garlic salt includes only about 30 per cent garlic in pure form and 70 per cent salt, the potency is limited. A good garlic powder is more satisfactory. A clove of prime raw garlic is equal to ⅛ of a level teaspoon of the best garlic powder.

Garlic Essence. Made from the garlic cloves, a powerful extract. A few drops of extract are equal to 1 clove garlic.

Garlic Salt. A combination of garlic and dairy or table salt, used for seasoning soups, salads, and spaghetti.

Gherkins. Tiny pickled cucumbers available either sweet or sour.

Grade Labeling. Is the summary of many quality factors, indicated on the package: "A," "B," "C," and "D" or "Fancy," "Choice," or "Extra-Standard," "Standard," and "Sub-Standard." The use of the letters *A, B, C,* and *D* is based on U.S. standards: *Grade A* or *Fancy:* the finest and most uniform vegetables or fruits obtainable; *Grade B, Choice,* or *Extra-Standard:* excellent product, but not quite as perfect or as uniform in color and size; *Grade C* or *Standard:* all sound and good, but the average run of the crop may be slightly irregular in color and size—*Grade*

C may not be so tender or as mature as the two top grades; *Grade D* or *Sub-Standard:* wholesome, but lacking in uniformity—some of it may be tough and may contain defects.

Grand Marnier. A clear, white, orange-flavored liqueur, similar in flavor to curaçao or Cointreau.

Green Chartreuse. There are two kinds of Chartreuse: green, which is most pungent and expensive; and yellow, which is almost as aromatic and much less expensive.

Gruyère Cheese. As sold in America, this is generally a processed Swiss cheese, most often cut into 1-ounce wedges and put up in 6- or 8-ounce packages.

Hearth Bread. A round, crusty loaf, generally of the Italian or French variety.

Herb Specialists. For herb plants, unusual herb seeds, and information about growing herbs, write to Herb Garden, Inc., Huntington Station, Long Island, New York, or Spice Islands (Frederick Johnson), 70 Pine Street, San Francisco, California.

Hock. A dry white German table wine. Excellent with fish. Should be served chilled.

Horseradish. A highly pungent root which is always shaved or grated. In all grocery stores, grated horseradish can be found in bottles put up in vinegar. Sometimes beet juice is added to the vinegar. There is also dehydrated horseradish, which should be soaked for a few minutes in water or milk before using.

Ketchup. (See Catsup.)

Kippers or Kippered Herring. Sea herrings, slightly salted and smoked, available in quick-frozen form or in cans. Kippers require only heating before they are ready to serve. Canned kippers are packed plain or in tomato sauce.

Kirsch or Kirschwasser. Made in Germany, France, and Switzerland, from small black wild cherries. Popular with fruits. Use with discretion, as too much gives a medicinal flavor.

Kitchen Bouquet. A bottled, trademarked coloring and flavor that adds a rich brown color to gravy, sauces, etc. Useful for giving color to meats roasted at low temperatures. Contains onions, carrots, parsnips, turnips, celery, parsley, and spices as well as caramelized sugar. Use very little, for it can impart a bitter flavor.

Lingonberry. A small, cranberry type of berry about the size of a red currant, popular in Scandinavia, and generally available in this country in a preserve. Also known as preiselberry.

Mace. The dried outer coating of the nutmeg seed. It is sold ground or in blade form and is used to flavor soups, sauces, cakes, and puddings.

Madeira. A fortified dessert wine used for flavoring desserts and cakes. Dry Madeira is used to flavor soups.

Mail Order. All kinds of specialty foods, flavorings, herbs, and spices, as well as unusual canned and prepared products, can be ordered by mail. Many of these shops have catalogs free on request. All are equipped to handle orders quickly and efficiently. Listing is alphabetical by states.

Albert Steinfeld and Co., Tucson, Arizona

Pfeifer's Home Center, Little Rock, Arkansas

E. Gottschalk and Co., Inc., Fresno, California

Baltzer, Los Angeles, California

Bullock's, Los Angeles, California

The Farmer's Market, Los Angeles, California

Holman's Department Store, Pacific Grove, California

City of Paris, San Francisco, California

The Emporium, San Francisco, California

D. F. May Company, Denver, Colorado

G. Fox and Company, Hartford, Connecticut

Edward Malley Co., New Haven, Connecticut

Shartenberg's, Inc., New Haven, Connecticut

W. W. Mertz Co., Torrington, Connecticut

The Epicure, Wilmington, Delaware

Karl the Caterer, Washington, D. C.

Magruder, Inc., Washington, D. C.

The Hecht Co., Washington, D. C.

The Little Caledonia Shop, Washington, D. C. (Georgetown)

Woodward and Lothrop, Washington, D. C.

Burdine's, Miami, Florida

Maas Brothers, St. Petersburg, Florida

Maas Brothers, Tampa, Florida

Davison-Paxon, Atlanta, Georgia

Rich's, Atlanta, Georgia

Carson Pirie Scott and Co., Chicago, Illinois

Marshall Field and Co., Chicago, Illinois

The Wm. H. Block Co., Indianapolis, Indiana

George Wymann and Co., South Bend, Indiana

The Killian Co., Cedar Rapids, Iowa

Younker-Davidson's, Sioux City, Iowa

The Stewart Dry Goods Co., Louisville, Kentucky

Baker and Hickman, Madisonville, Kentucky

D. H. Holmes Co., Ltd., New Orleans, Louisiana

Solari's, New Orleans, Louisiana

The Cuban Liquor Co., Inc., Shreveport, Louisiana

Freese, Inc., Bangor, Maine

The Senter Co., Bangor, Maine

Porteous, Mitchell and Braun Co., Portland, Maine

William Bouchee, Baltimore, Maryland

Jordan Marsh Co., Boston, Massachusetts

S. S. Pierce, Boston, Massachusetts

Newton House, % McAuslan and Wakelin Co., Holyoke, Massachusetts

Forbes and Wallace, Inc., Springfield, Massachusetts

J. L. Hudson Co., Detroit, Michigan

Paul Steketee and Sons, Grand Rapids, Michigan

Gilmore Brothers, Kalamazoo, Michigan

Hardy-Herpolsheimer's, Muskegon, Michigan

J. B. Sperry Co., Port Huron, Michigan

Dayton's, Minneapolis, Minnesota

Donaldson's, Minneapolis, Minnesota

Golden Rule, St. Paul, Minnesota

Natchez Department Store, Natchez, Mississippi

European Import Corporation, St. Louis, Missouri

Scruggs, Vandervoort, & Barney, St. Louis, Missouri

Miller and Paine, Lincoln, Nebraska

Bamberger's, Newark, New Jersey

H. M. Voorhees and Bros., Trenton, New Jersey

Arnold Constable, Trenton, New Jersey

McLean's, Binghamton, New York

Abraham and Straus, Brooklyn, New York

Weed and Co., Buffalo, New York

H. G. Munger and Co., Inc., Herkimer, New York

B. Gertz, Jamaica, New York

B. Altman and Co., New York, New York

Bloomingdale's, New York, New York

Charles and Co., New York, New York

Frazer, Morris & Co. Inc., New York, New York

The Vendome, New York, New York

Joseph Victori & Co., Inc., New York, New York

Beir Bros., Inc., Niagara Falls, New York

Bresee's Oneonta Dept. Store, Oneonta, New York

Sibley, Lindsay and Curr Co., Rochester, New York

Dey Brothers, Syracuse, New York

J. B. Wells and Son Company, Utica, New York

J. B. Ivey and Co., Charlotte, North Carolina

Ivey-Taylor, Raleigh, North Carolina

A. Polsky Co., Akron, Ohio

Canton Hardware Co., Canton, Ohio

H. S. Pogue, Cincinnati, Ohio

Halle Brothers, Cleveland, Ohio

Henry Taylor and Son, Cleveland, Ohio

Wm. Taylor Son and Co., Cleveland, Ohio

Rike-Kumler, Dayton, Ohio

LaSalle and Koch Co., Toledo, Ohio

Strouss-Hirshberg's, Youngstown, Ohio

Carl H. Meiser, Erie, Pennsylvania

Darmstaetter's, Lancaster, Pennsylvania

New Hope Craft Shop, New Hope, Pennsylvania

Gimbels, Philadelphia, Pennsylvania

Wm. Penn Fruit Shop, Philadelphia, Pennsylvania

C. A. Rowell's (Germantown), Philadelphia, Pennsylvania

John Wanamaker, Philadelphia, Pennsylvania

Joseph Horne Co., Pittsburgh, Pennsylvania

Kaufmann's Department Store, Pittsburgh, Pennsylvania

The Shepard Co., Providence, Rhode Island

The White House Dry Goods Co., Beaumont, Texas

Lichtenstein's Inc., Corpus Christi, Texas

Titche-Goettinger, Dallas, Texas

Frost Brothers, San Antonio, Texas

Zion's Cooperative Mercantile Inst., Salt Lake City, Utah

Charles Sterns and Co., Rutland, Vermont

Globman's, Inc., Martinsville, Virginia

W. G. Swartz Co., Inc., Norfolk, Virginia

Thalheimer's, Richmond, Virginia

The Anderson-Newcomb Co., Huntington, West Virginia

The Surprise Store, Parkersburg, West Virginia

Baron Brothers, Madison, Wisconsin

Malden Salt. (See Salt.)

Maple Flavoring. Usually, maple syrup fortified with lovage, fenugreek, and similar herbs. Maple extract can be used with sugar and water to make a maple-flavored syrup.

Maraschino. Originally, maraschino referred to a cherry liqueur richly flavored by the bruised cherry stones. Now the word usually refers to preserved cherries, brightly colored and flavored with coal tar derivative.

Marron. A large French- or Italian-type chestnut bottled with syrup and used principally for frozen desserts.

Marrons Glacés. A confection made from dried French marrons, cooked in sugar.

Meat Extract or Glaze. Concentrated meat juices available in the form of paste. Usually contain a sizable proportion of salt, some spices, and coloring. May be used instead of bouillon cubes. One teaspoon makes a cup of broth.

Monosodium Glutamate. A chemical generally known as MSG or by a number of trade names, it has no taste of its own, but seems to stimulate the taste buds and so accentuate flavors. Some brands contain salt, spices, and garlic; and this is stated on the label.

Mustard. There are two principal kinds of mustard seed: yellow or white, which is comparatively mild; and brown, which is pungent. Yellow or white mustard seed is sometimes sold in small packages for use in mustard pickles and other products. Dry mustard is the powder obtained by bolting the mustard flour through silk cloth after removal of the outer hull. *Prepared mustard* is the paste made by grinding mustard seeds and blending with salt, vinegar, and spices. The most popular prepared mustard is made from yellow mustard seeds; it is a mild mustard, often called *salad mustard.* Prepared mustard made from the brown seeds is sharper and is often described as Dijon-, French-, or German-type mustard because it is the color of the mustard prepared in European countries. *Horse-radish mustard* is a typical American mustard; it is a coarse-ground hot mustard with grated fresh horse-radish. In some sections sharp mustard is known as *English mustard.* This is usually bought in powder form and mixed.

Nectarines. A fruit that combines the flavors of plum and peach.

Nutmeg. The dried seed kernel of the fruit of the nutmeg tree, ground or whole. Used for flavoring milk drinks, custards, puddings, cakes, and mincemeat.

Onion Extract. Made from the concentrated juice of onions.

Onion Flakes. Prepared by controlled drying of selected onions, flakes have natural flavor and can be used in place of chopped fresh onions. One teaspoon equals one medium-sized onion for cooking purposes.

Onion Salt. Combination of dehydrated onion powder, rice flour, and salt, used for flavoring soups, meats, and dressings.

Oka. A Canadian cheese similar to French Port du Salut. It is a semi-hard variety with a delicate, spongy texture.

Orange Extract. Made from the oil pressed from fresh orange peels. A few drops of extract may be used to give the flavor of orange peel.

Orégano. An herb that imparts some of the flavor of marjoram and thyme as well as sage.

Paprika. The dried and ground fruit of capsicum plants used for enriching gravies, sauces, sausages, etc.

Peach Brandy. A distilled liqueur with a strong flavor of the peach, as well as the peach kernel.

Pepper. Black and white pepper comes from the same plant. The black is picked green and dries black. When left on the vine until mature, pepper turns white. Red peppers are from another plant. All pepper should be protected from moisture and sunlight.

Peppercorns. The whole berry of the pepper vine. Peppercorns are used in pepper grinders. Freshly ground black pepper has more flavor than commercially ground pepper.

Peppermint. Extract, or oil of peppermint, obtained by distilling leaves of the plant. A different extract from mint, for which the spearmint plant is used.

Pernod. An anise-flavored liqueur similar in taste to absinthe, but containing none of the harmful wormwood.

Pilot Crackers. Large crackers, very lightly salted, or unsalted, and traditionally used to thicken New England-type chowder or to serve as an accompaniment to chowder.

Pimiento. Sweet red peppers, seeded, flattened, and canned. Widely used as a flavoring in salads and sauces. To keep pimiento that has been opened, cover with olive or salad oil, place a lid on the dish and store in the refrigerator.

Pistachio. Small, oval nut with a thin, rosy-brown shell. Meat has characteristic pistachio-green color.

Pistachio Flavoring. An imitation flavor which also colors food pale green.

Poppy Seed. Very small seeds of the poppy plant, dark blue in color and used for garnishing bread and buns.

Port Wine. A full-bodied, fortified, dessert wine, particularly good with fruits and nuts. There are three kinds: ruby port, tawny port, and white port. White port is wonderful poured over peaches or grapes.

Processed Cheese. Natural, or bulk, cheese that has been heated, pasteurized, blended, and packaged for uniformity of flavor, texture and to provide better keeping qualities. Further ripening is impossible after a cheese has been processed. All cheeses of this type are marked as such.

Provolone. A smoked, Italian-type cheese. Widely used either sliced or grated in Italian dishes.

Pumpernickel. A bread made of coarse rye flour that is neither bolted nor screened. Has a distinctive flavor, a dark color. Russian pumpernickel is softer and more porous than Danish or German pumpernickel, which is black-brown, and moist.

Red Table Wine. Dry, nonsweet wine made of red grapes, traditionally served at room temperature, with red meat, game, goose, duck, or turkey.

Rhine Wine. Dry white table wine which should be served chilled, usually with white meats, cheese dishes, or fish.

Rice. *Brown rice:* This is not a special variety, but is any rice from which the hull has been shelled, but the kernel left unpolished. *Parboiled rice:* partially cooked before milling, also known as *processed or "converted" rice. White rice:* milled or polished rice of any variety. *Precooked packaged rice:* does not require any washing or draining and requires very little or no actual cooking. *Canned, cooked rice:* both white rice and wild rice are available already cooked in cans and need nothing but heating. *Wild rice:* is not a rice at all, technically speaking. It is greenish-gray in color; has a distinctive flavor and texture. Very expensive!

Romaine. A leafy vegetable of the lettuce family with long, pointed leaves. Delicious in salads.

Romano. A hard, salty, grating cheese.

Roquefort. A French cheese made of ewe's milk with a mottled appearance and a greenish-blue mold. Roquefort-type cheeses made in U.S.A., Denmark, and Argentina are generally called "blue" or "bleu" cheese.

Rose Extract. Prepared from the oil or attar of rose by distilling the petals of the flower. This is a highly concentrated, powerful essence requiring three thousand pounds of petals for the production of one pound of oil.

Rose Water. A dilute extract of roses, used for flavoring cakes, frostings, and beverages.

Rosemary. An herb that looks like a curved pine needle and has a sweetish taste. Rosemary is used for soups, stews, roasts.

Rum. A distillate of sugar cane. The light, brandy-type rums usually called white or white label rum; the darker, medium type referred to as golden or gold label rum; and the very dark, almost black, richly flavored type known as Jamaica or dark rum.

Saffron. Dried stamens of the purple crocus so concentrated that one ounce represents five thousand flowers. Used for coloring and flavoring foods.

Sage. The pleasantly bitter leaves of a shrub, used for flavoring soups, sausages, poultry stuffing, cheese.

Salad Oil. Oils, other than olive, widely used for making salad dressings: corn, peanut, soy bean, walnut, and cocount oils.

Salt. *Free-running salt*—harmless chemicals are added to keep the salt from caking; *iodized salt* to aid in the prevention of goiter; *Malden (or crystal) salt,* to be used in salt grinders. *Rock salt* is for killing weeds and freezing ice cream; it is also used as a bed for Oysters Rockefeller and other foods that should be held and served at a very high temperature.

Sauterne. A white wine. Dry types are used as table wines and are particularly good with chicken or other white meat. Sweet sauternes are best served with dessert.

Savory. An annual herb, the leaves of which are used for seasoning meats, poultry, stews, and salads.

Sesame. Small seeds that vary from grayish-white to black when unhulled. When hulled, the seeds are pearly white with a flavor that resembles toasted almonds. In the South these are called benne seeds, and are widely used in Charleston recipes.

Shallot. A small, bulbous plant, reddish in color. Since a shallot combines the flavor of onion and garlic, these two ingredients may be substituted, though the resultant flavor is not exactly the same.

Sherry Wine. The most popular wine for flavoring. Use the dry sherry to flavor soups and sauces; sweet, dark sherries for the flavoring of desserts and fruit.

Soy Sauce. A condiment of Oriental origin made from the soy bean and containing herbs, spices, and salt.

Sugar. (1) *granulated,* white sugar, the most widely used; (2) *superfine, or powdered,* a granulated sugar that is especially good for fruits or sweetening cold drinks; (3) *confectioners',* a pulverized sugar for uncooked frostings, icings, fondants, or candy; (4) *loaf, tablet, lump, or cube sugar—* principally used for sweetening hot tea or coffee; (5) *old-fashioned, dark brown sugar,* a moist, refined cane sugar in which some molasses has been allowed to remain. *Light brown sugar* or yellow sugar, lighter in color than the old-fashioned brown sugar, has a less-pronounced molasses flavor. *Granulated light brown sugar,* has rather coarse, separate grains. Pours; does not lump or harden.

Swiss Cheese. A mild, nutty cheese, having eyes or holes formed by gas-producing bacteria. The true Swiss product has the word "Switzerland" imprinted on the rind.

Tabasco Sauce. Trade name for a very hot, red-pepper sauce. Only a drop or two should be used.

Table Wines. Dry or nonsweet wines of the type usually served with the meal—not as a cocktail or dessert wine. There are three principal types of table wines: red, white, and rosé or pink.

Tarragon. An herb, whose leaves are used for flavoring vinegar, mustard, etc. Available in dried leaves, sometimes put up with peanut oil. Leaves are also preserved in vinegar. Tarragon vinegar can often be substituted for tarragon when vinegar flavor is not objectionable.

Truffles. A fungus that grows under the earth. Black truffles are imported from France; so-called white truffles from Italy. They have a distinctive, earthy flavor and fragrance. Truffle peelings, or a combination of mushroom and truffles, are available in jars. These impart some truffle flavor at much less expense.

Turmeric. A dried and ground root that combines well with mustard; an important ingredient in curry powder.

Vacuum Packing. Means that the can has been sealed in the absence of air to prevent deterioration or staling.

Vanilla. The most important of the extracts is prepared from vanilla beans, the seed pods of a climbing plant belonging to the orchid family and growing in tropical countries. *Vanillin* is the most prevalent of the imitation extracts. Its base is vanillin, which sometimes appears on vanilla beans in the form of frost-like crystals; it is also made synthetically from oil of cloves and from lignin (obtained from wood).

Vegetable Colorings. Available in liquid, paste, or pellets.

Vinegar. An acid obtained by the fermentation of cider, wine, or beer: (1) *cider vinegar,* made from apple juice; (2) *malt or beer vinegar,* made from malted grain, principally barley; (3) *tarragon vinegar,* cider, malt, or wine vinegar in which the leaves of the tarragon plant are infused; (4) *white (or distilled white) vinegar,* used in pickling, cooking, or for salads; because it is exceptionally strong, a lesser amount should be used; (5) *wine vinegar,* made from dry wines. Vinegar made from red table wine is red, while white wine vinegar has a light, golden color. Wine vinegars are often seasoned with basil, tarragon, garlic, shallots, or herbs

Water Cress. A pungent salad green, delightful for garnishing, to use in salads, in soup, or in sandwiches.

Wine. Used in cooking to accent and balance the flavors already present and to supply aroma, acidity, and smoothness. Properly used, the flavor of the wine in a cooked dish cannot be readily identified and the alcohol passes off as soon as the food is heated.

Wintergreen Flavoring. Made from oil of wintergreen, distilled from leaves of the checkerberry plant, and from the bark of the black birch.

Worcestershire Sauce. In addition to soy sauce, made from soy beans, Worcestershire sauce contains vinegar, lime juice, tamarinds, onions, red chili peppers, and garlic. Some types are flavored with anchovy or pickled herring.

Yogurt. A cultured milk product, yogurt is infant cheese. It is generally packed in individual jars or cartons.

Index